"In this carefully researched, thoughtfully framed, and beautifully written work, O. S. Hawkins has given us a fresh and illuminating look at two shaping figures in Baptist life and American Christianity during the first half of the twentieth century. Even for those who think they are familiar with these stories or who have an overview of Baptist life during this time period, *In the Name of God* will introduce new observations and connections that will provide eye-opening insights into the legendary lives of George W. Truett and J. Frank Norris. Truett, the ubiquitous leader and stately orator, and Norris, the fiery fundamentalist and Texas tornado, overlapped in so many contexts, yet understood their callings and purposes ever so differently. The first half of this book reads like a page-turning novel; the second half of the book offers a hermeneutical guide to the diverse and distinctive contributions of Truett and Norris, as well as to the longer-term implications of their approaches to life and ministry. Even if historians should quibble over some of the interpretive explanations offered, this book will be fascinating reading for all who are interested in twentieth-century religious movements and American culture, and will be essential reading for anyone interested in the various trajectories that Baptist life has taken in recent decades."

—**David S. Dockery**, distinguished professor of theology,
Southwestern Baptist Theological Seminary, and president,
International Alliance for Christian Education

"No one is better qualified to tell the untold story of Baptist legends J. Frank Norris and George W. Truett than my lifelong friend O. S. Hawkins. His own family roots run deep in the history of First Baptist Church in Fort Worth, and for several years he was one of George W. Truett's pastoral successors at the historic First Baptist Church in Dallas. This story of these entwining lives and legacies read like a page-turning novel. It reveals the dangers of elevating denominational loyalty over scriptural fidelity."

—**Jack Graham**, pastor, Prestonwood Baptist Church, Plano, TX

"Take two titanic personalities, two great cities, two famous pulpits, and two of the largest churches in the world—and then add two men shot dead, two rival visions of Christianity, two lasting legacies, and one earth-shaking feud, and you have O. S. Hawkins' book, *In the Name of God*. This is one of the most fascinating stories of our time, written by the one man who has a claim upon the entire story. It is incredibly well told and tremendously relevant. I recommend it eagerly."

—**R. Albert Mohler Jr.**, president,
The Southern Baptist Theological Seminary

"My roots are deep in First Baptist Church of Fort Worth, having been licensed and ordained to the ministry there. I have enjoyed every page of O. S. Hawkins' book. It is accurate in its history and has restored some balance to the life of a man who has too often been reviled. O. S. has brought the characters to life again—a few I actually knew and others whose stories I heard from eye-witnesses. Thank you for a great read."

—**Bill Monroe**, pastor, Florence Baptist Temple, Florence, SC

"This book by O. S. Hawkins, a Texas legend in his own right, is a marvelous read. It is well-researched, historically conversant, and written by a biographer who has a keen, almost barrel-aged, understanding of the human soul and psyche. Hawkins is close to his subjects in that he clearly honors and, in some ways, reveres them. However, his study of Truett and Norris is never hagiographic. It presents each man in full color, and works in colorful and arresting portraits of their peers, Baptist titans like L. R. Scarborough, W. A. Criswell, and more.

In the Name of God is indeed clear-eyed about how both Truett and Norris failed in different ways. The study of two contrasting styles yields much wisdom in the gleaning, and reminds this reviewer of the outstanding juxtaposition of Hitler and Churchill by elite biographer Andrew Roberts.

In sum, I regard this work with considerable respect and interest. It is academic and well-grounded in historical disputation but eminently readable and arresting. I learned numerous details from each man's career, and I found the material edifying and engrossing. Rehabilitating J. Frank Norris to some degree is a job for which there are few takers, but Hawkins succeeds in that task, and thus performs a service to the historical guild. All in all, *In the Name of God* is a rich study, and should make a real contribution to the conversation over this most vaunted of Baptist eras."

—**Owen Strachan**, associate professor of Christian theology, Midwestern Baptist Theological Seminary

"O. S. Hawkins' best-selling Code books are already considered devotional classics. His *In the Name of God* will become a primary source for those who want to understand Southern Baptist history in general and the Conservative Resurgence in particular. Dr. Hawkins reveals in a new and fresh way how the issues in the Conservative Resurgence simply reflected the earlier controversies of the 1920s in SBC life.

Some today, like George Truett of old, still place denominational loyalty over doctrinal fidelity while others, as Hawkins so skillfully shows, keep their priority grounded in doctrinal truth. Frank Norris' rallying of thousands of pastors from the "folks from the forks of the creeks" was simply a harbinger of the mobilization of the masses of pastors supporting the inerrancy debate during the 1980s. No one yet has connected these dots as Hawkins so effectively does in this volume. Dr. Hawkins' unique perspective as a Fort Worth native and as the much-loved pastor of First Baptist Church, Dallas qualify him to give us this vital resource."

—**Jerry Vines, pastor emeritus**, First Baptist Church, Jacksonville, FL, and two-time president, the Southern Baptist Convention

IN THE NAME OF GOD

IN THE NAME OF GOD

*The Colliding Lives,
Legends, and Legacies of
J. Frank Norris and George W. Truett*

O.S. HAWKINS

ACADEMIC
NASHVILLE, TENNESSEE

To Susie.

CONTENTS

INTRODUCTION

History repeats itself. At least, that is what the well-worn expression has taught us through the years. As we look back at events of decades gone by, we often view them through our own prejudicial lenses. Sometimes the distance can serve to sharpen our focus today. Perhaps this has never been truer than when we revisit the lives and legends of two iconic figures, J. Frank Norris and George W. Truett, who dominated so much of the first half of twentieth-century ecclesiology and culture—not just in Texas and the Southwest, but in the whole of America.

The turn of the twentieth century found two cities in Texas in stark contrast and in fierce competition with one another. Fort Worth and Dallas have grown up side by side—one, Dallas, like an older sophisticated sister and the other, Fort Worth, like a younger sibling intent on sowing her wild oats. Arising out of these two cities were two churches that had no peer in the first five decades of the century. In our modern world of megachurches in every city, it is difficult to capture how legendary the First Baptist Churches of Fort Worth and Dallas became in their day. They were the two largest churches in the entire world in the 1920s and the 1930s, and the Fort Worth church actually pioneered many of the approaches and programs still in play today in thousands of congregations.

Arising out of these two churches were two men, Norris and Truett, who ruled and reigned from their respective pulpits for almost fifty

1

years. They shared much in common. Both had the near unanimous and unquestioning following of their flocks. Both lived lives of impeccability in moral and financial matters. Both shot and killed a man, one by accident and the other in self-defense. Both died while still in their pulpits as pastor. Yet their years were spent in almost constant conflict and controversy with each other, while at the same time enjoying the following of multiplied thousands both at home and across the country.

J. Frank Norris was the pastor of the First Baptist Church in Fort Worth from 1909 to 1952. He was the most colorful and controversial figure of his day, and whoever was in second place was so far behind it would scarcely deserve mention. He was indicted and tried for arson, perjury, and even murder, but he was quickly acquitted by sympathetic jurors in each case. He was a curious mix of brilliance and belligerence. He was an antagonist par excellence and loved nothing more than getting under the skin of and taunting those he considered his enemies. He had a spy network that his personal friend J. Edgar Hoover, then head of the Federal Bureau of Investigation, would envy. Some despised him and thought of him as the devil incarnate, yet masses of people loved him with sincere devotion and would have followed him straight into hell with a water pistol.

George W. Truett was the pastor of the First Baptist Church in Dallas from 1897 to 1944. If ever there was the human antithesis to Norris, it was Truett. He was almost universally beloved, respected, and even revered by the masses of those both in the church and out of it. Today, three-quarters of a century after his death, the name Truett is etched in stone over massive entrances to hospitals, seminaries, universities, public schools, and various other institutions that are all called by his good name. He abhorred controversy and sought by every means to live in peace with those around him.

My own history and heritage afford me a unique opportunity to lead us on a journey of revisiting these two legendary lives. My own family's spiritual roots are found in Norris's church. It was at the altar of that church that my own father, as an eighteen-year-old young man, knelt with Dr. Norris himself and had a life-transforming spiritual experience.

My great uncle, Harry Keeton, served for more than forty years as one of Norris's most loyal and dedicated deacons, and his wife served as one of the pastoral secretaries. Then, it was my high privilege for several years to preach week by week in the same pulpit as did Truett, my own pastoral predecessor, when I served as pastor of the First Baptist Church in Dallas. I was the pastor to many of his sweet family members, including nieces and nephews who essentially grew up in his home.

This volume is gleaned from hundreds of primary sources, including personal letters and numerous interviews with people who witnessed these long-ago days. It contains many yet-to-be revealed stories and includes "the rest of the story" regarding many of the defining moments of each of these men's lives. At the same time, it is the perplexing and paradoxical story of two men whose lives are forever entwined and who both changed their world for the good in so many ways. Some may be offended that anything unkind could be said of Truett. Perhaps no one life has been written about with as much bias, and perhaps no one has achieved in death the level of near-human worship, adoration, and reverence as he. Others may be offended that anything good could be said of Norris. While Truett has been universally revered, Norris has been virtually reviled by those who have sought to recount their lives and legacies. As the old cliché says, "The half has not been told." That is, until now. These two lives present to us a panoply of intrigue, espionage, confrontation, manipulation, plotting, scheming, and even blackmail. And yes, it was all carried out . . . *in the name of God!*

1

Two Cities, Two Churches, Two Pastors

Two Cities

The cities of Fort Worth and Dallas have lived side by side in perpetual competition throughout the decades. Since their respective inceptions, they have lived in rivalry with one another. Their constant competition, whether in commerce, athletics, education, or the arts, has been fierce. The Ballpark at Arlington, home of the Texas Rangers; Cowboy Stadium, home of the Dallas Cowboys; and the mammoth Dallas-Fort Worth International Airport all sit in the middle of the "Metroplex" as statements of the standoff and compromise between these two cities.

In their adolescent years, Fort Worth and Dallas fought over the railroads. To this day they continue to fight over commerce, industry, and athletics. Before Major League Baseball arrived in the area, the Fort Worth Cats and the Dallas Eagles of the old Texas League were bitter rivals. Their universities, Texas Christian University (TCU) in Fort Worth and Southern Methodist University (SMU) in Dallas, have fought it out for generations, with TCU emerging victorious most years. TCU had more wins than any football team in the nation in the 1930s and won national titles in 1935 and 1938. The Fort Worth school's dominance has continued with eight out of ten wins in the last decade.

Dallas

In 1841 Dallas superseded Fort Worth when John Neely Bryan settled on the east fork of the Trinity River and opened a trading post to serve passersby on the old Indian trails of North Texas, which later became the first highways of the Republic of Texas. Neely was convinced the forks in the river would make an ideal spot for a town and trading post. He built a log cabin that, with some restoration, still stands on the old courthouse lawn in downtown Dallas.[1]

No one knows for certain where Dallas derived its name—most likely from either George Dallas, vice president of the United States from 1845 to 1849, or from Joseph Dallas, who settled near the new town in 1843.[2] Because of its water source and prime location, it did not take long for the new little village to become the hub of the surrounding rural areas. Within just ten years of its founding, Dallas boasted insurance agencies, dry goods stores, shoe shops, numerous small industries, and even a weekly newspaper, *The Dallas Herald*. By the eve of the Civil War in 1860, the population had grown to almost two thousand and was experiencing an infusion of European immigrants and African Americans.[3] One year later, the residents voted to secede from the Union and become a Confederate Army outpost. After the war the city boomed with an influx of freed slaves, and by 1870 the population had risen to more than three thousand.[4]

Knowing that transportation lines are the key to economic growth and expansion, many people attempted to navigate the Trinity River. Most of them failed due to the impracticality of crossing the river. Thus, the city fathers focused their efforts on attracting the railroads. Things came together quickly, and by 1873 they had brought the rail traffic to their new city. In fact, by enticing the Texas and Pacific Railroads to their city, they made Dallas one of the first significant rail crossings in the entire Southwest. Along with the Texas Central line, they had now positioned themselves to transport goods, not just north and south, but also east and west. Cotton became king and Elm Street became its throne, making Dallas the cotton capital of the country. By 1880, in less than a decade, the population had tripled to more than ten thousand.[5]

The natural outcome of this explosion of commerce was the growth of the banking industry, and with this Dallas was set to become the mega city it eventually became. Insurance quickly followed, and with the addition of electricity and telephones in the 1880s, the city again tripled her population in the next decade. On New Year's Day 1890, Dallas officially boasted forty thousand citizens.[6]

However, the 1890s did not roar in Dallas as the national financial crisis brought the failure of several Dallas banks and a number of industries. Cotton prices bottomed out, and the job rate plummeted. But by the turn of the century, the resilient new metropolis had rebounded and was leading other cities in the Southwest in nearly every venue. In 1910, with a population now soaring to more than ninety thousand people, Dallas boasted the world's leading inland cotton market and led the world in the manufacture and distribution of leather goods and saddles.[7]

Fort Worth

Meanwhile, something new was arising on the clear fork of the Trinity River, thirty miles west of Dallas. In 1849, a small contingency of Texas Rangers brought Army Major Ripley Arnold to a strategic bluff above the Trinity River. From this elevated perspective, Major Arnold could readily see that this was an ideal spot to establish an army outpost to help ward off the increasing Comanche raids on the area. On June 6, 1849, Major Arnold officially established a United States Army Post on the exact spot:

> Major Arnold commanded the outpost of Fort Worth at the age of thirty-two. Six feet tall, slender and graceful, gray eyes, a dominant forehead topped with auburn hair, a good chin and

a mouth set in purposeful lines—he had the bearings of youth. He was symbolic of the trait that would dominate Fort Worth's city pioneering.[8]

This fort marked the original founding of what would later be known as the city of Fort Worth. This new city was named after General William Jennings Worth, a national hero of the Mexican-American War of 1846. Not only did General Worth never visit the city named in his honor, he died before its official establishment. Today his body rests in a tomb within a large monument on one of the busiest intersections in the world—Fifth Avenue and Broadway—at Worth Square in the Manhattan borough of New York City.[9]

The city of Fort Worth was incorporated in 1873, and by 1878, "the great American buffalo slaughter was underway, and hides began to arrive in Fort Worth. Wagon freighters often hauled full loads on each round trip, taking supplies to the Plains and returning with buffalo hides."[10] At the peak, sixty thousand hides awaiting shipment would be piled on the platform near the railroad; two hundred thousand hides were processed during the year, making Fort Worth the largest direct buffalo hide market in the world.[11]

During this same period the Chisholm Trail had become the super-highway for Texas cattle drives on their way to the slaughterhouses in Kansas City, going straight through the middle of town. From the "first days of spring until late summer, cattle was the heartbeat of Fort Worth. Northern cattle buyers with ready cash gathered in Fort Worth . . . thousands of cattle from sunrise until late afternoon passed through in continuous procession."[12] Fort Worth became the prominent rest stop for weary cattlemen along the trail. The last stop before the final destination in Kansas, the city became a virtual oasis for cowboys in search of rest and relaxation. Not surprisingly, hotels, saloons, gambling halls, and houses of ill repute sprung up on almost every corner. Thus, Fort Worth earned the name that has stuck throughout all these years—"Cowtown, Where the West Begins." When Amon Carter founded Fort Worth's most prominent newspaper, *The Star-Telegram*, he placed the slogan on the masthead: "Fort Worth . . . Where the West Begins."[13] This slogan has been the rallying cry for the growth and progress of the city until today.

By 1902, the Swift and Armour packing plants had moved their operations to Cowtown, and the economic fortunes of the city were running on all cylinders. The young upstart city was standing toe to toe with Dallas, its rival sister city on the east fork of the Trinity River. Fort Worth had focused every effort on enticing the lucrative company to their new and growing city. Optimism soared as the local paper prophesied that Fort Worth was destined to become "the greatest packing house center in the entire Southwest."[14]

Dallas had its nationally known industrial center, and Fort Worth now had its own nationally known enterprise—a red light district known as "Hell's Half Acre." Made wildly famous by the likes of Butch Cassidy and the Sundance Kid, along with their female sidekick Etta Place, Hell's Half Acre actually covered about two acres of the southeast quadrant of downtown and quickly became the home away from home for thousands of cowboys and gunslingers who, from time to time, made their way through Fort Worth. The area was inhabited by dozens of one- and two-story saloons, gambling joints, dance halls, and of course, the sporting houses (more commonly known as "places of ill repute," among other slang terms). Fort Worth became a popular hideout for desperados, stage coach and train robbers, and every other type of motley character that can be conjured up in the mind. Hell's Half Acre had a law unto itself. One law enforcer after another failed miserably to maintain any semblance of peace and order. For decades Hell's Half Acre was a haven for debauchery and depravity. As late as 1911, J. Frank Norris led the First Baptist Church board to approve a statement that no member would be retained on the church rolls "who has any interest, directly or indirectly, in a disorderly house of any kind or class."[15]

In 1878, C. K. Fairfax opened the luxurious and lavish three-story El Paso Hotel on the southwest corner of Third and Houston Streets. The El Paso was not only the city's first three-story structure but also its first genuine first-class hotel. The hotel "boasted eighty rooms, each with solid walnut furniture and Brussels carpet."[16] The El Paso became the favorite attraction for the likes of Bat Masterson, Doc Holliday, and the legendary Wyatt Earp. Quanah Parker, the famous Comanche chief who persuaded his tribe to give up their battle with the white man, was a frequent visitor.[17] When Earp visited Fort Worth, he always requested the room on the third floor of the old El Paso Hotel, located in what is today Sundance Square. From there, he had a direct view into one of the most popular sporting houses at night, and from that vantage point he got a free show put on by the prostitutes and their customers.[18] This also provided Earp with a way to ensure that his own men were not availing themselves of the extracurricular activities of the evening hours.

Dallas got her big break when a nationwide financial crisis in 1873 brought about a national depression. This brought a stark halt to the building of the Texas and Pacific Railroad, which was supposed to run tracks to Fort Worth but was now forced to stop in Dallas due to failed funding.[19] The people of Dallas could not hold back their delight in the assumed demise of their sister to the west. The Dallas media mocked Fort Worth with a caustic report that downtown Fort Worth was so sleepy and empty "a panther had been seen sleeping on the streets in the dying city of Fort Worth."[20] The city fathers in Fort Worth seized upon this and took it as a rallying cry. Fort Worth has been known as "the Panther City" ever since.[21] For decades their minor league baseball team carried the mantle of "the Cats," and a large bronze statue of a watchful panther can be seen to this day across the street from the courthouse in downtown Fort Worth.

Thus, these sister cities emerged in the twentieth century with distinct personalities. The rivalry and competition have grown fiercer over time. John Nance Gardner, former vice president of the United States, was quoted in the November 11, 1938, edition of the *Saturday Evening Post* as saying, "Amon [Carter, one of the most influential of all Fort Worth's city fathers] wants the government of the United States to run for the exclusive benefit of Fort Worth and, if possible, to the detriment of Dallas."[22] Carter was "Mr. Fort Worth," and as owner of *The Fort Worth Star-Telegram*, WBAP radio, and what is now KXAS (NBC5), he framed and fashioned public opinion and thought in Fort Worth for a half century until the time of his death in 1955.[23] One of his most well-known position statements about Fort Worth was, "Fort Worth is where the West begins . . . Dallas is where the East peters out."[24] Of the life-long rivalry between Fort Worth and Dallas, Carter was fond of saying the two cities "have tried to bury the hatchet many times but somebody always leaves the handle sticking out."[25] Former CBS television news anchor Bob Schieffer, himself a Fort Worth native and TCU graduate, once even wrote a song that contained this lyric:

> Dallas, Dallas how we love you,
> But why's our airport known as DFW?
> Move that D. Shift that letter.
> FWD sounds so much better.[26]

These two cities, Dallas and Fort Worth, have grown up together across the decades with diametrically opposite personalities. Dallas is cosmopolitan and extremely class conscious. Fort Worth still strives hard to live up to her reputation of "Where the West Begins" and maintains her former pride as a haven for oil wildcatters and gunslingers bent on protecting second amendment rights. Dallas emits an image of sophistication and social awareness; Fort Worth is like a larger-than-life old friend with open arms and a warm, welcoming smile.

Stark differences show up in myriad ways to illustrate this truth. The two department stores that emerged from the downtown cores of these two cities are examples. In Dallas, the erudite Herbert Marcus and his brother-in-law A. L. Neiman teamed up to launch what would become Neiman Marcus. Today, more than one hundred years later, Neiman Marcus is internationally acclaimed for its high prices and cosmopolitan flare. In 1918 in Fort Worth, the Leonard brothers, J. Marvin and Obadiah (Obie), founded the department stores that, for decades, bore their names and to which the masses from all over North Texas descended to explore their massive offerings and low prices. Their commitment to low profit margins and high volume quickly turned Leonard Brother's Department Store into the largest retail establishment in Fort Worth and a recognized leader in retail in the entire Southwest. Across the street from their mammoth store was their subsidiary, Everybody's Department Store, where the common man felt at home shopping for bargains and saving money on seconds and other slightly damaged goods. Leonard Brothers and their cut-rate cousin Everybody's dominated Fort Worth shopping for decades.[27] Although Leonard Brother's Department Store closed its doors when downtown shopping fled to neighborhood malls, their good name still exists, and a museum in honor of their success is a popular attraction in Fort Worth today. Taking a not-so-subtle shot at Dallas, Oliver Knight, in the original preface to his volume *Fort Worth, Outpost on the Trinity*, wrote on September 10, 1953: "Fort Worth does not have the supercharged atmosphere of a city that is conscious of itself. Nor is it particularly conscious of culture."[28]

Two Churches

Arising out of the downtowns of these two cities were two churches that had a dominating influence on early twentieth-century ecclesiology. In the modern world of megachurches in every city, it is difficult to capture how legendary the First Baptist Churches of Fort Worth and Dallas were in their day. By the 1920s, they became two of the largest churches in the world. The Fort Worth church pioneered many of the approaches and programs that are still utilized in thousands of churches today.

Baptist historian Leon McBeth relates that in the summer of 1868:

> . . . a tall young man rode into the city of Dallas sitting in his saddle awkwardly. Dismounting near the center of Main and Jefferson, he hitched his horse to a rail and headed toward W. L. Williams's law office. His saddle stance was graceful compared to his ludicrously ungainly walk. This was W. W. "Spurgeon" Harris, Baptist preacher-evangelist, and part-time missionary of the Elm Fork Baptist Association. He was on his way to see Williams, who had invited him to come to discuss the possibility of holding a revival in Dallas.[29]

They secured the lower floor of the local Masonic Lodge build-ing at the corner of Lamar and Ross Avenue for the services. Lasting two weeks, the revival recorded one conversion.[30] At the conclusion of this feeble beginning, eleven persons—three men and eight women—presented themselves for membership and constituted the First Baptist Church in Dallas.

If one person could be called the founding force behind this new beginning, that man was W. L. Williams. However, equally important, his wife, Lucinda, was the driving force behind many of the programs in this new congregation. They prevailed upon Spurgeon Harris to stay in Dallas, and he became the first pastor in the long and illustrious his-tory of this great church. Harris was followed by a succession of pastors for almost thirty years, most serving the church for only two or three years before moving on. In 1897, the church called young, thirty-year-old George Truett as pastor, and for the next forty-seven years he shep-herded the Dallas congregation, as Asaph, the psalmist, wrote of King David in Psalm 78:72, "with the integrity of his heart and the skillful-ness of his hands."

Meanwhile, a year earlier over in Fort Worth, a group of Baptist pio-neers busily established their own Baptist church. They struggled over the years until, meeting in the old Tarrant County Courthouse, twenty-six charter members officially constituted the First Baptist Church of Fort Worth in 1873. Like their friends to the east, they began meeting in the Masonic Lodge building in Fort Worth. They were driven from their previous meeting place at the courthouse because of the constant noise, dust, and odors from the cattle drives down the middle of Main Street, immediately outside the open windows of their Sunday services.[31]

J. M. Masters is recognized as the founding pastor of First Baptist Church in Fort Worth. His successor, W. M. Gough, led the church to build a new brick meeting house on Jennings Avenue in 1876. A parade of short-tenured pastors followed, and in 1886 Morgan Wells heeded the call to the church. His pastorate saw the church grow to 541 members and witnessed the building of a magnificent 1,100-seat sanctuary at the corner of Taylor and Third Streets. The national Southern Baptist Convention

(SBC) was held in this building in 1890.[32] Wells was greatly loved by the congregation, and after his death in 1896, three short-term pastors served the congregation until 1909 and the arrival of J. Frank Norris, who would lead from the Fort Worth pulpit for the next four decades.

Two Pastors

Arising out of these two churches were two men, John Franklyn Norris and George Washington Truett, who led from their respective pulpits for almost fifty years. Like their adopted cities of Fort Worth and Dallas, these men passed the years in almost constant competition and conflict with each other, while at the same time endearing themselves to thousands of followers at home and across the entire United States as radio broadcasts and their printed sermons propagated their ministries. Their personal correspondence reveals close and intimate friendships with people in high places, not the least of whom was President Harry Truman, who on occasion would call upon them for advice and counsel.[33] If ever two men took on and lived out the personalities of their two cities, it was Norris and Truett. Norris was a pioneer and a provocateur who often shot from the hip. Truett sought to be a prophet and peacemaker, always proper in public conduct with an air of sophistication.

J. Frank Norris was pastor of First Baptist Church in Fort Worth from 1909 to 1952. He was one of the most colorful and controversial figures of his day. He built the largest church in the world and at the same time was indicted and tried for arson, perjury, and even murder—yet was quickly acquitted by sympathetic jurors in each case. He was a curious mix of brilliance and belligerence. He was an antagonist par excellence and loved nothing more than taunting those whom he considered his enemies, yet masses of people loved him and followed him with unabashed love and unqualified loyalty. There were also numbers of people who despised him and thought of him as the devil incarnate.

Norris arrived in Fort Worth when the town was rapidly growing. The new meat packing plants were processing five thousand hogs and three thousand cattle a day, and the demand for jobs brought about a growing employment rate.[34] The multiplied hundreds of new laborers who were flocking to Fort Worth for good-paying jobs were just the type of people who were attracted to Norris's confrontational and sensational approach to ministry, enlisting in his army of followers that eventually grew into the multiplied thousands.

Frank Norris was tailor made for the Wild West, moving to Cowtown just a few years after one of the most famous gunfights in western lore took place. Luke Short, the infamous gambler and gunslinger, shot and killed the city marshal, Long Hair Jim Courtwright, on Main Street between Second and Third Streets, directly in front of the White Elephant Saloon. Courtwright drew first, but before he got his Colt 45 out of his holster, Short shot and Courtwright fell. Short fired again, hitting the marshall in the chest, then standing over him, fired three more times at point-blank range.[35] A bronze historical plaque marks the spot today in downtown Fort Worth. Not long after, Short met the same fate on the same street, gunned down by an unnamed desperado passing through town.

Norris arrived in this raucous environment in Fort Worth and was introduced to a city that boasted sixty saloons, more than a dozen sporting houses, and only nine churches. Against a backdrop such as this, many were not surprised when Norris himself shot and killed a man in his own pastoral office in 1926. No man ever took on the personality of his city and fit its wild and woolly times as did Frank Norris. He was the true "lone star" in the Lone Star State.

George W. Truett was pastor of the First Baptist Church in Dallas from 1897 to 1944. He was the human antithesis of Norris. He was universally beloved, respected, and even revered by the masses. He abhorred controversy, avoided conflict, and sought by every means to live in peace with those around him. However, in the case of Norris it was a futile effort. Truett never mentioned Norris by name and reverted, when having to refer to him, as simply "that man in Fort Worth." Yet their lives and influence are forever entwined in the building of the largest non-Catholic denomination in the United States, the Southern Baptist Convention.[36]

Truett and Dallas were a perfect match, and, like Norris, he took on the personality of his own city. He was cultured, sophisticated, and proper in every respect. He was tall and stood erect with a stately demeanor and a sophisticated presence that filled every room he entered. It is said that often upon his entrance into a banquet room or a civic function, "suddenly without warning the entire group arose and applauded."[37] A well-known Houston civic leader often said that Dallas had only two things that Houston envied: "Neiman Marcus and George W. Truett."[38] Always immaculately dressed and refined in character, his very presence demanded awe and respect from the humblest man on the street to the most prominent person in the city. And Truett loved them all. He often would be without an overcoat in the winter, and his wife, Josephine, would discover he had given it to someone he had passed on the street.

George W. Truett was the epitome of a Christian gentleman and statesman. He graced the pulpit in the historic First Baptist Church at Ervay and Patterson Streets Sunday by Sunday for forty-seven years. In a twenty-first-century culture, it is difficult to appreciate the level of stature and respect this solitary Baptist pastor demanded in his day. Hospitals, public schools, seminaries, libraries, and hundreds of individuals have all been assigned his good name. Truett Cathy, founder of the enormously successful fast food franchise Chick-fil-A, says, "My parents named me after George W. Truett, the great preacher and evangelist of the first half of the twentieth century, for whom the theological seminary at Baylor University is named."[39] George Truett was a paragon of faithfulness and stability. However, he thrived on denominational unity, often at the cost of doctrinal compromise.

While both Norris and Truett moved off the scene in the middle of the twentieth century, their influence on Baptists is felt to this very day. There is a sense in which they both morphed into the titular head of the Conservative Resurgence of the SBC.

W. A. Criswell, at only thirty-four years of age, became Truett's successor shortly after his death in 1944. Criswell was born in 1909, the year Norris assumed the pastorate of First Baptist Church in Fort Worth. He grew up in a home where his father was a devout follower of

Norris and his mother was a passionate devotee of Truett. As a young boy he sat at a multitude of dinner tables listening to the debate that would inevitably ensue between his mother and father as to whether Norris or Truett was the greatest preacher. Criswell rose to succeed the legendary Truett and would lead the Dallas church to unparalleled heights during his own fifty-year pastorate. In theology, scriptural affinity, and practice he aligned with Norris. He employed Norris's strident fundamental theology but managed to wrap it in Truett's more compassionate and relational ministry philosophy, thereby leading First Baptist Church in Dallas to become the father of all modern megachurches. He ascended to become the undisputed leader of the "Battle for the Bible" in the Southern Baptist Convention. Like a rose bush in a chain-link fence, these three lives are forever entwined with one another. Loved by most and despised by some, Criswell left a lasting legacy as did his two mentors before him, Norris and Truett.

2

J. Frank Norris:
The Texas Tornado

No man ever lived up to the nickname "The Texas Tornado" more than J. Frank Norris. He was one of the most interesting and intriguing figures in Texas history. From his pen and pulpit in Fort Worth, he would swoop down out of his own dark cloud, strike with dastardly force, and often leave the ruins of lives and even legacies in his wake. When Texas Baptist leaders like George W. Truett sighted his sudden strikes, they would seek shelter from his damage. Others would stand outside and shake their fists in his face, to their own destruction. This perplexing personality lived a life of perpetual paradox. His memory is a strange mixture of both fact and fiction. Certainly, he left his mark on the Baptists with whom he engaged. In fact, his influence among many Baptists persists. No one remains neutral when it comes to J. Frank Norris. People either loved him and followed him with abandon, or they despised him and stayed as far away from him as possible. His pastoral successor, Homer Ritchie, said, "Dr. Norris was a classic example of a schizophrenic. He could be the kindest, most loving person, but if you ever crossed him or embarrassed him, he could be as mean as the devil himself."[1]

Norris possessed a complex personality. He was a preacher and a polemic, a pragmatist and a politician, a publisher and a provocateur. Norris was known as a trailblazer in every sense of the word. He preceded all megachurch pastors. In the 1920s, First Baptist Church in Fort Worth gathered several thousand people every week to their worship services. He enjoyed, by far, the largest crowds of his day. Baptist historian Robert Baker quotes him saying that he had set out to "build the biggest church in the world."[2] By the mid-twenties, Norris's Sunday school had become "the largest Sunday School in the nation."[3] He was the first national media personality. Long before television, much less Christian television networks, Norris preached on virtually every major power radio station in America. Additionally, he personally owned one of the largest, KFQB, in Fort Worth.[4] Long before the creation of the internet and the craze of social media, Norris shared his thoughts and pet peeves through his weekly tabloids, *The Searchlight* and *The Fundamentalist*, which found their way into the hands of scores of thousands of readers weekly.[5]

The Early Years

J. Frank Norris, the Texas Tornado, spawned out of the dark cloud of a father, Warner Norris, and a godly mother, Mary Davis Norris. He was born on September 18, 1877, in Dadeville, Alabama. His father toiled as a sharecropper and could never seem to make ends meet. During Norris's childhood, his father became an alcoholic. Once on a Christmas Eve, in a drunken stupor, his father beat him so severely that a doctor had to be called to the home to treat his injuries. Later, his sobered father knelt by his bed and wept profusely. The next day, Mary Norris hitched their buggy to a horse, drove into town, and with a horsewhip beat the bartender that sold Warner the liquor.[6] Whereas Norris's father acted like shifting sand, his mother became his solid rock.[7]

Norris frequently recalled a vivid and traumatic event of his childhood:

I was about eight years old, one day I was standing on the porch of the public school when two boys came up, one was 12 and the other 14, and each of them had on a nice suit of clothes, a nice overcoat. I had on a little cotton suit, no overcoat . . . these boys, sons of a banker, came up, looked at me and said, "Your coat is too little"—well, I knew it. Then one of them pointed his finger at me while all the boys gathered around and said, "Your daddy is a drunkard and mine is a banker." I turned, went into the school room, and buried my face in my hands. The dear school teacher came up to me, put her arm around my shoulder and said, "Frank, what is the matter?" I couldn't say a word . . . I fairly flew home—when I got home, mother said, "Frank, are you sick? What are you crying about?" I wouldn't tell her what happened but that night after I had gone to my room she came in and said, "Tell Mother what is the matter. I must know so we can cry together." I told her what happened. Mother said, as she put her tender arms around me and brushed away my tears, "Son, it is all right, some day you are going to wear good clothes—some day you are going to make a man—some day God will use you." I said, "Mother, please don't make me go back to that school." She said, "You don't have to go back, Mother will teach you." And it was a great blessing to me. I read all the histories and memorized whole chapters of the Bible.[8]

And so, at the feet of his godly, nineteenth-century, homeschooling mother, Norris prepared for what would later become his valedictorian status.

The Move to Texas

In 1888, at the age of eleven, Norris moved with his family to a farm outside of Hubbard City, located in the hill country of central Texas. At the age of thirteen he accepted Christ as his personal Lord and Savior in a Methodist revival meeting, and a few years later Catlett Smith, pastor of Hubbard Baptist Church, baptized him. Smith quickly became a mentor and pastoral role model.[9] After his baptism, Norris's mother shared with him how she took him as a baby to the banks of the Tallapoosa River back in Alabama, held him up to heaven, and said to God, "This is the best I have to give You." She said she felt the Lord reply, "You have given the world a preacher." Then, turning to the young teenage Norris, his saintly mother said, "You are going to preach the gospel of Jesus. I have known it all my life."[10] Norris's mother's influence, coupled with the power of her convictions, shaped him throughout his lifetime.

Poverty and hardship caused more adolescent trauma within young Norris as he arrived in Texas. Although Fort Worth found itself in the throes of earning its reputation as "Cowtown" in the 1890s, cattle rustling began to spread with abandon across the state of Texas. On a given afternoon, and quite by accident, Warner Norris rode upon a cattle rustling operation and recognized two of the townspeople involved. Feeling he was unnoticed, he continued on his way home, steering clear of the controversy. He took his horse to the barn, unsaddled him, and upon looking around, was suddenly confronted by the two men, who had followed him home.

Frank, now a young teenager, chopped cotton in a nearby field. The sound of shouts and loud voices startled him; several gunshots followed the loud voices. He rushed up to the barn and found his father lying on the ground, bleeding. He jumped between the men who had shot his father with only a small pocketknife in his hand. They fired more shots, and young Norris was hit three times. The rustlers quickly fled the scene. The elder Norris's wounds were somewhat superficial, but young Norris's were life threatening. By the time they could summon a doctor from Hillsboro to rush to their home, gangrene had spread and the prognosis was bleak. The doctor informed his mother that her son most likely would not survive, and if he did, he would be an invalid the rest of his life.[11]

He lived with excruciating pain for the next several months. As the young lad lay bedfast, his mother hovered over him with tender care. She read the Bible continuously to him. She convinced herself and her son that he was destined to recover and to be used mightily in God's kingdom's service. By the age of eighteen he had learned to walk again. A few years later and fully recovered, he left the farm for Baylor University. No evidence exists to show how he acquired the resources for this journey and his initial college expenses; nevertheless, he prepared for ministry and fulfilled his destiny.

College and Seminary Years

Norris's Baylor years were among the most formative of his life. At the university, John S. Tanner, his Hebrew and Greek professor, invested in him. Prior to his marriage, Norris lived in the Tanner home, where he rented out a small bedroom along with fellow student and roommate J. M. Dawson. Dawson later became the longtime pastor of First Baptist Church in Waco and a leader in the Southern Baptist Convention. At Baylor he also came under the tutelage of one of the towering giants of Baptist theological education, Benajah Harvey "B. H." Carroll. A few years later B. H. Carroll would lend his voice and influence in recommending Norris to the pastorate of the First Baptist Church in Fort Worth. Other Baylor notables, such as S. P. Brooks and J. B. Gambrell, also became the young theologue's mentors—both of whom in later years found themselves on the receiving end of some of his most scathing and vicious attacks.

Norris's lifelong proclivity for conflict and confrontation, which later characterized his life, began to sow seeds of growth in two defining events at Baylor. First, Norris decided to join a campus organization of young preachers. He recounts:

> On the first day I was fool enough to stand up before that bunch of pious cadavers called ministers and say to them, "I'm going to preach in the greatest cities and churches in the world. And, I am going to build the greatest church in the world." The first thing you know, they wanted to pray for me. Well, they didn't want to pray for me, they wanted to cuss me out. They kept praying for me because I was too ambitious. While they were still praying . . . I tiptoed out and left them there.[12]

The second incident occurred during a chapel service on the third floor of the administration building. Some fellow students smuggled a dog into the meeting. When the dog began to bark and howl, the erudite and Ivy League–educated president of Baylor, O. H. Cooper, became so irritated that on impulse he picked up the dog and threw it forcefully out of the third-story window. The next day he profusely apologized, but a campaign was underway to have him fired. The leader of this effort, in the words of J. M. Dawson, was "a gifted pugnacious youngster named J. Frank Norris."[13] Norris led a student protest against the president, notified the board of trustees, and made sure the Society for the Prevention of Cruelty to Animals was aware of the act. Pressure mounted, which ultimately resulted in Cooper's resignation as president of Baylor.[14]

While at Baylor, Norris met Lillian Gaddy, the daughter of J. M. Gaddy, a highly respected pastor and Texas Baptist leader. He was a sophomore and she was a senior. Norris fell in love with her at first sight. He wrote of the "long quiet walks amidst the calm, colorful life of nature and pleasant evenings filled with conversation and expression" in the ensuing months after they met.[15] Lillian graduated valedictorian of her class, and J. B. Gambrell performed their wedding ceremony in 1902. After Norris's graduation, the newlyweds moved to Louisville to pursue graduate work at the Southern Baptist Theological Seminary. Humanly speaking, Lillian was the best thing that ever happened to Frank Norris. She stood steadfastly by his side through fifty years of marriage, taught the Bible with skill and clarity, and nurtured the four Norris children, Lillian (1903), Jim (1906), Frank Jr. (1910), and George (1916). Guy Thompson, Fort Worth's legendary funeral director and an icon in his own right, observes, "There was a real touch of genius in all the Norris family."[16]

Norris preached and served as a pastor through his college years at First Baptist Church in Mount Calm, Texas. It gave him the practical experience to couple with his academic knowledge, which prepared him for more expanded ministry opportunities in the future. Ray Tatum explains:

This pastorate meant a source of physical sustenance, meager as it was, and it came at a time when he did not know how he would finance his second year at Baylor. He could now, with the weekly salary . . . commute by railroad from Waco, the twenty-six miles to Mount Calm each week and then back to Baylor on Mondays. . . . The style of his preaching, the metaphors, clichés, and pathos of his messages were developed in the Mount Calm pulpit.[17]

Upon graduation and narrowly losing valedictorian honors to his former roommate, J. M. Dawson, Norris resigned his four-year pastorate in Mount Calm. In a final service of sentimental farewell, the church presented the beloved young pastor and his new bride with a large white envelope. When he opened it, he found the large sum of six hundred dollars for a farewell gift.[18]

At Southern Seminary, Norris sat at the feet of two of the greatest minds in all of Baptist history, A. T. Robertson and E. Y. Mullins. He forfeited a Sunday pastorate in order to focus on his studies, completing the challenging three-year Master of Theology program in only two years, graduating at the top of his class and delivering the valedictorian address to the graduating class in 1905.[19]

The Call to Dallas

With a stellar education and both college and seminary behind him, Norris found himself ready to reemerge into the pastorate. The "call" came from McKinney Avenue Baptist Church in Dallas. Norris and his young family arrived on the scene and were greeted at his first service by thirteen faithful members meeting in a wooden tabernacle on McKinney Avenue on the north side of downtown. Just a mile away, in the heart of the city, George W. Truett had already been presiding over the First Baptist Church for a decade. Truett was preaching to growing crowds and building a stellar reputation in the city. These two legendary figures entwined for the next forty years in such a way that they would, at times, border on near obsession with one another.

In Norris's own words:

When I graduated, the McKinney Avenue Church at Dallas called me; they called me sight unseen before I graduated— and I accepted sight unseen. Talk about marrying by corre- spondence, that is nothing. They thought I was some pumpkin, and I thought they were some pumpkins because they were in Dallas. No young Roman Catholic priest ever looked with stron- ger devotion toward St. Peter's in Rome than I looked at the denominational headquarters in Dallas. What disillusionment was awaiting me.[20]

Norris's brilliance and pulpit prowess immediately began to take hold. From a feeble start of thirteen congregants, the church grew to a crowd of one thousand on his first anniversary, and by his sec- ond anniversary, a huge and stately Greek-columned church edifice was under construction on McKinney Avenue.[21] This rapid success caught the attention of all Texas Baptists, not the least of whom was Truett, since many of Norris's new flock had formerly been members at First Baptist Church, leaving Truett for Norris.[22] Truett complained to his friend J. M. Dawson about the young newcomer's techniques, as Dawson's future wife, Willie Turner, was among those lured away from Truett's First Baptist Church by the persuasive and winsome power of young Norris.[23] Thus began the constant and continuous strife between Norris and Truett, which would extend over the next four decades.

Having established himself in the church, the ambitious young pul- piteer now set his eyes on the *Baptist Standard*, one of the largest weekly papers in Texas. Norris stated:

Right in the midst of the rapid growth of the church, Judge T. B. Butler, former business manager of the Baptist Seminary and a director at the time of the *Standard*, called me before a group of men to take over the management of the *Baptist Standard*. I was not thirty years old and had never written an article in my life for a paper.[24]

Norris quickly moved to acquire 54 percent of the voting stock, later moving on to purchase both S. A. Hayden's *Texas Baptist Herald* and J. B. Gambrell's paper, *The Advocate*. The purchase money came from an inheritance he received following the death of his father-in-law, Rev. J. M. Gaddy.[25] Norris and Gaddy were alone late at night in the back Pullman of a train en route to Austin when Gaddy fell from the train to his death.[26] This event is not without controversy:

> Norris's erstwhile critic, J. M. Dawson, has advanced the possibility that Norris pushed his father-in-law, J. M. Gaddy, off the rear platform of a train and used the insurance money to buy the *Standard*. This, of course, is a rather grave charge, and thus far nothing has been proved which could stand up in a court of law.[27]

Norris assumed sole charge of distributing Baptist news to the Lone Star State and beyond, all the while serving McKinney Avenue as pastor—while not yet thirty years of age. This expanded platform provided Norris instant notoriety with Texas Baptists and exponentially multiplied his influence among the pastors and the churches.

The Move to Fort Worth

In 1909, the prestigious and influential First Baptist Church in Fort Worth was in search of a new pastor. B. H. Carroll, Norris's old Baylor mentor and the founder of Southwestern Baptist Theological Seminary, leaned on the church's pulpit search committee with passionate persuasion to look east to Dallas . . . to young Frank Norris. Near midnight on a Wednesday in September 1909, Judge R. H. Buck, chairman of the search committee, telephoned Norris in Dallas to exclaim excitedly, "I am happy to tell you, you have been called to the pastorate of the First Baptist Church in Fort Worth."[28] The congregational vote was nearly unanimous. Only one family, that of J. T. Pemperton, voted against him. Pemperton was an influential bank president who stated:

> I am not opposed to J. Frank Norris; I am for him, but this church is in no condition for his type of ministry. If he comes,

there will be the all firedest explosion ever witnessed in any church. We are at peace with the world, the flesh, the devil and with one another. And this fellow carries a broad axe and not a pearl handled pen-knife.[29]

As the years unfolded, Pemperton turned out to be more of a prophet than anyone could imagine, and ironically, when many of the staid church leadership eventually abandoned the church, Pemperton remained through the ensuing decades to be one of Norris's most vocal and vociferous friends and defenders.

Norris was met in Fort Worth by a congregation he described as "reformed sinners, socially and financially elite, conservative, unproselytic, liturgically housebroken, a tamer breed of Baptists, almost like regular Christians."[30] The church possessed the reputation as "the church of the cattle kings" and boasted that "millionaires hung in bunches."[31] Norris was young, brilliant, successful by every measure, well connected, and filled with potential and promise. He was "tall and gawky, slender to the brink of emancipation. Norris seemed an innocuous Ichabod Crane figure until one was transfixed by his messianic eyes. Eyes of absolutism, pale blue and painful, mesmerizing. Old Testament eyes that trespassed on other men's souls."[32]

For the first two years, nothing of note happened in the church. Norris seemed to fit the mold of old First Church, a servant of the upper crust, and one those who inhabited the high-steepled, stained-glass edifice could control. In fact, Norris described himself during those years in the following way:

> I was a typical city pastor. I was the chief after-dinner speaker. I had tuxedos, swallow tail coats, a selection of "biled" shirts, several of them, and I would give $10.00 for the latest joke. I was, as I said, the main attraction at all the gatherings of the Rotarians, Lions, Kiwanis, and Eagles. I was Will Rogers and Mark Twain both combined; they thought so, so did I.[33]

In the early months of the Fort Worth pastorate, Norris avoided confrontation at all costs. He actually fulfilled what he had written earlier in an editorial when still editor of the *Baptist Standard*: "The *Standard* takes no part in petty quarrels. It will not indulge in harmful controversy, personal or otherwise. There is something in this life better than mud-slinging, the constructive work of Baptists."[34] In a few short years, his lasting legacy would become the very antithesis of these words.

A New Beginning

Discouraged with his lack of spiritual power, one evening young Norris desperately said to his wife, Lillian, "I think I will just quit the ministry."

The wise young woman replied, "When did you ever begin?"[35]

At this strategic moment in his life, Charles Carroll, the son of his mentor, invited him to come to Owensboro, Kentucky, to conduct a series of revival meetings.

This trip proved to be one of the defining moments of Norris's life and provided a new beginning for him. While in Kentucky, spending time alone with God on the banks of the Ohio River, Norris decided to "enter the ministry."[36]

He returned to Fort Worth and began preaching like a modern-day John the Baptist. He started slinging that "broad axe" that Pemperton had prophesied. He "lost his dignity and became demonstrative with his own emotions, and he wept, exhorted, shouted, pleaded, and persuaded his listeners."[37] The results occurred instantaneously. Sixty-two new converts made their way down the aisles and to the altar for salvation the first Sunday after he returned from Kentucky. J. Frank Norris was never the same. Soon the church averaged one hundred new members every week.[38] By 1920, "membership of the First Baptist Church reached twelve thousand," and the five-thousand-member Sunday school was the world's largest.[39]

Norris's desire, as his tombstone would say, "to do anything to keep a man out of hell," soon led him to the sensational. He would advertise dramatic topics to attract great crowds and then always preach the gospel to the large assemblies, which included many unsaved souls.

Harry Keeton became one of these early converts. He was a successful textile merchant and avid fan of the Fort Worth Cats baseball
team. In the biggest game of the year, the Cats lost the championship
game to their archrivals, the Dallas Eagles. Keeton walked on a downtown street when he saw a banner stretched across a building that said
in flaming red letters, "Why Dallas beat Fort Worth in Baseball . . . Hear
J. Frank Norris Sunday Night at 7:30 p.m."[40] Out of curiosity, Keeton
attended and found the auditorium packed beyond capacity, with standing room only. Norris referred to the ballgame with one introductory
remark, "Dallas beat Fort Worth because they were better prepared for
the game." From that introduction, he launched into a message on salvation and the importance of preparing to meet God in judgment. Norris
"pulled away his tie and celluloid collar, threw off his jacket, ran about
the church, up and down the aisles," pleading with the crowd to pre-
pare to meet God.[41] He then invited the people who desired to come to
Christ to make their way to the front of the auditorium. The aisles filled
with men and women, many in tears, making their way to Christ. Among
them was Harry Keeton, who for the next forty years would become one
of Norris's leading layman and closest confidants.[42]

Such sensational tactics soon became the norm at First Baptist
Church. One of his most effective crowd-gathering, attention-getting
sermon titles came from information he received from one of his
church members. A Sunday school teacher at First Baptist Church
worked as a clerk in one of the downtown department stores. She
alerted the pastor that a certain well-known banker, who had publicly
spoken out against Norris on occasion, had purchased a dozen pairs of
expensive women's silk stockings. The very next day, a woman, not the
wife of the banker, brought the same stockings in to exchange for a different size. Norris drew a standing-room only crowd the next Sunday
after widely advertising in the local papers that he would be preaching
on this question: "Should a prominent Fort Worth banker buy high-
priced hose for another man's wife?" Norris claimed that, before the
sermon was preached, three different bankers called him that week to
beg for mercy.[43]

The Exodus

In due time, the dignified, upper-crust parishioners became vocal opponents of Norris and wanted their church back. Every Sunday, masses of common men and women were converted, and before long they became the majority. Norris's new approach to ministry attracted the common man, while the religious establishment began to oppose him vehemently. The old church establishment caucused and decided the pastor needed to be terminated. The deacon chairman, an imposing, dominating individual, warned Norris to change his sermons. When his warning fell on deaf ears, he summoned Norris to his office. Norris said, "I went to that office like a lamb led to the slaughter." The deacon chairman put it bluntly: "Norris, you are a damned fool! And this is to notify you that you are fired." Norris continued:

> I walked up close to him, and if ever the Lord helped a poor
> preacher He helped me that noon. I was made over. There was
> something beyond human power and wisdom that shot through
> my soul. I looked him straight in the eyes, and I wasn't afraid of
> him. I had already come to the point where it mattered little at
> all what happened to me. All sense of fear was gone. I said, "No.
> You have made a mistake . . . you are the one that is fired!"[44]

Norris later revealed that instead of his preaching, the deacon chairman's principal complaint centered on the fact that a "notorious street walker was baptized in the very same baptistery where I was baptized."[45] The pastor took the fight to the entire church, and the masses of new converts, totally loyal to him, gave him an overwhelming vote of confidence over the disgruntled, longtime congregants in a church-wide vote.[46] Afterward, the First Baptist Church never had regular business meetings, and by the end of Norris's life and ministry, no official deacons served the church—only a finance committee.[47]

An exodus soon followed, and hundreds of longtime First Baptist members sought a church home elsewhere. The new Norris and his sensationalism clashed with the dignified congregants. Many of them moved their membership to Broadway Baptist Church in Fort Worth. Even his mentor, B. H. Carroll, stood up in an open meeting to call for his and his wife's letters and walked out of the church.[48]

Norris, now in complete control, turned his attention to several other sensational approaches. When preaching against evolution, he had a monkey dressed in a suit and tie sitting on a stool by his pulpit. Periodically, during his message, he looked down at the monkey and asked him absurd questions while the creature just stared at him—to the delight of the crowd.

During Prohibition, when he was preaching against the liquor crowd, he sent out his secret agents to buy moonshine. He would bring these pint jars of illegal liquor to the pulpit and, after publicly exposing those who were selling it, he would ceremoniously break open the jars and pour out the contents in large wash tubs. Norris knew little and cared less about the art of conflict resolution. His confrontational efforts would not subside until he returned from Florida in a coffin forty years later.

Hell's Half Acre

Frank Norris lived in constant fear that he was going to miss some contentious confrontation or fierce fight. With the struggle for control of the church now over, he turned his attention to Hell's Half Acre, the infamous cesspool of iniquity on the south side of downtown Fort Worth. Norris launched an all-out war, not only on "the Acre," but on the city government for its failure to enforce the city laws and ordinances regarding the unbridled prostitution and promiscuity that was running rampant downtown. In 1911, houses of prostitution operated in the city with little restraint, and Norris used his widely advertised Sunday evening services to expose this sin.

Norris discovered that many of the publicly respected "city fathers" actually owned properties in Hell's Half Acre—properties that were openly functioning as saloons and houses of ill repute. He hung up huge banners all over town and placed large advertisements in the local papers announcing his Sunday sermon topic: "The Ten Biggest Devils in Town and Their Records Given."[49] In the midst of his sermon, Norris named these property owners one by one along with the city officials who were in league with them.[50] The city of Fort Worth found itself in an intense conflict. Moving on his momentum, Norris next erected a large tent right on the border of the Acre and began preaching nightly on the city's sins, calling upon the city government to begin enforcing laws already on the books, which they were conveniently and completely ignoring.[51]

Simultaneously, Norris heightened his attack on the entire liquor industry and on Mayor Bill Davis, charging him with the misappropriation of city funds. The situation became so contentious that Mayor Davis publicly threatened to have the preacher hanged vigilante style.[52] As with most of Norris's early fights, he won. The property owners retreated or sold out, and the city began to enforce the laws. Today, a beautiful city water park sits on the site of Hell's Half Acre, and a bronze plaque at the entrance marks the spot and credits J. Frank Norris with its demise.

Indicted for Arson

Among the more defining moments of Norris's life were his infamous indictments and public trials. Frank Norris was indicted for arson in the burning of the First Baptist Church in 1912 and indicted for murder in the death of D. E. Chipps, whom he shot dead in his office in 1926. He was found not guilty on both accounts. On February 4, 1912, a night watchman heard an explosion and saw flames rising from the First Baptist Church in Fort Worth. The same night, antagonists tossed oily rags on the back porch of the Norris home, doing only minor damage. By the time the sun rose on the morning of February 5, Fort Worth's most ornate church edifice was lying in a pile of smoldering ashes. Less than a month later, another fire heavily damaged the Norris home, and the family escaped by jumping from a second-story window.[53]

Four weeks later the district attorney indicted Norris on two counts of arson and one count of perjury.[54] The following day's front-page story in the *Fort Worth Record* carried a story defending the pastor's innocence and was signed by sixty-eight of his leading laymen. The church not only stood with their pastor, but they also raised money for his defense. J. B. Gambrell, one of his mentors from his college days and now editor of the *Baptist Standard*, stated that "not in the history of America was there ever an indictment brought by a grand jury on such a flimsy and shadowy piece of evidence."[55]

At Southern Baptist's mother seminary, the Southern Baptist Theological Seminary in Louisville (Norris's alma mater), President E. Y. Mullins joined Gambrell in jumping to Norris's defense. In a piece of personal correspondence that became very public, Mullins wrote to Norris, "I have read Dr. Gambrell's review in the *Standard* and I quite concur with his judgment that it was a 'colossal frame up.' May this sorrow turn to the deepening of your spiritual life and thereby enlarge your ministry."[56]

L. R. Scarborough, who would become Southwestern Seminary's second president upon the death of Carroll in 1914, had his doubts. Scarborough told W. W. Barnes, Southwestern's renowned history professor, that one Sunday morning after the worship service Norris had mentioned to him his dissatisfaction in feeling as though Morgan Wells, the beloved former pastor of the First Baptist Church in Fort Worth, was looking over his shoulder each time he preached. Wells, under whose ministry the elaborate eleven-hundred-seat sanctuary had been constructed in 1889, made known his desire to be buried outside the church under one of the stained-glass windows. Upon his death, and by special permission of the city council, he was buried beneath one of the beautiful stained-glass windows. Soon after his death, a large stained-glass portrait of the beloved pastor replaced the one above his grave. Norris felt that, even in death, Wells dominated the upper-crust membership of the church.[57] Scarborough related to Barnes what Norris said to him: "Lee, I will never be able to do anything with this church as long as that face looks down on me." He continued, "This whole thing would have to burn down to the ground and let us start over again."

Dr. Barnes said to Scarborough, "And sure enough it burned down." He replied, "Yes, it did."[58]

This was more than a mild insinuation of Norris's guilt by Scarborough, who was about to become his new nemesis.

During the arson trial, Norris sat stoically at the defense table with his hands folded atop a worn Bible. Church members packed the courtroom to overflowing and spilled out into the courthouse hallways. At the moment of the verdict, heartbeats seemed to pound in unison. "Innocent on all charges" was the unanimous verdict of the jury.[59] The courtroom immediately turned into a revival meeting. The singing of hymns of praise erupted in the courtroom and echoed through the courthouse.[60] The outcome only empowered Norris. He likened his ordeal to that of Martin Luther at the Diet of Worms—and even the apostle Paul before King Agrippa.

After his acquittal, Norris began to feel and act as though he were invincible and untouchable. The verdict served as a turning point in the explosive growth of the church, as more new members flocked to the Sunday services.[61] The church held services in the Byers Opera House downtown while its new and elaborate five-thousand-seat preaching palace was under construction.[62] Norris held court in this beautiful, massive sanctuary Sunday by Sunday until it, too, burned to the ground a few years later in 1928.

Indicted for Murder

The single most defining moment in the Texas Tornado's life came on a Saturday afternoon, July 17, 1926. In big, bold, black letters, the front page of the local paper announced the news the next morning: "DR. NORRIS SLAYS D. E. CHIPPS: Lumberman dies after shooting in church office."[63] The story behind the headline was H. C. Meacham, then-mayor of Fort Worth and a well-known citizen due to the popular and successful downtown department store that bore his name. He was also well known locally for his sympathies and association with the Roman Catholic Church.

A controversy arose at city hall related to the accusation that some of the city funds had been siphoned off to benefit Ignatius Academy, a

Catholic institution, through the purchase of a piece of property that was appraised at $62,000 and for which the city of Fort Worth paid $152,000. The property was used to build a street that ran directly by Meacham's Department Store.[64]

Norris jumped into the middle of the fray, immediately seizing upon the controversy. He printed sixty-two thousand copies of a sermon he had preached calling Meacham nothing more than a Catholic puppet. He stationed several church members outside Meacham's Department Store to hand out copies to all potential customers when they entered the premises.[65] Meacham retaliated by firing six employees, all of whom were members of Norris's church.

Norris announced he was putting the mayor on trial the next Sunday evening at the First Baptist Church. The church was filled to overflowing with thousands in the auditorium. One by one, Norris interviewed the six church members previously employed at Meacham's Department Store. In true Norris fashion, he did not retreat. The next Sunday, while pounding the pulpit with fierce gestures, he made a direct assault on the mayor's character. He shouted:

> Mr. Meacham's record is well known. Up here in Judge Bruce Young's court a few years ago it is a matter of record that H. C. Meacham had to pay to one of his employees—a young lady— $12,500, and he gave the lawyers $10,000 besides to settle it. . . . I say to this great audience it is a shame on the name of Fort Worth that a man of that kind should be mayor for one minute.[66]

This public disclosure of Mayor Meacham's moral failing brought the conflict to a new level of engagement.

Dexter Elliot Chipps, a local lumberman and close friend of Mayor Meacham, had heard enough. Chipps, known for his heavy drinking and carousing, began making death threats about Norris to people downtown. At 10:00 a.m. on Friday, July 16, 1926, two police officers, Harry Conner and Fred Hollond, visited Norris in his office to warn him of the threats, relating to him what Chipps had said the evening before at the Hotel Texas on Main Street: "I am going to kill J. Frank Norris."[67] On the following afternoon at 3:30, Chipps telephoned Norris at his office from his room in the Westbrook Hotel, where he lived. The hotel switchboard operator, Fannie Tom Greer, placed the call through the PBX switchboard at the hotel and listened in. She later testified that Chipps was angry and abusive, and everyone who worked at the Westbrook Hotel was afraid of him. In a sworn affidavit, she stated under oath that she heard Chipps call Dr. Norris many vile names with repeated profanity. She said, "I heard him repeat several times, 'You blankety-blank-blank, I am coming over there to kill you.'"[68]

Within minutes Chipps made his way the two blocks from the hotel to the First Baptist Church and stormed unannounced into Norris's inner office. L. H. Nutt, a church deacon and teller at the Farmer's and Merchant's Bank where J. T. Pemperton was president, sat with the pastor in his office. Because of some recent church break-ins, the night watchman had been carrying a loaded pistol, and after his shift he placed it in Norris's top desk drawer for safekeeping.

Chipps burst into the office wearing a trench coat on a hot July day, and he made a move toward his hip pocket. Instantly, Norris grabbed the night watchman's gun and fired four times. One bullet lodged into the ceiling, and three found their mark in the body of D. E. Chipps, who fell dead in a pool of blood on the office floor.

The police arrived and cordoned off the room. Their report indicated that Chipps was unarmed. However, Nutt testified to seeing a gun on the floor beside the hulky lumberman before the police arrived.[69] Jane Hartwell, the pastor's longtime secretary, was sitting in her office with the door open into Norris's office, and in a sworn affidavit, under penalty of perjury, testified:

I was present on the afternoon of July 17, 1926, when D. E. Chipps came into the office of Dr. Norris and was killed. He did not knock on the door but just kicked the office door open and spoke in a loud, rough voice, using much profanity, so that all the office force could hear him, and said: "I am going to kill you." He ran his hand into his hip pocket and pulled out a gun.

Dr. Norris, who was standing by his desk, fired several shots first. Chipps fell to the floor of the office.[70]

The police report failed to mention these two testimonies, and later, when photographers appeared to capture the scene, the gun had either been removed or was never there in the first place.

Police arrested Norris, and within ninety minutes, thirty men from the church had posted his bond and he was released on his own recognizance. J. Frank Norris stood before his congregation the next Sunday morning and offered his resignation as pastor. They immediately refused it, and the congregation jumped to their feet in unified support of their greatly loved pastor. Over the next few days, the sensational story was carried on the front pages of newspapers across America. On the following Sunday, a crowd of more than six thousand gathered to hear Norris. He made no mention of the shooting and preached from the text, "There is now no condemnation to them which are in Christ Jesus" (Rom. 8:1).[71] Rumors began to spread that Meacham had sent Chipps to kill Norris. Stories appeared to this effect in the major papers in Los Angeles and Chicago, from coast to coast.[72] The prosecutor, knowing the near impossibility of finding a jury in Fort Worth that did not have some opinion of J. Frank Norris, convinced the judge to move the trial to Austin, the state capital, set to begin in January 1927.

Meacham felt no confidence in the abilities of the district attorney or his prosecution team. In a rare and somewhat unprecedented move, he hired his own private prosecutors to assist the district attorney's office. When questioned by Defense Attorney Marvin Simpson at the change of venue hearing, Meacham admitted "that he had retained the law firm of Scott, McLean and Sayers as special prosecutors at a fee of $15,000 and had already advanced them $6,500."[73]

Dayton Moses and Chester Collins joined Marvin Simpson to serve as Norris's defense team for the trial. Jury selection began with 182 potential jurors subpoenaed. Hundreds of spectators crowded into the courtroom and spilled into the halls of the courthouse to witness the trial.[74] After four days of intense scrutiny, the jury was selected and the trial began. The state called several key witnesses and argued that

Norris provoked the confrontation with Chipps and that Norris shot an unarmed man in order to gain more publicity for himself. The defense's star witness was L. H. Nutt, who emotionally reenacted Chipps's last act of rushing toward the pastor while reaching toward his back pocket as if he were reaching for a gun. He continued by telling how Norris, in self-defense, fired four shots, three of which hit Chipps.[75]

The climax of the trial came when J. Frank Norris took the stand in his own defense as the final witness. He told his story through tears, his voice quivering, sometimes hardly articulating his words. He told his testimony with deep emotion. Through a racking cough and with hand-kerchief in hand to wipe his brow, Norris told his story. Then, under intense cross-examination, he never wavered in his story.[76]

After fourteen days of testimony and media frenzy, the jury reached their verdict on January 25, 1927. In less than an hour of deliberation and with one unanimous ballot, they found J. Frank Norris not guilty of the murder of Dexter E. Chipps by reason of self-defense. Norris received total vindication.

The pastor returned triumphantly from his murder trial in Austin to Fort Worth, more the hero to his followers than ever before. Arriving by train at 6:40 p.m., Norris found that:

> the station was thronged with multitudes to meet him; the streets were lined with crowds from there to the church. Regardless of the bitter cold night, long before the arrival at the church the massive auditorium was packed to standing room, and multitudes were turned away.[77]

When the pastor arrived in the church, the crowd began to cheer, but his eyes were filled with tears as he began:

> If there is anything at all that can be construed as a celebration, you certainly misread and misunderstand the feelings of our souls tonight. I want to ask you, therefore, that there be no demonstration. . . . I ask that there be no hand clapping . . . the occasion is too solemn for applause. . . . I shall be brief tonight and then I hope I may slip out with my family.[78]

Despite his pleas for solemnity, "they interrupted his talk with hand-claps and cheers, being unable to restrain their joy in having their pastor back."[79] Norris referred to this episode as "the unfortunate dark tragedy that fell across my life."[80] He told his people:

> I had no hate, I had no malice, there was no murder in my heart and never has been against a single human being. I never saw the unfortunate man until he broke into my study. It is a matter of record as to who sent him there and for what purpose. I repeat it was a great sorrow, a life-long sorrow, but not one tinge of remorse . . . but a Gethsemane of sorrow. A great preacher in Dallas, Dr. Truett, killed a man—it was not murder, it was accidental, inevitable . . . it was a deep sorrow and always will be.[81]

Norris had no remorse because he viewed the tragedy as purely an act of self-defense.

J. Frank Norris and the Southern Baptist Convention

Norris began his ministry known by many as a consummate denominational loyalist. But after his awakening in the Kentucky revival of 1910, he returned to Fort Worth ready to do battle with the denomination that he now considered to be sliding down the slippery slope into modernism. Many of those he had considered partners in ministry, like L. R. Scarborough, found themselves in the crosshairs of some of his most vicious attacks. One confrontation led to another, from his confronting and exposing the teaching of evolution at Baylor to his perceived strong-arm tactics against Truett and Scarborough in the national SBC's 75 Million Campaign—the battle continued on several fronts.[82]

Norris realized quickly that these Southern Baptist leaders were not going to allow him to run over them. In 1922, in a brazen act of defiance, the local Tarrant Baptist Association, led by L. R. Scarborough and Forrest Smith, expelled Norris and the First Baptist Church in Fort Worth from its fellowship by a vote of 135 to 6.[83] The larger state group, the Baptist General Convention of Texas, followed suit in 1924 by refusing to seat messengers from First Baptist Church in Fort Worth at their annual meeting.

While publicly Norris may have worn this among his independent Baptist friends as a badge of honor, privately it was a blow. J. T. Pemperton, Norris's loyal member and well-known bank president, wrote to Dr. Scarborough on July 24, 1924, pleading for a second chance. Pemperton writes to his "Dear Brother," "I do not wish to engage in any unseemly or unbrotherly controversy; my prayer and hope is for unity and harmony among our Baptist brethren, and most especially in the Association that I love."[84] The national body of Baptists, the SBC, never formally dealt with Norris—although he responded to years of being ignored by holding competing meetings near their national convention sites. Norris seemed to thrive on these denominational confrontations. This battle would consume most of the rest of his life and was destined to be the one conflict in which he could never claim legitimate victory.

The Second Church Fire

After the murder trial in Austin, Norris found his refuge back in the safety of his fundamentalist fold in Fort Worth among those who, for the most part, were more convinced now than ever that he was a true saint of God. However, his next major challenge was only a year away. A 1928 fire destroyed the magnificent multi-thousand-seat church, its radio tower, and the printing presses that issued his weekly tabloid, *The Searchlight*. *The Searchlight* spread Norris's weekly sermons and diatribes into thousands of homes every week. All his necessary ministry tools—from his pulpit, to his radio station, to his magazines—were now lying in a pile of ash at his feet. Earlier on January 2, 1928, the Norris family home went up in flames. Most of the family was in church. Mrs. Norris, her eighty-four-year-old mother, and their youngest son, George, were at home due to illness. They saved only a few treasured family keepsakes, and Norris lost his entire library. A generous response followed from the church and friends, and soon the family moved into a new nine-room, fully equipped home without a dime of debt.[85]

These fires were immediately followed by the stock market crash in 1929. The timing could not have been worse for Norris. With masses of his congregants out of work and little possibility of raising the needed funds for rebuilding, the First Baptist Church met in wooden tabernacles hastily erected in various places across the city. These activities effectively legitimized the ministry of the First Baptist Church in the eyes of the city. Through these tabernacles dispersed around the city, they provided life's necessities—including food, cots, showers, and medical treatment—to the poverty-stricken victims of the Great Depression.[86] Eventually, in 1932, the church managed to construct a very large, no-frills auditorium on the corner of Fourth and Taylor Streets. Norris preached at that location until his death in 1952.

Norris's public image never quite recovered after he walked through these dark valleys. In 1935, he was called to the pastorate of the Temple Baptist Church in Detroit, Michigan. He accepted this assignment with the understanding that he would pastor both the Fort Worth church and the Detroit church simultaneously, something he did for the next fifteen years. In Detroit, he attained a degree of social acceptance that he had not enjoyed in Fort Worth since his beginning days. The Detroit congregation had high visibility, and its prominence was associated with the fact that it had a number of extremely wealthy members, including many executives of the booming automobile industry of the 1930s and 1940s. This visibility and prominence became an ever-increasing help and kept the Fort Worth ministry thriving until Norris's declining years.

Seeing the need for a more fundamental training center for future pastors, Norris founded the Fundamental Baptist Missionary Institute in 1937, later renamed the Bible Baptist Seminary in Fort Worth. He founded the school because, in Norris's own words:

> What is needed is a school that teaches the whole English Bible. What is needed is a school that will take men from engine cab, from between the plowshares, and teach them the Bible. What is needed is a school that is free from modernism. What is needed is a school that will teach a man how to go out with a Bible under

his arm, faith in his heart, and in the power of the Holy Spirit, begin in a vacant lot and build a church to the glory of God.[87]

He lived to see the Bible Baptist Seminary train multiplied hundreds of preachers and missionaries who literally went to the ends of the earth spreading the gospel message.[88]

The Family Feud

Not long after Norris's Southern Baptist conflicts and confrontations in the 1920s and 1930s, some of his own family and loyal friends found themselves the objects of his wrath. His youngest son, George, had "a real touch of genius about him."[89] Educated at the United States Naval Academy, Texas Christian University, and the University of Michigan, young George was the Norris child who heard the call of God to follow in his father's footsteps as a gospel minister.

But then, in Frank Norris's thirty-fifth year of ministry, his church named young George Norris pastor—successor to his famous father. In fact, the June 19, 1944, headline in the *Fort Worth Press* stated, "Son is named Pastor—But Norris has not resigned."[90] It was an ominous omen. Behind the scenes, the elder Norris had consulted no one—not the church or even the new pastor. He simply announced the decision on a Sunday morning.

George Norris had a bright mind and a winsome personality and immediately gained acceptance and favor among the church members. However, his father could not let go of the major decision-making. Over his lifetime Norris had perfected a domineering leadership style, which had characterized his ministry for decades. The family tension became so intense that after only seven months, young Norris wrote his letter of resignation to the church on January 26, 1945. He then took Horace Greeley's advice, "Go west, young man."[91] He journeyed two miles west of downtown on Camp Bowie Boulevard and started the Gideon Baptist Church. Three hundred of the best Bible teachers and church workers at First Baptist Church followed him.

Homer Ritchie observed that J. Frank Norris was a "classic case of a schizophrenic," an evaluation supported by a series of letters that Norris wrote to George over the next several months.[92] Christian fathers seldom speak to a son of their own flesh the way Norris berated and belittled his own grown son. As the family contention came to a head, Norris wrote to his son a series of caustic comments:

> We would not have near the sorrow over you and your future as if you were a corpse today. . . . Everywhere you drive in these streets and everywhere you go you will meet people who will not say a word to you openly, but they'll say, "There is the young man who stabbed his own father and mother in the back." . . . My pity is deep for you . . . that you would stab your own mother in the back—your own mother who carried you for nine months and nursed you. . . . The day will come in the course of human events when your mother and I will lie cold in death—and before the casket lid is pulled down over the faces of those who gave you life you certainly would remember you stabbed us both in the back.[93]

As in his other conflicts and confrontations, Norris never accepted any personal responsibility for his estrangement from his son. Someone else was always to blame. Believing himself to be especially anointed, Norris exhibited a messianic complex, concluding, "God has raised me up for this age."[94]

Just two days later, Norris wrote George another letter—one of the most loving and tender letters ever to come from his prolific pen. In it, he reached out to George:

> Mother and I are very happy over the tremendous and happy attitude of the church toward you. It's all one way. If possible, they love you more tenderly today than ever before and, of course, that makes us deeply grateful. . . . The people have the deepest appreciation of you as well as love for you—and that goes for Martha [George's wife] also. . . . Yours with abiding love, Dad.[95]

Sensing a major church split in the making, Norris sought to cover himself with this kind and gracious letter. Or, as Homer Ritchie believes, it might have been a true expression of his being "the kindest, most loving person."[96]

With damage control now in full force, the next day Norris had one of his faithful henchmen write to George seeking to encourage him to reconsider resignation from First Baptist. An ever-loyal layman, Harry Keeton, in a letter dated January 12, 1945, wrote to George to plead with and assure him that the church "holds a very tender love for you . . . you no doubt have a firm place in the hearts and affections of the whole church, and I believe that all look forward to the day when you will be at the helm again."[97]

Less than two weeks later, true to form, Norris returned to attack George in a letter dated January 25, 1945. In this particularly long and rambling epistle, he prophesies to his son: "Some of your supposed friends would now laugh at you in your day of calamity."[98] Paragraph to paragraph, his double-mindedness reveals itself. He continues, "Anytime you want to come back, the door is off the hinges. Anything I can do to assist you in any way I would consider a privilege." He concludes, "I feel certain God has his hand upon you, and since He did He will not permit you to play the fool always."[99]

George Norris ended the charade the last week of January 1945 in a letter of resignation to the First Baptist Church, which listed all his father's broken promises relating to his father's leadership at the church. Then, in a conciliatory spirit, George concludes his letter:

> I want you to know that I shall be praying for each of you individually, as well as praying that God's richest blessings shall continue on you as a church, and when we stand together in His presence to give an account of all things done in the body whether good or bad, we shall stand unashamed and unafraid with a harvest of souls to lay at His feet.[100]

With those words, George Norris ended his brief tenure as pastor of the First Baptist Church. His father resumed the reins of leadership, which, of course, he had never relinquished.

True to his fighting nature, Frank Norris could not surrender. Norris wrote to his son again: "People everywhere believe that your resignation was insincere and that it was an Absalom revolt."[101] This charge was not without merit. Young Norris had proposed in a fall business session that the church reinstall his father as pastor, thinking that they would reject this notion and put George in total control. This maneuver backfired, and the church, ever loyal to Frank Norris, voted to do just as the motion stated. Norris concludes this letter to his son, saying, "You don't need me . . . and certainly I don't need you. I would pay the $500.00 necessary for you to get the legislation to change your name, because every time your name is advertised it is a constant reminder of the revolt that you led against your father's great ministry. . . . Yours in deepest sorrow, J. Frank Norris."[102] Sadly, he could not find it in himself it sign the letter "Dad."

Unity in the Norris household never fully recovered. All four children and their families would still gather at the Norris home for the holidays, but the family dynamics had forever changed. George's son, George Norris Jr., an insurance salesman in Vernon, Texas, acknowledged that "Grandmother could never really bring herself to forgive my dad."[103] George Norris successfully served as pastor of the Gideon Baptist Church in west Fort Worth for years, wrote a few inspiring books, died of cancer, and is today buried a few feet from his father at Greenwood Cemetery in Fort Worth.

Conflict Continues

Strident fundamentalism has a history of drawing its circle smaller and smaller until most everyone is shut out. Having fought his earlier battles with the church, with the city fathers, with the seminary, with the culture, with the denomination, and with his own family, Norris could now only turn to his longtime friends and associates. After witnessing the ugly family fight, his friends must have known they were next in line. With the exception of his decades-long associate Louis Entzminger, Norris eventually spewed out his vitriol on everyone with whom he had been associated in ministry. He had no more loyal partner in ministry than Beauchamp Vick, his trusted associate at both the Temple Baptist Church in Detroit and at Bible Baptist Seminary in Fort Worth.[104] In fact, so close and trusting were these two men that Vick had become like a son to Norris.[105]

For years Norris's ministries in both Fort Worth and Detroit grew and enjoyed unparalleled success, reaching a combined membership of twenty-two thousand and an average Sunday school attendance of more than eight thousand, making Norris the pastor of the "largest church in the world."[106] However, after the episode with his son George, the ministry began to unwind rapidly. In the 1940s, hundreds of people left the Fort Worth congregation, and Norris's own health began to fail. The Premillennial Baptist Missionary Fellowship, a national organization founded by Norris, split apart in 1950. The same month, after a serious conflict with Beauchamp Vick, Norris was fired from the pastorate of the Detroit church, with the deacons voting 25 to 0 and the church affirming the decision by a vote of 3,000 to 7.[107]

The reason for these fractures in fellowship came from Norris's caustic public attacks and undermining of Vick. Norris turned on his longtime ministry partner with vengeance. He saw Vick as a growing threat to his own power base and autocratic leadership. Norris's declining health and loosening power influenced his thinking. In a letter to the Temple Baptist Church members regarding the dismissal of Norris as pastor, deacon chairman Ralph Pew accused Norris of indulging in "low, vile gossip and innuendo" and of "repeatedly distorting facts and deliberately misrepresenting" the issues at hand.[108] Norris overplayed his hand in seeking to terminate Beauchamp Vick and was not used to laymen like Ralph Pew taking a strong public stand against him.

An exchange of letters between Beauchamp Vick and Frank Norris in May 1950 reveals how bitter the battle had become. Norris pounced on the recent divorce of Vick's daughter with a venomous attack. Vick fought back, and things got nastier. However, this time Norris had finally met his match. Vick wrote to Norris calling him "bull headed" and stating, "Altho [*sic*] when you couldn't get your way one time, here at the church, you flew into a rage and told an official of the church that as far as you were concerned Temple Church could 'go to hell.'"[109] Norris responded by threatening legal and even criminal action. Finally, settled by the unanimous vote of the deacons and the near unanimous vote of the entire congregation, Temple Baptist Church of Detroit, in its own way, told Norris to "go to hell."

The Detroit confrontation and defeat injured Norris and his ego, but an even larger battle was looming back in Fort Worth. Norris became disenchanted with the by-laws of the Bible Baptist Seminary and with Vick, who served as Norris's own appointed head of the seminary. In typical Norris fashion, he had abruptly written new by-laws and ousted Vick without the knowledge or consent of the board of trustees.[110] Vick and his followers soon broke from Norris, moved to Springfield, Missouri, and established the Bible Baptist Fellowship International (BBFI). In the coming years, BBFI would train and educate thousands of ministers and missionaries, including Jerry Falwell.[111]

While Norris fought hard to maintain his strident public persona, he would often, very quietly and always privately, attempt to protect his image and smooth out his major conflicts. Realizing that he was now, at seventy-two years old, on the losing end of several significant and public battles and that his influence was also waning among his peers, he made a final fleeting attempt to keep Vick and his followers from splitting with him. Homer Ritchie remembered the event vividly. As the seminary conflict came to a head, young Ritchie, then a student at Bible Baptist Seminary, went to a popular café on Fourth Street across from the church for lunch with a small group of students. He recalls:

> There were booths with little swinging doors. We sat down in one and soon began to hear a conversation between two men in the booth next to us. The voices were unmistakable. The voices were those of Dr. Norris and Mr. Vick. Norris was not confrontational. He never raised his voice. His tone was conciliatory, as if his head was bowed and his hat was in his hand. He

was begging and pleading with Vick not to leave the seminary, to forgive him, and to not lead the split that by now seemed inevitable. In a tender voice he was beseeching the man, who he had just earlier publicly and shamefully accosted, to give him a second chance and stay with him and the school. Vick replied in a calm voice that it was too late. He said there were too many broken hearts and battered lives in Norris's wake.[112]

Thus Beauchamp Vick, along with his entourage of Bible fundamentalists, left Fort Worth to begin again in Springfield, and Norris's school and reputation were never the same.

Not lost in this sad saga is the irony that "while Norris never successfully split the Southern Baptist ranks, he shattered his own quasi-denomination," the World Baptist Missionary Fellowship and his Bible Baptist Seminary, just two years before he died.[113]

Billy Graham Comes to Town

At about this time, a young preacher named Billy Graham burst on the evangelical and national scene after a wildly successful crusade in Los Angeles, California.[114] A group of Fort Worth pastors invited him to Fort Worth for a large revival meeting, and Norris did his best to get to the party, albeit late. He jumped on the Billy Graham bandwagon, and in a letter to Graham dated March 2, 1950, he sent him a transcript of his recent radio address, which was also published in his weekly tabloid, *The Fundamentalist*. The address was filled with profuse praise of Graham, putting him on a parallel with some of the greatest names in all of church history. Norris said, "As it was in the days of Irenaeus, Athanasius, St. Bernard, Martin Luther, John Wesley, and other great spiritual dynamos, Billie [sic] Graham is the man for this hour."[115]

He followed this letter with a series of flattering epistles to young Graham, none of which were answered; Graham was concerned how they might be manipulated or reprinted in Norris's tabloids. Sensing Graham's suspicions, Norris conceded in one of these letters that when Graham came for his 1951 Fort Worth Crusade, "the best thing for me to do is to stay in the background . . . the thing to do is keep me out of it."[116] Billy Graham finally wrote Norris, and the first line of the letter admitted, "One of the reasons I have purposely not answered your letters is because I was afraid you would print them in your magazine. . . . I must confess that I have disagreed with many of your methods in days gone by."[117]

Soon after Graham arrived in Fort Worth for the crusade, Norris made repeated attempts to leverage Graham's growing and prominent popularity. However, the local pastors and Graham himself managed to keep Norris at arm's length during the protracted revival services. Norris maintained a calm and sweet spirit, seemingly understanding their reasoning. In a letter addressed to Mr. Graham at the Loring Hotel on Seventh Street, where he was staying during the revival, Norris acknowledged that he had been in attendance and heard all but two of the sermons during the month-long campaign. Then he added, "I am not joking when I say that I will be glad to make you president of the [Bible Baptist] Seminary."[118] In a small irony, Mr. Graham placed his church membership in the First Baptist Church in Dallas soon after the Fort Worth Crusade, and it remained there for the next half of a century.

The Latter Years

Meanwhile, at the First Baptist Church in Fort Worth, Norris's health and crowds both declined, and a parade of copastors who worked alongside him in his declining years grew. Most prominent of these copastors was the respected Luther Peak. For a few months, Peak sought to pastor his own church, Central Baptist Church in Dallas, and the Fort Worth congregation at the same time. Norris wrote to Peak on February 14, 1952, expressing his approval of the arrangement, "I am delighted beyond words with the progress of things. Instead of the church going down, it is going forward. When you average 200 additions a month under a new pastor, you are progressing. There has never been a deeper, abiding conviction and spirit in the church than now."[119]

However, in the end, the arrangement simply did not work. Peak had a greater capacity to tolerate the aging Norris's antics than any of the others, but ultimately the relationship ended in the same way George Norris's did. Peak went his way with grace in a kind letter of resignation dated June 8, 1952.[120] He showed respect for Norris as long as he lived, but after Norris's death Peak made a clean break from the fundamentalist movement and led Central Church out of the independent Baptist movement and into the Southern Baptist Convention in 1956.[121]

Shortly before he died, Norris called upon young Homer Ritchie to take over the leadership of the church. Ritchie had been Norris's prized seminary student and former staff member at First Baptist. He was now the energetic, winsome, and articulate twenty-five-year-old pastor of the Central Baptist Church in Athens, Texas. During the first week of July 1952, Norris called young Ritchie and told, not asked, him to be at his home near Eagle Mountain Lake on the following Tuesday morning at six o'clock sharp. At the appointed time, Homer Ritchie knocked on the pastor's front door. Mrs. Norris came to the door still dressed in her gown and led Ritchie to the back porch, where Norris was waiting for him. Ritchie relates:

> He had me drive from Athens at that early morning hour to test me to see if I would be on time. Had I not been punctual that morning I doubt I would ever have been the pastor of the First Baptist Church.

The pastor wasted no time. "Homer," he said:

> I want you to be my successor. There was never a Sunday when you were on my staff that you didn't bring young people to Christ and His church. You doubled the young people's department. I have been watching you for years, and you are the man to pastor the church.

Ritchie began to weep, "But, I am only twenty-five years old. I don't know if I can do it."

"I will help you," the pastor replied, and then he began to weep along with Ritchie.

Ritchie then pledged to honor Norris and his wife in his words, "as long as you live." Unbeknownst to either of them, Norris had only two weeks to live.[122] Four days after Norris's death, the church officially called Homer Ritchie as pastor. He served for almost thirty years but never saw the church regain her former glory.

Norris: Two Distinct Personalities

Homer Ritchie framed Norris's personality thus:

> He was a classic case of a schizophrenic. He could be the kindest, most loving person, but if you ever crossed him or embarrassed him, he could be as mean as the devil himself. I saw the good side of him so many times. He would take his last dime out of his pocket and give it away. He cared for widows. I never knew him to be anything but full of integrity with theological, moral or financial matters.[123]

Louis Entzminger, his associate of almost four decades, attested to this truth in the newspaper article announcing Norris's death: "If there was ever an honest soul in financial matters I believe Dr. Norris is one."[124] He elaborated:

> Explosive! Enigmatic! Indomitable! Those are but a few choice adjectives one might use to describe the man who has been hated, loved, revered, despised, praised, and maligned by people who knew him, to say nothing of those who only "knew what they had heard." The preaching of Norris was one of his finest assets, and in it he excelled more than in any other area of his many talented life. Possessed of a God-given ability to speak, his messages held his audiences spellbound, motivating them to yield to the moving of the Spirit. Norris was unsurpassed in eloquence. His messages appealed to the rich and the poor, the learned and the unlearned, the good and the bad. Crowds sat in

rapt attention to hear the man who "came from the farm" to the forefront of American religious life.[125]

J. Frank Norris raised the use of exaggeration and hyperbole in the pulpits and the pens of some preachers to a higher art form.[126] He became notorious for cutting, pasting, and doctoring the pictures of his crowds to make them appear larger than they actually were before printing them in his self-promoting tabloids.[127] Such tactics struck at the heart of his character and insecurities. Norris biographer Ray Tatum astutely observes that "regardless of his success, the emotional hunger, the sensational craving for a larger and larger ministry was never satisfied."[128] His enemies constantly accused him of fabricating and grossly exaggerating his successes, and his own people just smiled and looked the other way. He lived with virtually no accountability. Frank Norris garnered the biggest crowds of his day by far, but it failed to satisfy him. He always wanted more. It is a sad commentary for someone who also seemed genuinely to believe and passionately proclaim that one's identity and worth are found in Christ alone.

Nevertheless, he possessed a sensitive, selfless, and sacrificial side for which those who lived with him or have studied his life find themselves rooting to overcome. He loved people—especially those many deemed unlovely. Ritchie tells of visiting a home when he was on the church staff:

> Many times I went into homes and watched Dr. Norris win men to Christ through his own genuine tears and weeping before them. I once visited an older man in a small frame home on the south side of town. As soon as I introduced myself, he asked if I was from the same church as Frank Norris. When I replied in the affirmative, he began to curse and slammed the door in my face. I told Dr. Norris about the experience. The next Saturday he called me and said, 'Son, I want you to take me to that home on the south side.'
>
> We drove up to the house, got out of the car, walked up on the porch and knocked on the door. The man came to the door,

and when he noticed Norris he seemed to recoil. The pastor pleaded with him to let us come in for just a few minutes. Finally, he acquiesced and the three of us sat down in his living room. Norris began to make eye contact with him with those piercing blue eyes and he opened the Scriptures to him. Then Norris started weeping, real and genuine tears. The man's hardened heart melted before our eyes; he gave his life to Christ and was baptized in the First Baptist Church the very next evening.[129]

In the End

In the end, the stress created by the divisions in the church, his seminary, and his worldwide fundamentalist movement succeeded in breaking Norris's health physically and most likely mentally as well.[130] In a heartfelt letter dated July 21, 1951, he wrote to the entire church family:

> I have never known the effectiveness of your prayers like I have the last month. I have never been so sick, had pneumonia, and my condition was much worse than I thought [sic]. I am going to take a sabbatical next year and am going to Battle Creek. I expect to be stronger than ever.[131]

He took a sabbatical in 1951 to rest and quietly checked himself into the sanatorium at Battle Creek, Michigan, for an extended stay. John Rawlings believed that Norris had a series of strokes and that "several of them, apparently, had injured his mind, and I don't think he was the J. Frank Norris of 20s, 30s, and early 40s" in his later years. His communicational abilities began to show signs of "forgetfulness and incoherence."[132] A few months later, and a few weeks before his death, he wrote Luther Peak, telling him of a recent doctor's visit in which the doctor confirmed "the diagnosis that I have Parkins [sic] disease."[133]

Sickly and growing weaker, Norris continued to preach at every opportunity. On a warm August day in 1952, Homer Ritchie drove Norris to Meacham Field in Fort Worth, where he was flying to a preaching engagement at a youth camp in North Florida. Ritchie recalls

Norris had only $1.75 in his pocket: "I had $21.00 and I gave it to him, watched him slowly walk up the steps to the plane, disappear inside, and I was the last one in Fort Worth to see him alive."[134]

The great pastor died alone in a small motel room outside of Jacksonville on Wednesday, August 20, 1952. The next Sunday, Homer Ritchie stood in Norris's pulpit, preached from the biblical text "Moses, my servant, is dead," and the church called him as pastor just as Norris had earlier prophesied.

Two days after his death, Norris's body returned to Fort Worth by train, arriving at the old T&P train station downtown right on time, as Norris would have wanted it, at 8:45 a.m. The *Fort Worth Star-Telegram* reports, "J. Frank Norris came home Friday. The smiles and handshakes that usually greeted him when he stepped out of an airplane on his return from his many travels were missing. Instead there were muffled sobs and audible laments."[135] He was greeted by hundreds of mourners. When the plain box bearing his body emerged from the baggage cart, pulled by a crying baggage carrier, the crowd began to sing hymns.[136]

Undertaker Guy Thompson personally met Norris at the train station and took him to his funeral home on Eighth Avenue, where he meticulously dressed the preacher in his blue suit, white shirt, and red tie. Lillian, his wife, requested a private funeral the day before the huge public memorial service at the church. There, at this private service, the family and a small circle of intimate friends spoke and prayed together. The evening before the larger funeral, Lillian fell in her home, broke her hip, and was unable to attend the church memorial. She never left the confines of her home again. In the ensuing months she died, and upon the family's request, Guy Thompson went to the home, prepared her body for burial there, and took her straight to the cemetery, where she was laid to rest alongside her husband in a private family graveside service.[137]

Upon Norris's death, the *Fort Worth Star-Telegram* editorialized him:

> The force of his personality was enormous. The controversies surrounding him were frequent and noisy. He had the faculty of binding his friends and followers to him with hoops of

steel, and the kindred quality of making implacable opponents, whom he always needled and sometimes frustrated. But deep in his character, whatever the controversies, was the spirit of a builder. He built in belief, in numbers and in stone. These monuments remain.[138]

In the end, even his son George, who had borne the biggest brunt of his father's wrath, attested:

The thing that highlights his memory to me was how he could sweep himself to veritable mountain peaks. I remember a man sorely hurt under the stress of great conflicts. I can see him as he brought his family around him and with a broken heart would tell his wife and four children, "I have erred, I have sinned against God—have mercy on me." The name of J. Frank Norris will bring mixed reactions to different groups, but at the peak of my memory, I remember that man as a man who yearned for lost souls, "I'd rather have the souls that these hands have baptized than all the riches of the world. I would rather have the certainty that God wanted me to preach than any office in the world."[139]

Homer Ritchie, recalling Norris's death more than fifty years later, said:

He, arguably, was one of, if not *the*, greatest preacher of the twentieth century. He had the boldness of Melanchthon or Luther or any of the Reformers. He also preached through tears. He was a powerful defender of the truth. He never wavered. Contrary to what many thought, he had a very compassionate heart. He wept when he preached and when he counseled, and the people wept with him.

Then, true to his own balance and character, Ritchie added, "But there was a streak of meanness and vindictiveness in him which went beyond description and caused enormous problems, displeasure, and hurt with those who crossed him."[140]

3

George W. Truett:
The Eternal Optimist

George W. Truett, the polar opposite of J. Frank Norris in almost every sense, served as pastor of the First Baptist Church of Dallas from 1897 to 1944. Truett lived a life of character and integrity, and his ministry stood above his peers. Tall and stately in frame, he kept himself above the fray of disputes of all kinds. His life was consistently characterized by dignity, integrity, and all those other virtues for which good men strive.

Early Life

On May 6, 1867, George Washington Truett entered the world in a rural farmhouse in Clay County, North Carolina, as the seventh child of Charles and Mary Truett. The family resided on a two-hundred-fifty-acre farm just two miles west of the mountain village of Hayesville. The Truetts farmed half the land for crops, and the other half was mountainous, so young Truett's boyhood was spent cutting down trees, splitting rails to make fence posts, and preparing the timber logs to be taken to the local saw mill. These activities were in addition to his other chores: tending to the wheat and hay crops and feeding and caring for hogs, sheep, and a few cattle.

Even in those nineteenth-century days, Charles and Mary valued their children's education. For ten years, young George made a four-mile roundtrip walk to attend the Hayesville Academy with his siblings. Truett became obsessed with reading, devouring every book and periodical to which he had access. By his early teens, he was well-versed in the writings of many preachers of his day, including John Broadus, James Boyce, Charles Spurgeon, and Dwight Moody.[1]

Even from childhood, Truett's presence and demeanor made lasting impressions upon those with whom he came in contact. His mountain neighbors knew him as "that big-faced boy of Charlie Truett."[2] His authorized biographer and son-in-law, Powhatan James, said:

> He has an open face, an Anglo-Saxon face, a balanced face with strength in every feature. It is a handsome face because it is so well proportioned. In repose, he is serious and even stern, but when his blue-gray eyes light up with laughter and his lips lift into a smile, his true character shows forth.[3]

Throughout his adolescence, young George saw his need for a Savior, but not until he turned nineteen did he make what he referred to as the "supreme decision" of his life.[4] The next morning, alone with his mother at the breakfast table, he told her of a soliloquy he had had with himself the evening before:

> What if Christ should now come visibly into this room and put you to this question: "Are you willing for Me to have My way with your life, from this time on? I will not indicate to you what that way is to be—it is enough for you to know that My way is always right and safe and best. May I have your consent, without evasion for reservation, to have My way with you now and always?" To such tests I gave my unreserved, "Yes," and a great peace filled my heart.[5]

Upon his conversion, he publicly expressed his Christian faith to the assembled church and was joyfully received as a candidate for baptism and church membership.

The School Teacher

Upon his graduation from Hayesville Academy, Truett set out to start a school of his own. He named his new school the Hiawassee Academy and planted it in Towns County, Georgia. In a short time, enrollment exploded to three hundred students, becoming the talk of that entire mountain region. In spring 1888, the annual meeting of the state convention of Baptists in Georgia met in the town of Marietta. The moderator of the meeting called upon young Truett to come to the platform, saying to the assembled crowd, "This is George Truett. He can speak like Spurgeon. George, tell them what the Lord has done for you and what you are trying to do up in the mountains."[6] His presence and passion immediately captured their attention. Within moments the people became mesmerized by his voice and vocabulary and began to weep. J. B. Hawthorne, one of the great pulpiteers in America and pastor of the historic First Baptist Church in Atlanta, was seated among the crowd. He later said:

> I have heard Henry Ward Beecher and Phillips Brooks and others of the world's famous speakers, but never in all my life has my soul been more deeply stirred by any speaker than it was that day in Marietta by that boy out of the mountains. My heart burned within me, and I could not keep back my tears.[7]

The Move to Texas

In 1889, Charlie Truett heard reports of the rich fertile farmland in north Texas. He sold his unprofitable farm in North Carolina and headed west. Young George Truett followed his parents, and they settled in Whitewright, Texas, just south of the Red River.

Soon after their arrival, they joined the local Baptist church, and before long George became the Sunday school superintendent and an occasional preacher in the Sunday services. However, feeling completely unfit for ministry, he refused to preach behind the pulpit, taking his place on the floor in front of it. He achieved success for himself by starting another school in Whitewright, and things were going wonderfully for him until a special called meeting of the membership on a Saturday in 1890 to encourage him to enter the ministry.

No one, least of all Truett, knew what the meeting was about. Unexpectedly, the senior deacon arose from his seat, walked to the podium, and made a passionate speech. After a persuasive appeal as to the qualifications of young George Truett to the gospel ministry, he concluded his remarks by saying:

> There is such a thing as a church duty when the whole church must act. There is such a thing as an individual duty, when an individual, detached from every other individual, must face duty for himself; but it is my deep conviction, as it is yours—that this church has a church duty to perform, and that we have waited late and long to get about it. I move, therefore, that this church call a presbytery to ordain Brother George Truett to the full work of the gospel ministry.[8]

The motion took Truett by complete surprise. Before he could stand to protest the deacon's motion, someone seconded it.

"Wait six months," Truett pleaded.

"We can't wait six hours," they responded.[9]

After a sleepless night immersed in prayer, Truett accepted the will of the people, convinced the will of the Lord Himself was revealed through them. Soon thereafter, the church "set him aside" for the gospel ministry. A few weeks later, at age twenty-three, he preached his first official sermon, titled "Let There Be Light," at the First Baptist Church in Sherman, Texas. Remembering this event, Truett often recalled his text and exclaimed with a twinkle in his eye, "My own light went out in around ten minutes."[10]

The Baylor Years

Meanwhile, one hundred fifty miles to the south on the banks of the Brazos River, a stifling indebtedness was crippling Baylor University. B. H. Carroll was assigned the task of finding someone to lead a financial campaign to save the school and get it back on firm financial footing. A statewide call to prayer went out to all the Texas Baptist churches on behalf of the state's signal Baptist college. R. F. Jenkins, pastor of the Whitewright church, took this call to pray for Baylor to heart. The more Jenkins prayed, the more he became impressed to recommend young Truett to Carroll, even though he was still in his early twenties and a virtual unknown throughout the state of Texas at the time. Finally, acting on this gnawing inner impulse of his heart, he wrote to the legendary Carroll, saying, "There is one thing I know about George W. Truett— wherever he speaks, the people do what he asks them to do."[11]

In late fall 1890, during a preaching assignment in north Texas, Carroll met Truett. A bond immediately developed between the two men that lasted a lifetime, in spite of their quarter-century age difference. A short time later, Truett traveled to Waco, consumed with the awesome responsibility of traversing the entire state to raise large sums of money from the Baptist faithful in what Carroll and Truett began to call "the great battle to save Baylor."[12]

For most of the next two years, Truett journeyed from El Paso to Texarkana, from Brownsville to Amarillo, and many cities and towns in between. He preached everywhere and anywhere, often finding his pulpit in churches, associational meetings, civic rallies, county halls, and anywhere else the people would give him a hearing. He journeyed by train, on horseback, in buggies, and even by foot. For years Truett had been saving his money to attend college. In order to demonstrate his own commitment to those he asked for funds, he gave his entire savings of $500 to the Baylor cause. His lead gift built huge momentum around the state, and the campaign took on wings of its own.

However, the financial campaign experienced a number of challenges and concerns. In the middle of the campaign, with prospects of success looking somewhat discouraging, the young leader wrote to his mentor, Carroll, from Sulphur Springs, where he was speaking. In a letter dated February 18, 1891, Truett wrote, "I am continually cheered by the consciousness that I have your gracious counsel and your most fervent sympathies and prayers. The Lord helping me, I will do my very best for His own glory and leave every result to Him. The one impulse of my heart is to do His will."[13] These four one-syllable words became the theme of Truett's life—"Thy will be done."[14]

While at home, Truett spent his time writing countless letters encouraging various individuals he had met around the state to give to Baylor. S. P. Brooks, who later became president of Baylor from 1902 to 1931, was enrolled as a student at the university during the financial campaign to eliminate the debt. He recalled on many occasions seeing Truett in his office writing "hundreds of letters on behalf of the university."[15] By early 1893, twenty-three months into the campaign, Truett and Carroll had reached their goal of raising almost $100,000 to retire the debt.

Upon Truett handing Carroll the last check of $500, Carroll lifted his head toward heaven and said, "It is finished."[16] Truett wept.[17]

During the months of the financial campaign, Truett stayed in Carroll's home in Waco from time to time. As the months passed, his admiration for his mentor grew, leading him to often refer to Carroll as "the greatest personality I ever touched."[18] All the matchmakers in Waco, including Carroll, found themselves of one accord that Truett should meet young Josephine Jenkins, whose father, the greatly respected Judge W. H. Jenkins, was serving as the chairman of the board of trustees at Baylor. After the huge success of the financial campaign, Truett and Josephine began to spend considerable time in one another's company. Over time they fell deeply in love with one another. They married on June 24, 1894, at the First Baptist Church in Waco, with Dr. Carroll officiating. This began fifty golden years of love and life together.

Truett enrolled in Baylor University and began his studies toward his bachelor's degree. During this time, the East Waco Baptist Church called him to become their pastor, and membership and attendance doubled in the few years of his student pastorate there. He was fond of saying that he found "the shepherd's heart" during these years of work and study.[19]

The Move to Dallas

In 1897, the First Baptist Church in Dallas was in search of a new pastor. The pulpit committee was in the capable and trustworthy hands of W. L. Williams, one of the church's founding members. Williams sought the advice of the respected editor of the *Baptist Standard*, J. B. Cranfill. Without hesitation Cranfill replied, "I think George W. Truett of Waco is your man."[20] Other men of stature in Texas, including B. H. Carroll and J. B. Gambrell, followed suit with glowing recommendations. Through the summer, letters of encouragement flooded Truett's post office box from Dallas church members and outstanding citizens of the city at large.

On August 4, 1897, the church voted seventy-four to three in favor of calling Truett as pastor,[21] so, at age thirty, George W. Truett became pastor of the First Baptist Church in Dallas. His youthful enthusiasm coupled with a wisdom and maturity beyond his years gave him instant appeal with the people. He and Josephine were welcomed into one of the most established and notable churches in the state with a stately, brand-new, and beautiful sanctuary that serves the congregation still today. His starting salary was $1,800 a year—quite a sum in those days! In fact, the salary represented over half of the entire annual contributions of the church.

When Truett assumed the pastorate, the church had debt of $12,000 and no provision or real plan for its elimination. The church had a longstanding policy that no special offerings could be taken for missions, benevolences, building funds, or the like. These needs were to be supplied from the regular tithes and offerings through a percentage basis. Truett found this policy unacceptable. He flatly told the church, "I must be free to take special offerings whenever the need for them appears. If I am to become your pastor, then you must agree that I can be free to present an appeal for missions and benevolence wherever the denomination program calls for it."[22]

Somewhat reluctant, the church acquiesced, and in a short period of time news came that a man, not even a member of the church, had died and left his property to the church. When the property was liquidated, the church received a check for $12,800, which paid off the debt and left a hefty sum for local church ministry.[23] Truett and the First Baptist Church were off and running on a forty-seven-year partnership that did not end until his death.

Immediately, the people of Dallas accepted their new pastor with waves of optimism and expectancy filling the atmosphere of every worship service. Crowds swelled and new members joined the church in growing numbers. As the coming years unfolded, the reputation of the pastor and church extended far beyond Dallas; it was a nationally known ministry. For a period of time, the church was the largest in the world . . . until its numbers were eclipsed in the 1920s by the ever-present J. Frank Norris at the First Baptist Church in Fort Worth. In 1919, membership in the First Baptist Church in Dallas stood at 3,036.[24] The same year, on September 12, at the tenth anniversary of Norris's pastorate in Fort Worth, the local newspaper reported "total attendance for the day was more than 12,000 with at least two thousand turned away and two hundred converts were added to the church."[25]

According to Trevin Wax of the Gospel Coalition, by 1924, First Baptist Church in Fort Worth was the "largest Protestant church in America."[26] By 1928, Norris's numbers had doubled those of Truett's in Dallas. The Fort Worth congregation numbered more than twelve thousand members, in contrast to the Dallas membership of a little more than six thousand the same year.[27] Numerically speaking, not until the height of the Criswell years in the 1950s and 1960s would the church in Dallas regain its stature as the largest in the country.[28]

A Deep and Abiding Sorrow

If coming to Dallas was a defining moment in the great pastor's life, what happened in his second year of ministry at First Baptist proved to be even more so.

What began as a relaxing getaway for J. C. Arnold and his new pastor ended in a life-altering tragedy for them both. Arnold, formerly a captain in the famed Texas Rangers, had for nearly twenty-five years been serving as the Dallas Police Chief and was a faithful member of the First Baptist Church. He invited his new pastor on a two-day quail hunting trip to Johnson County. On February 3, 1898, the two men traveled by train to Cleburne, where they were met by George W. Baines, pastor of the Baptist church in Cleburne and uncle of Lyndon Baines Johnson, future president of the United States. From the train station, the trio of friends traveled by horse and carriage to a farm eight miles outside Cleburne, near the small community of Venus. They hunted with little success that afternoon and the following morning. On the afternoon of February 4, they headed from the field to the farmhouse to hitch up the carriage for their return to Cleburne. Truett walked behind Arnold along a beaten path. As the pastor was shifting his shotgun from one arm to the other, the weapon accidentally discharged twice, striking the police chief in the back of his right calf.

Upon hearing the shot, Baines ran from the house to the scene. Using his leather suspenders as a tourniquet, he was able to stop the bleeding. A doctor was called to the farm and dressed the captain's wound.

On Saturday morning, February 5, Baines accompanied his friends to Dallas, arriving by train at 8:00 a.m. Arnold settled into his home, where his local physician tended to him. However, that evening at 8:10, Captain J. C. Arnold died of coronary thrombosis, most likely brought on by the stress of the accident. The news of Arnold's death devastated Truett as well as the entire city of Dallas.[29]

Even though everyone ruled it an accident, Truett was devastated. He castigated himself for his "carelessness and his inexcusable awkwardness."[30] In the ensuing days he paced the floor, not eating or sleeping, and finding no comfort. Repeatedly, he said to his wife, Josephine, "I will never preach again. I could never stand again in the pulpit."[31] His parents came from Whitewright, as well as Judge and Mrs. Jenkins from Waco, seeking to comfort him but to no avail. The families prayed and wept together, and finally, the night after Arnold's funeral, Truett slept.[32]

That night Truett had a recurring dream, the content of which was not publicly revealed until 1939.[33] He woke Josephine from her sleep to tell her he had seen the Lord Jesus standing alongside his bed looking at him. With a tender voice, the Lord said to him, "Be not afraid. You are my man from here on."[34] This same vivid dream awoke him three times in rapid succession. This great tragedy, along with this accompanying dream, proved to be the turning point in Truett's life.

Frank B. Spangler, in attendance the day Truett returned to the Sunday pulpit for the first time, described the scene this way:

> His face was drawn and his eyes were so sad. When he stood to preach, he remained silent for a long moment. You could have heard a pin drop. When he began, somehow he sounded differ-ent. His voice! I shall never forget his voice that morning as we heard for the first time the note of sadness and pathos which later we came to know so well. It seemed to carry the burden of all the grief in the world.[35]

Though some in Dallas found the explanation of the vision hard to believe, Truett never doubted it and was never the same again. He had seen the Lord, and he rested upon His promise.

In the aftermath of this great tragedy, invitations abounded for Truett to leave Dallas and find a new beginning of ministry elsewhere. The very next year he was invited to become the president of Baylor University. In 1901, the First Baptist Church in Waco invited him to follow his mentor, B. H. Carroll. Other invitations came regularly, but Truett stayed where God had placed him, touching the world from the Dallas pulpit over the next four decades.

The Hayden Controversy

During the early years of Truett's Dallas ministry, he found himself in a controversy not of his own making. This conflict, one of the few contro-versies of his life that could not be blamed on J. Frank Norris, involved Samuel Hayden, editor of the widely circulated *Texas Baptist Herald* weekly tabloid. The controversial Hayden never shied away from a good fight and seemed to live in constant fear that he might miss one. He possessed an extremely combative disposition and lived for controversy, which served to keep him and his paper in the public view.[36]

Hayden, in an unprecedented attack in 1896, accused J. B. Cranfill, then treasurer of Texas home mission work, of embezzling money from the state convention funds. A convention inquiry and an accompanying investigation showed no grounds for such claims. The convention of Texas Baptists asked Hayden to withdraw his charges. Instead of doing so, Hayden stepped up his attack on Cranfill and other convention leaders with continued innuendo, filled with sarcasm and ridicule.

Texas Baptist leaders lost their patience. Truett took the matter personally. The even-keeled Truett lost patience, fearing that Hayden's continued attacks would irreparably damage Texas missions. When the annual convention met in San Antonio in 1897, the state convention refused Hayden a seat as a messenger. Several leaders, including the state board chairman, W. H. Jenkins (Truett's father-in-law) along with Truett, signed a resolution directed at his exclusion. Truett publicly read the resolution of exclusion on the convention floor. The following conventions in Waco (1898) and Dallas (1899) also refused to seat Hayden. The Baptist General Convention of Texas (BGCT) finally and decisively removed him from the fellowship of Texas Baptists in Dallas by a vote of 1,181 to 557.[37]

Samuel Hayden responded by filing multiple lawsuits against Truett, Cranfill, and other leaders, totaling over $100,000. Over six grueling years, four trials, several appeals, and two hung juries, the matter persisted until finally reaching the Texas Supreme Court in 1904.[38] In 1905, Cranfill put an end to the case by agreeing that his party would pay damages. This decision cost Truett several hundred dollars.[39] In the aftermath of the decision, and in true Truett form, he enlisted several men who helped Cranfill fulfill his financial obligations from the extended litigation.

Hayden's strident fundamentalism and caustic attacks had a profound effect on Truett and prepared him for the relentless conflicts and confrontations with J. Frank Norris that were still to come. Norris, unlike Hayden, developed a massive and loyal following and was a force to be reckoned with for the remainder of Truett's life.

A National Prominence

Two events catapulted George W. Truett onto the national scene and made him a household name among Christians in the United States. The first came in 1918 when President Woodrow Wilson requested that Truett spend a few months encouraging and preaching to the United States Armed Forces battling the Germans in the European theater. Truett readily accepted his nation's call to "preach to the soldiers in the camps and in the blood-sodden trenches beyond the Atlantic."[40]

On July 31, 1919, Truett sailed from New York to England, eventually headed for the battlefields of Europe. He wrote in his diary, "The German Bastille must fall. . . . The Am [sic] people have their minds made up about this war, and they unhesitatingly believe that our Allied Armies are God's instruments to right the greatest wrong in all human history."[41] Truett doubtless believed that the war was just and must be won at all costs.

In October, he arrived in France. For several weeks he spoke to the troops in the camps, in mess halls, and out in the trenches, as close to the front lines as chaplains were allowed to venture. The war revealed Truett's true human spirit. He lived in the primitive camps with the men, ate their food with them, got wet and cold alongside them, and slogged through the mud and freezing winter temperatures to minister to them. He saw more than his share of suffering and death and wrote repeatedly in his diary of the "horribleness of war" and "the awful desolation of war on every hand."[42] Truett wrote in his diary daily and never closed a day without writing a letter to Josephine. On January 8, 1919, near the end of a particularly hard and bitterly cold day, he wrote, "My thoughts and heart turn homeward, with inexpressible yearning. God be gracious to my loved ones, giving them every needed mercy. And to the church, making my very absence to fall out for their best good."[43] The personal tone of his letters to Josephine reveals his commitment to his loving marriage relationship.

George Truett sailed for New York on January 31, 1920. He arrived in Dallas by train, and a crowd of city officials and church members welcomed him home, grateful to God for answering their prayers for his safe return. The fact that the distinguished and statesman-like Truett left the comforts and confines of home and hearth, family and friends, in order to live with the ploughboys of the infantry in the muddy trenches of a faraway war zone, did more to thrust him into national prominence and appreciation, legitimizing his ministry more than anything else had.

The second event that led to Truett's fame was his famous address on religious liberty, delivered on the steps of the United States Capitol in 1920. In the midst of the early challenges of the 75 Million Campaign, Southern Baptists were in need of a word of encouragement as they gathered in the nation's capital for their annual meeting in May 1920. Truett was chosen to represent the Baptist faithful in delivering a major address on religious liberty. He rose to the occasion. Fifteen thousand people gathered outdoors to hear his address from the east steps of the United States Capitol. The crowd was a who's who of American dignitaries, including Supreme Court justices, military leaders, cabinet officials, members of the Congress and Senate, ambassadors, and thousands of Baptist faithful who had traveled to Washington, DC, for the annual convention. Robert Coleman led the crowd in singing "My Country 'Tis of Thee," followed by several hymns, including "Rescue the Perishing" and "My Faith Looks Up to Thee."[44]

J. B. Gambrell introduced Truett to the vast assembly. Gambrell later wrote about the event in a booklet of Truett's speech:

Since Paul spoke before Nero, no Baptist speaker ever pleaded the cause of truth in surroundings so dignified, impressive, and inspiring. The shadow of the capitol of the greatest and freest nation on earth, lately made so by the infiltration of Baptist ideas through the masses, fell on the vast assembly. . . . There was no trimming, no froth, and not one arrogant or offensive tone or word. It was a bold, fair, thorough-going setting out of the history and life principles of the people called Baptists. And then, logically and becomingly, the speaker brought the Baptist brethren to look forward and take up the burdens of liberty and fulfill its high moral obligations.[45]

Without the aid of a public address system and without notes or a teleprompter, Truett delivered the most famous address of his long and illustrious career. He spoke of the past, the present, and the future, and he emphasized that the foundation of all religious liberty is found in the absolute lordship of Jesus Christ. Truett spoke of the incomparable apostasy that resulted from church-state unions and warned against such in America's future. He viewed every state church on earth as a spiritual tyranny. Near the end of his remarks, he boldly proclaimed the exclusivity of Christ, stating that evangelism is the primary task of the church. He declared, "Salvation for sinners is through Jesus Christ alone, nor is there any other name or way under heaven whereby they may be saved."[46] Such declarative statements, delivered from the steps of the nation's capitol, seem unimaginable in today's crumbling culture.

This major address forever branded George W. Truett as the champion of the separation of church and state. In a strange bit of irony, his immediate pastoral successor, W. A. Criswell, would declare that "the concept of the separation of church and state is the figment of some infidel's imagination and brought about by a misapplication of Jefferson's letter to the Danbury Baptists."[47] First Baptist Church of Dallas's present pastor, Robert Jeffress, is equally convinced and has bluntly stated, "There's no such thing as the separation of church and state."[48]

While Truett's address on the separation of church and state expanded his fame, his approach can only be understood when viewed in the light of its historical context. In the 1920s, Southern Baptists were virtually blind to the reality of racial inequality. According to *D Magazine*, Truett's city of Dallas was the most racist city in America in the 1920s. At that time, the Dallas chapter of the Ku Klux Klan included one out of every three eligible men in the city and was the largest branch in the country.[49] The bulk of Dallas's Klan membership was made up of "Protestant churchmen, especially those with a more fundamentalist outlook."[50] J. M. Dawson, Truett's closest pastor friend and pastor of the First Baptist Church in Waco, spoke out boldly on the issue of race in spite of the reality that "nearly all the men in his church were members of the Klan."[51] Truett's own congregation contained members of the Klan, some of whom served on the deacon body. When the city finally took a public stand against this radical group with a statement in the local newspaper denouncing the Klan, most of the prominent leaders of the city added their names—with one glaring exception: the pastor of the First Baptist Church, George W. Truett. Dawson lamented "the silence of his peers" and expressed "disappointment in the silence of a particular friend."[52] Since Truett was well known for his warm relationship with Dawson, and because little record exists of Truett speaking out against the evils of racial hatred, people likely assumed that Dawson's "particular friend" was George W. Truett.

In Truett's religious liberty address, he spoke of Baptists being the "unwavering champions of liberty, both religious and civil." He continued, "Whoever believes in Christ as his personal Savior is our brother in the common salvation. . . . God wants free worshippers and no other kind."[53] Yet, even as those words escaped his lips, Blacks in Dallas were not allowed to be "free worshippers" within the membership of the First Baptist Church—and would not be until a full two decades after Truett's death.

Leon McBeth speaks of Will and Agnes, "a Negro couple who helped the Truetts for thirty-five years."[54] Agnes cooked and worked in the house, and Will took care of daily household chores, kept the Truett car in good repair, and served as a chauffeur. In their later years, Will's eyesight failed and Agnes fell into poor health. The Truetts kindly cared for them until their deaths. Nevertheless, Agnes and Will could not be members of the church, "free worshippers," where George W. Truett preached Sunday by Sunday.

Southern Baptists' sinful positions on race relations were certainly not confined to George Truett. Over in Fort Worth, J. Frank Norris and his First Baptist Church were known to be openly sympathetic to many of the policies of the local Ku Klux Klan. Norris alternately criticized and praised the Klan, often pitting them against the Catholic interests expressed in the Knights of Columbus, where he was convinced the real threat to Southern culture resided.[55] How otherwise great men could be publicly indifferent to such human indecencies is one of the imponderables of Almighty God. Throughout their ministries, neither Norris nor Truett expressed outrage over the sins of racial hatred, while often speaking out loudly against social ills such as alcohol, gambling, and the violation of Sunday laws. Joseph J. Davis lists the most visible Texas Baptist supporters of racial reconciliation in the twentieth century, which include J. M. Dawson and T. B. Maston—but not George W. Truett or J. Frank Norris.[56]

The Wise Builder

Building proved the greatest of all of Truett's attributes and lasting accolades. He built things that lasted. He built a great church. He started other churches in Dallas, such as Gaston Avenue Baptist Church and Cliff Temple Baptist Church, which grew into megachurches in their own right. The *Baptist Standard,* the Baptist General Convention of Texas, Baylor Medical Center, the Relief and Annuity Board of the Southern Baptist Convention, Buckner Orphan's Home, and many other organizations all have one thing in common: George Truett was a vital factor in their founding or development. He served on the boards of each of these entities and helped raise vast sums of money for their support.[57] His signal part in the founding of two of them, Baylor Medical Center and the Relief and Annuity Board, has changed the lives of millions of people over the past century.

The modern and far-reaching ministry of the Baylor Hospital System found its roots in the mind of Truett, and his shadow still permeates every square foot of its sprawling reach. In 1903, the world-renowned Austrian physician Adolf Lorenz visited Dallas at the invitation of local physician Charles Rosser to hold clinics on his famous manipulation technique, which replaced surgery to correct congenital joint and bone deformities. On May 23, the city of Dallas honored Lorenz at a large banquet held at the Oriental Hotel on Commerce Street. Among the Dallas dignitaries invited to speak at the gala event was George Truett.[58]

In his address, Truett said, "Whatever makes for the betterment of the race has its origins in Christianity. The Christianity of the Divine Physician does not stop at bandages and medicine but takes the sufferer to a hospital where every attention, care, and kindness may be bestowed." Then, he closed his address with the following, resulting in a large and appreciative ovation:

> With our magnificently growing city, with our young though promising medical school, with our splendidly equipped medical profession, I raise this question: Is it not time to begin the erection of a great humanitarian hospital, one to which men of all creeds and those of none may come with equal confidence?[59]

Colonel C. C. Slaughter, the greatest cattle baron the world had ever seen and a deacon at the First Baptist Church, was seated in the audience that evening. At the conclusion of the banquet, he sought out his pastor and said, "I will give the first $50,000 toward the building of a hospital such as you've described in our city of Dallas."[60] Truett, buoyed by Slaughter's gift, helped raise additional funds, and Baylor Medical Center became a reality in the city of Dallas. Shortly after Truett's death in 1944, additional funds were raised to build another tower as an addition to the hospital, which is called the Truett Memorial Hospital to this day.

What Truett started eventually became the Baylor Scott and White Health System, one of the largest health systems in the United States. It includes forty-eight individual hospitals, more than nine hundred patient care sites, more than six thousand active physicians, and more than forty thousand employees.[61] Truett described it as "a great humanitarian hospital, one to which men of all creeds and those of none may come with equal confidence." The large shadow of George W. Truett continues to cast itself over every patient who comes through the admitting offices of the Baylor system and over every square foot of its vast and sprawling campuses.

One of Truett's many lasting legacies was born in the heart of a Tennessee pastor, Dr. William Lunsford. Lunsford was born in Virginia on May 22, 1859. As a young man, he set off to "Mr. Jefferson's University," the University of Virginia, to study law. After earning his law degree, he settled in Roanoke and over the years established a successful law practice and was elected mayor of the city.[62] At the height of his professional aspirations, Lunsford began to feel the Lord had other plans for him and was calling him to enter the gospel ministry. He left his law practice and enrolled at the Southern Baptist Theological Seminary in Louisville, where he earned a degree in theology. This was followed by successful pastorates in Asheville, North Carolina; Waco, Texas; and Nashville, Tennessee.[63]

Lunsford was pastoring in Nashville during the days of the First World War. He watched as young men returned from the war—lame, some maimed for life, others dead—and took note of how the United States government was caring for their needs. Lunsford felt a burden for the increasing number of aged pastors and their wives and widows who had spent their lives serving smaller churches in out-of-the-way places with little pay, ending up destitute in their declining years. He brought the issue before a Nashville pastor's conference, expressing his passion about somehow taking care of these old "soldiers of the cross" and asking who was going to care for them.[64] The answer was obvious—no one.

Lunsford called upon George Truett, whom he had befriended during his days of pastoring his Waco congregation, and he shared this burden with him. Truett immediately moved into action, contacting his friend John D. Rockefeller in New York. Lunsford and Truett traveled by train to New York for what proved to be one of the most God-led appointments for the betterment of the lives of hundreds of thousands of pastors and church workers over the years to come. After hearing Lunsford so passionately share the burden for these pastors in need,

Rockefeller opened his heart and his wallet to them. Over the next two years, 1918 to 1920, he transferred one million dollars' worth of stock in his Standard Oil Company to seed the ministry of the Relief and Annuity Board of the Southern Baptist Convention, known as GuideStone Financial Resources today. Lunsford resigned his pastorate, moved to Dallas, and established the first SBC entity west of the Mississippi River. Truett served as a member of the board of trustees until his death in 1944.

Lunsford launched the ministry of the new SBC board with this promise to the pastors: "Give yourself wholeheartedly to the work. We'll stand back of you. If you fall in the work, we'll care for you; if you die, we will not allow your family to suffer. If you grew old in the work, we'll comfort you in your declining years."[65] Today, more than one hundred years later, due to the energies and efforts of George W. Truett and William Lunsford, GuideStone Financial Resources has kept its founder's promise. GuideStone has grown to become the largest Christian-screened mutual fund in the world, with assets under management approaching $20 billion, serving more than a quarter of a million individual participants with their retirement and benefit service needs. True to its founder's vision, Mission: Dignity, the relief arm of GuideStone, distributes over $10 million annually to those pastors, their wives, and their widows living near the poverty level.

Biographers and historians have said that among George W. Truett's greatest attributes was his keen ability not only to envision new and innovative ministries, but also to inspire the masses to adopt his vision and see it come to fruition. He built things, and the things he built have lasted over several generations.

The Latter Years

Over the course of his forty-seven-and-a-half-year ministry at the First Baptist Church in Dallas, George Truett had the unqualified and near-unanimous support of the church. He was, arguably, among the most respected citizens of the city of Dallas. He maintained a spotless reputation, and his character remained beyond reproach. The two people from whom Truett gained strength and to whom he was fully committed and indebted were his wife, Josephine, and his partner in ministry, Robert Coleman.

More than just a life partner, Josephine served as his life protector as well. The Truett home was completely harmonious and happy largely due to her dedication and devotion to "Georgie," as she affectionately called him. After their three daughters were grown, Josephine gave herself completely to Truett. In addition to her wifely duties, she served as his "chauffeur, business manager, social secretary, and a general barrier against unnecessary interruptions and irritations. She sought in every possible way to release her husband from all minor worries that he might devote himself to his ministry."[66]

During his declining years as he became progressively ill, she became his food taster, tasting every morsel of food herself before allowing him to indulge. "The stately, dignified Dr. Truett would simply sit quietly until Josephine had conducted her culinary examinations. He would then look at her, as unobtrusively as possible, and she would indicate what he could eat and what he was not to touch."[67] Truett believed that "raw" milk was more nutritious than pasteurized milk. Therefore, Josephine made sure the Truetts had a cow in the backyard from which he could drink his fill of milk straight from the source each and every morning.[68] When he traveled, she was with him. Like a loving hen on her nest, Josephine Truett cared for her husband every moment of every day until he breathed his last breath.

By the time Robert Coleman joined the First Baptist Church in Dallas in 1901, he had already enjoyed several successful careers. By the age of thirty-two, he had owned and operated a drug store, worked in a bank, edited a small-town newspaper, and managed a YMCA facility. In 1903, at the invitation of Dr. Truett, he became the assistant pastor of the church. For the next four decades he would serve the pastor and the church with excellence and integrity. Coleman's specialty was music, and he was "without doubt the Baptist's greatest song leader of his generation."[69] Although he was the perennial song leader at the annual meetings of the Baptist General Convention of Texas and the SBC, he was at his best when leading the worship music at First Baptist before Truett preached. On the side, he was an extremely successful publisher and entrepreneur. Over the course of his life he published more than thirty different hymnals and songbooks that sold into the countless millions of copies.[70]

Though vastly different, Truett and Coleman remained fiercely loyal to one another. Greatly adept in business matters, Coleman became a valued teammate of the pastor. Coleman handled the administration of the church, and Truett tended to the spiritual dimension. Coleman out-lived Truett by eighteen months, just enough time to provide a smooth transition to the new pastor, who was destined to lead the church to its greatest glory for the next half century, W. A. Criswell.

Truett spoke so often and accepted so many varied and sundry invitations that it is said he averaged preaching or speaking once a day for more than forty years.[71] This began to take its toll in the latter years of his Dallas ministry as the church sank into a steady decline. Over the entire course of almost fifty years of his ministry at First Baptist, Truett was absent from the city of Dallas an astounding 40 percent of the time.[72] He gave himself to the evangelical world beyond the doors of his own church. He served as president of the Southern Baptist Convention (1927–1929) and as president of the Baptist World Alliance (1934–1939).

Truett's diary entries from the early 1940s often contain notations of his preaching to "vast throngs" at the church services in Dallas.[73] However, observers who were there noted that the lower floor was never full and the two balconies were empty.[74] Leon McBeth observes that in Truett's latter years the "church had become staid . . . their program became structured primarily to mature adults. . . . Most of the dea-cons were over sixty years of age . . . the staff . . . though loyal . . . was advanced in age."[75]

Over the last twenty years of Truett's pastorate, the church con-tinued to sink into the quagmire of a steady decline; the older people were dying, and Truett's inability to reach and attract new generations for Christ became more and more apparent. In his later years, Truett "tended to gloss over problem areas in the church . . . [R]ather than respond to the church's inability to attract younger couples, Truett merely resigned himself to the role of the status quo and ministered to his own aging congregation."[76] The problem resulted in his failure to maintain the status quo, and the church continued year after year in a steady decline. Sunday school enrollment in 1926 stood at almost seven thousand; by Truett's death in 1944 it had fallen into the three thousands.[77]

Upon accepting the pastorate of the church in October 1944, young Criswell took a private tour of the church property. He found the sanctuary to be one of the most beautiful preaching centers anywhere, but the buildings that housed the Sunday schools and other ministries of the church spoke volumes of the church's long decline. In his own words:

> [W]hen I walked out of the sanctuary, the whole world changed. The first room I entered was dark, dank, and dusty. There were signs that children met there for Sunday school. A few rather primitive pictures of Bible times were pinned haphazardly to the walls. An old flannelgraph had remnants of last Sunday's lesson clinging to its stained and wrinkled surface. The room was a mess, and even when I switched on the lights, the place was dark and rather grim. With the help of a custodian I went from room to empty room, unlocking doors that had been closed for a quarter of a century, or so it seemed, dusty rooms filled with old furniture stacked against the walls and piles of outdated Sunday school materials and unread Baptist papers.[78]

Criswell said the first few months he felt like he was "preaching to wood." He said, "I looked out over the lower floor from the pulpit and all I saw was wood, the wooden backs of one empty pew after another. I just preached to wood. I looked up into the balcony and all I saw was wood, the empty wooden backs of the seats in an empty balcony."[79]

And in Death

During the spring of 1938, Truett became ill and was out of the pulpit for an extended period of Sundays. He recovered and continued much of his travels as president of the Baptist World Alliance. Then again in 1941, an undiagnosed sickness caused him to miss the majority of Sundays in his home pulpit. In late 1943, he became seriously ill in what would be his final fight. While the family released no official medical diagnosis, his niece Josephine Nash reports that the sickness that finally confined him to his home was

> . . . a form of bone cancer that afflicted his left thigh leaving him in excruciating pain. Uncle George seemed to have a stigma about anyone hearing he had cancer, so we kept it quiet. To complicate the matter, he was allergic to any of the pain medication and spent his last months, day and night, in constant and excruciating pain.[80]

The family drew the circle closer in the final weeks. No one was given admittance to the Truett home except his doctor, his family, and, of course, Bob Coleman.

In winter 1944, the great pastor took a radical turn for the worse. Periodically, he would preach to his gathered Sunday morning congregation from his home via a special telephone hook-up. Then a particular Sunday came when he had rallied enough strength to return to his pulpit for what would be his last public moment with the people who had been his life and love for almost half of a century.

His longtime, faithful deacon, A. B. Tanco, relates the scene of Truett's last sermon with a photographic memory of minute detail—although almost fifty years removed from the moment. Remembering this high hour, Tanco says:

> We had not seen the pastor in over three months due to his home confinement. Everyone knew this would be the last time the great George W. Truett would speak to us from his pulpit. The service had begun and, in the course of a congregational

hymn, Truett entered the sanctuary through one of the choir doors. After the conclusion of the singing a noticeable hush swept over the entire congregation as gently, with the aid of a walking cane, he slowly made his way to his pulpit chair.

We all wanted to somehow express our love to him in a tangible way. Someone, rather softly, began to clap and then the entire congregation broke out in a loud and long applause as we all stood to our feet. The pastor never approved of applause in the worship service, but that morning a broad and appreciative smile swept over his face. He preached a powerful sermon and then the choir began to sing the invitation hymn, "He Leadeth Me." After the singing of the first two verses, the pastor raised his arms and the music stopped. Slowly and haltingly, with cane in one hand and Bible in the other, he descended the platform steps and in the holy hush of the moment, standing beneath his pulpit, he quoted the last verse of the hymn—"And when my task on earth is done, when by Thy grace the victory is won, even death's cold wave I shall not flee, since God through Jordan leadeth me." Then, without another word, he turned and walked out the side door. And those were the last words George W. Truett, our great pastor and friend, ever spoke in that room.[83]

At the monthly meeting of the church deacons on July 5, 1944, Coleman reported to the men the seriousness of Truett's condition and how, by all human appearances, he was near the end of his earthly sojourn. Two days later, at precisely 11:50 p.m., Truett died. The July 10 funeral was one of the most widely attended in the history of Dallas. City flags were flown at half-mast as the entire city mourned the death. County and city employees were given time off on the day of the funeral. District and county judges closed their courts early as they gathered to pay their last respects to this giant of a man who often said, "I fear not death. Oh, what a wonderful thing it will be to be face to face with my Maker!"[84]

The funeral was directed by Bob Coleman. Louie D. Newton, former president of the Southern Baptist Convention and a lifelong friend of Truett's, of Atlanta, Georgia, delivered the main message. A three-mile-long procession of cars followed the hearse to Grove Hill Cemetery, where years earlier Truett and Coleman had bought adjoining plots for themselves and their wives. Through the years they had made it a well-known fact within the church that their life wishes were, having shared their lives in ministry for forty years, to remain by each other's side even in death. At the graveside, Bob Coleman had the final word. With tears streaming down his cheeks, he quoted Mark Twain's eulogy for his daughter, Susan:

Warm summer sun, shine brightly here.
Gentle southern breeze, blow softly here.
Green sod above, lie light, lie light.
Good night, great heart, good night.
We'll see you in the morning.[85]

The mourners returned to their cars and back to their lives, leaving the physical remains of their beloved pastor behind to await the resurrection. The words of one of his previous sermons must have been echoing through their minds:

You shall hear someday that the preacher before you is dead. Oh, no! His tongue will be quiet, his lips will be still, his heart will have ceased its beating, but he will be alive—more alive than he is now, more alive than he has ever been in this world! He will have gone from this life; he will be where the conditions of life are perfect because God gives those who trust Him eternal life.[86]

Just three short summer months after Truett's death, the church called W. A. Criswell as pastor. Criswell was thirty-four. After completing his PhD at Southern Seminary, he had enjoyed successful pastorates in Chickasha and Muskogee, Oklahoma. Identified as the pastoral antithesis of George Truett, young and full of enthusiasm, he stood in sharp contrast to what the church had known for the last several years under their aged and sick pastor. Criswell was a premillennialist. Truett was postmillennial. Criswell preached expository sermons, verse by verse, digging deep into the text and making use of the biblical languages of Hebrew and Greek. On the other hand, Truett was a topical, textual preacher who seldom dealt with the text at hand in any depth but carried the day with his presence, voice, and ability to use his words to hold people in rapt attention. Criswell was expressive, moving from one side of the pulpit to the other, using violent hand and arm gestures and raising his voice in loud inflections. Truett was stoic in the pulpit, almost never gestured, and seldom smiled. Not long afterward, the "wood" that Criswell lamented preaching to each Sunday was filled with new, young families captivated by the dynamic preaching ability of the new pastor of the First Baptist Church. In his first year, 888 happy new members joined First Baptist, the largest number in any single year in the church's long and illustrious history.[87]

Leon McBeth reports that Mrs. Truett "died in 1956 at the Live Oak home at the age of eighty-four, loyal to the last to the First Baptist Church and its new pastor, Dr. Criswell."[88] Unfortunately, McBeth misrepresents "her loyalty." In public and in print, Criswell always honored the Truetts and spoke highly of Mrs. Truett. However, in private, another story often emerged among his closer confidants.[89] Whether motivated by her intense desire to continue to be his protector even in death, by the sheer optimism that flooded the church over its new pastor, or by some other factor, Mrs. Truett began to subtly undermine Criswell to some of the Truett loyalists within the church. In an interview in 1994, Criswell stated:

> After a while it began to be reported to me that Mrs. Truett was criticizing some of the changes that I was implementing in the church. She ceased speaking to Betty and found an accomplice in Deacon Car P. Collins. Collins picked up her mantle and began to publicly challenge me on several fronts.
>
> Judge Ryburn, God forever bless that sweet man, was our longtime chairman of deacons. Car Collins went to him, invoking

Mrs. Truett's name, and laid out many grievances against me, most finding their origins, I strongly suspect, in Mrs. Truett. Judge Ryburn gave Collins an ultimatum, "Car, he said, we are behind our new preacher so you can do one of two things. You can get in or you can get out."

No one had ever talked to Car P. Collins like that before. Why, he was the most influential business man in the whole city, powerful, and used to always getting his way. So Car P. Collins got out. He left our church and joined the Park Cities Baptist Church and that beautiful building you see on Northwest Highway today came about through the major gift of Car P. Collins.[90]

According to Joel Gregory, Criswell's immediate pastoral successor, Criswell often contended that "the widow Truett did him great harm. . . . She could not stand the fact that anyone might successfully follow her husband."[91]

McBeth also writes, regarding the aftermath of Truett's death, that "some months later Truett's body was removed to the Hillcrest Memorial Cemetery, where more adequate space was available to develop a suitable marker."[92] Keith Durso repeats this excuse to exhume Truett's body in his brilliant, extremely detailed, and definitive work on Truett, *Thy Will Be Done*.[93]

However, Criswell, on numerous occasions, argued another motivation:

> She [Mrs. Truett] dug him up! She had him to herself in life and could not stand the thought of sharing a grave site along with Bob Coleman in death. So, in opposition to his lifelong desire to be buried alongside Coleman, she dug him up and moved him to Sparkman's.[94]

A careful visit to either cemetery readily shows that the size of the marker that sits today above Truett's grave at Sparkman-Hillcrest Cemetery could easily have fit on his original grave next to Bob Coleman's in the Grove Hill Cemetery. Removed from their wishes and from each other, Bob Coleman still awaits the resurrection at Grove Hill and Truett resides eight miles away, next to Josephine—and Josephine only—at Sparkman-Hillcrest.

In spite of the issues that arose in death, George Truett lived a life of spotless character, and his legacy of love has only grown throughout the decades.

4

Conflict and
Controversy

The seeds of the intense personal and sometimes public conflicts between George Truett and Frank Norris grew out of the context of both controversy and competition. Much of Southern Baptists' history in the first half of the twentieth century centered on or arose from the intense relationship, or lack thereof, that existed between these two prominent pastors of the two largest churches in the SBC. Their interactions served as a microcosm of the larger conflicts facing Baptists, including the struggle to move the new Southwestern Baptist Theological Seminary from Waco to Fort Worth, the Baylor evolution controversy of the 1920s, and the 75 Million Campaign.

Truett centered his approach in cooperation and unity. Norris thrived on conflict and uniformity. However, Baptist historian Leon McBeth advises that those who examine Norris must ask, "Which Norris? The one who helped establish the seminary, or the one who later tried to destroy it?"[1] While Norris began as the consummate denominational supporter and loyalist, he evolved into a constant source of agitation for those who were intent on keeping the waters of the SBC smooth at all costs.

Truett, often to his detriment, avoided conflict with Norris, trying never to mention his name. However, when forced to do so, he would simply refer to Norris as "that man in Fort Worth."[2] Truett's early biographers, Powhatan James and Leon McBeth, followed his example. While many of the denominational conflicts during the first half of the twentieth century included Norris and Truett, James never mentions the name J. Frank Norris in his biography of Truett.[3] In his volume *The First Baptist Church of Dallas*, McBeth makes only a casual reference to Norris in the long section devoted to George W. Truett.[4]

The source of Norris and Truett's rivalry stemmed from a difference of opinion concerning how leadership in the local Baptist church should be expressed. Norris was convinced that his view of strong pastoral leadership aligned more closely with that found in the New Testament church than Truett's more tolerant, less authoritative approach did. This tension existed in the historical context of Texas Baptists during the early days of both their ministries. Landmarkism played a part in this conflict.[5] This movement, begun by J. R. Graves, A. C. Dayton, and J. M. Pendleton, "militantly sought to preserve the purity of the church."[6] B. H. Carroll, founder of Southwestern Seminary and mentor to both Norris and Truett during their college days at Baylor, was sympathetic toward Landmarkist ecclesiology.[7] Norris emerged as a militant separatist and strong advocate of this approach. Truett, on the other hand, "became the quintessence of the tolerant good-ol'-boy."[8]

Norris's constant and often hostile crusades against the SBC establishment, specifically against Baylor University and Southwestern Seminary, led the Tarrant Baptist Association, as well as the Baptist General Convention of Texas (BGCT), to ostracize him. Norris convinced himself that Truett was responsible for much of this opposition, as attested in Norris's archived letters.[9] On January 6, 1931, in a letter to Louis Entzminger, Norris acknowledges that Entzminger affirmed this view in their early conflicts. He writes, "You were the first man to say that George Truett was the cause of the whole trouble, but multitudes now agree with that position."[10] In a later letter to Victor Masters, editor of the *Western Recorder*, the weekly newspaper of the Kentucky Baptist Convention, Norris affirms Masters's own suspicions:

> Your judgment years ago has been vindicated, namely that Truett is the main cause of the trouble . . . everybody knows that Truett and his crowd went in to destroy me. As far back as 1913 when I was fighting the fight of my life he came to Fort Worth . . . and put his feet under the table of my enemies.[11]

Norris's suspicions about Truett's private campaign against him continued until his death. In 1949, Masters wrote to Norris, "I knew Truett and admired his single but great gift—in the pulpit. Out of it he was an intolerant bullwhip."[12]

Norris did everything in his power to intimidate and coax Truett into an open confrontation, but Truett never obliged him. Before Norris's move to Fort Worth, while serving as editor of the *Baptist Standard*, his combative approach so infuriated and frustrated Truett that he declined to contribute any more of his popular columns to the *Standard*. Norris retorted that he did not care because he "needed the space anyway."[13] Truett's modus operandi was to remain under the public radar and encourage others to do his bidding. McBeth describes it bluntly: "Truett worked behind the scenes, enlisting others to carry the ball in public."[14]

In 1924, when the First Baptist Church in Fort Worth was denied messengers at the Baptist General Convention of Texas's annual meeting, Truett crafted a resolution to oust Norris. However, he refused to join other members of the committee by adding his signature to it, preferring to hover "serenely above the fray."[15] Norris confronted Truett for the manner in which Truett sought to undermine him behind the scenes. He wrote Truett a caustic epistle accusing the Dallas pastor of throwing his

> . . . weight of great influence, and that at the time when you were at the zenith of your power and influence—throwing the weight of a great denominational machine against one man according to all the rules of the game was calculated to destroy

that man. I have always known that you were the moving force behind such schemes.[16]

Norris never learned how to deal with a man who wouldn't answer his constant, caustic attacks.

Norris spent much of his life attacking his denomination for its slow slide into modernism. He railed on educational institutions, particularly Baylor, for allowing heresies to infiltrate their faculties, which certainly posed the threat of diluting the faith of the young men and women who studied under them. Over the years, his relentless methods often resulted in his being increasingly ignored by the establishment. Truett's main weakness was his "tendency to be loyal to a fault, defending causes and friends who were clearly in the wrong."[17] As great a leader as Truett was, his main weakness also expressed itself as "his inflexibility and his tendency to ignore problems."[18]

McKinney Avenue Baptist Church

The first conflict between Norris and Truett occurred in 1905, shortly after Norris's arrival in Dallas to pastor the McKinney Avenue Baptist Church. Less than one mile away, Truett had a head start, having been pastor of the large and influential First Baptist Church for eight years. Nevertheless, Norris's brilliance and pulpit prowess took hold quickly and captured the admiration and attention of Baptists in Dallas. His reputation spread rapidly throughout the Lone Star State. After a feeble beginning of thirteen in attendance on his first Sunday, Norris preached to a growing crowd of one thousand on his first anniversary as pastor.[19] By his second anniversary, the explosive growth of the church saw a new huge, stately Greek-columned church edifice under construction on McKinney Avenue. Powerful in the pulpit, better educated than Truett and most of his peers, and leading a growing church, Norris quickly rose atop the ranks in the SBC.

Tension built as Norris's zealousness to enlist members for his new congregation resulted in many leaving the First Baptist Church of Dallas to join the new and growing church on McKinney Avenue. In his biography of Truett, Keith Durso attests that "several of the new members at McKinney had come from Truett's congregation."[20] Truett took the loss of these members to someone like Norris personally. This sense of betrayal came to light when his best friend, J. M. Dawson, lamented that even his fiancée and future wife was among those who left First Baptist. Willie Turner, a bright and popular young lady whom Truett had baptized at First Baptist—and whom he and his wife "regarded . . . almost as a daughter"—became enamored with Norris and was among those he persuaded to join his church.[21] The reality of members leaving his established First Baptist Church to associate with Norris became a major irritant to Truett. A few years later, after Norris had left Dallas for Fort Worth, Truett was "still mad at Norris for coaxing several FBC members to join McKinney Avenue Baptist Church when Norris pastored the church."[22] This episode began the personal rivalry that would characterize their broken relationship through the coming years. For Norris, the McKinney years set the stage for his future ability to grow the largest church in the world and to attract massive crowds.[23]

The *Baptist Standard*

Norris acquired the *Baptist Standard* in April 1907.[24] The *Standard* was the most widely read statewide, Baptist weekly paper, with thirty-eight thousand subscribers at the time.[25] The twenty-nine-year-old Norris had never written an article for a paper in his life, by his own admission.[26] He quickly and strategically moved to consolidate the paper's competitors by purchasing Samuel Hayden's weekly tabloid, *The Texas Baptist Herald*, as well as J. B. Gambrell's *The Advocate*. By doing so, Norris became the single recognized voice for all Texas Baptists, and in the process he became an icon of denominational loyalty and promotion. Norris's purchases ended the bitter newspaper wars that had divided Texas Baptists so deeply, uniting all communication under one banner of loyalty.[27]

Almost overnight, young Norris became one of the most recognized and popular figures among Baptists in the Lone Star State. He controlled denominational communication for the entire state while serving as pastor of one of the fastest growing churches in the denomination. The widely respected J. B. Gambrell heaped praise upon him, saying that Norris was "young, cultured, has a good outlook, is active, has a business turn, and is committed to the whole program of the Baptists in Texas and throughout the South."[28] Gambrell also challenged Norris to remember that "denominational loyalty goes directly to matters doctrinally."[29] These words and this challenge would become the North Star of Norris's philosophy for the rest of his life, as well as the motivating factor of his decision-making, elevating doctrinal loyalty above denominational loyalty. To J. Frank Norris, denominational loyalty consisted of two matters: doctrinal fidelity and denominational faithfulness—always, and in all ways, in that order.

While Norris served as owner and editor of the *Baptist Standard*, the tension between Norris and Truett continued to build. "Although professing to shun publicity, Truett and his associates worked hard at creating a positive public image" by way of the *Baptist Standard*, the most well-read weekly periodical among Baptists of the day.[30] Norris revealed that everywhere Truett traveled he would regularly send daily local news clippings with glowing reports of his great crowds and meetings to the *Standard*. According to Norris, "There would be no comment, just a large envelope of clippings from the daily papers. And the 'folks in the forks of the creek' wondered how I got hold of these papers. Of course, Dr. Truett 'detested the publicity.'"[31] The controversy between Truett and Norris continued and increased when B. H. Carroll publicized his own desire to move his new seminary to Fort Worth.

Southwestern Baptist Theological Seminary

In Waco, Norris's mentor, B. H. Carroll, envisioned a great theological seminary that would arise out of the Southwest to become the crown jewel of Baptist theological education for generations to come. His dream entailed moving the Bible department from Baylor University to the booming and growing metroplex of Dallas-Fort Worth, incorporating it as a standalone, fully fledged theological seminary.[32] Carroll's passion to separate the seminary from Baylor contributed to his strained relationship with Baylor president S. P. Brooks, ultimately leading him to move to Fort Worth.[33]

Historians have failed to credit Norris's primary and pivotal roles in the founding of Southwestern Baptist Theological Seminary in 1910 as well as the establishment of its eventual home on a hill in south Fort Worth, where it exists today. Although George W. Truett later served as both a Southwestern Seminary trustee and board chair and became memorialized in a campus auditorium named in his honor, he originally tried to form a coalition with A. J. Barton, J. B. Gambrell, and S. P. Brooks, among others, to oppose and prevent Carroll's dream from coming to fruition.[34] According to Southwestern historian Leon McBeth, Carroll "encountered massive opposition" from this coalition of respected Texas Baptists led by Truett.[35] Truett simply "did not want the seminary in Dallas, preferring that the school remain tied to Baylor and perhaps fearing that it would interfere with his efforts to fund the sanitarium and support Buckner Orphans Home."[36] Even though he strongly opposed the move, by the sheer power of his personality, Truett was appointed the chairman of a committee tasked with finding a new site for the fledgling institution. In hopes of dampening the spirit of the move away from Baylor and Waco, Truett recommended two small lots in the Oak Cliff section of Dallas, which infuriated B. H. Carroll.

In a lengthy letter dated March 30, 1909, Carroll let Truett know in no uncertain terms that he considered this recommendation of only two small lots, less than a city block, an insult. He let him know that he did not intend the new seminary to be, what he then typed in all capital letters, "A TWO BY FOUR INSTITUTION."[37] Norris seized the moment. He loved Dr. Carroll, revering him since his days at Baylor. In 1907, while on a brief visit to Dallas, Carroll asked Norris to come to his room at the Oriental Hotel.[38] Norris writes:

> I went to his room and was happy to do so. What a giant figure he was, standing way above six feet and with that long venerable white beard—and I thought I was standing in the presence of Samuel. And, he was, indeed, a prophet for his day and

generation. . . . He said, "Frank, how much stock of the *Baptist Standard* do you own? And, what is your legal relationship to it?"

I said, "Dr. Carroll, I own the majority of the stock, and can control its policies."

"What do you think of the establishment of a seminary here in the Southwest? You were my student for four years, and you took my English Bible course. . . ."

I was for it and I told him so. . . .

He said, "All I want is plenty of space in the *Standard* . . . if you will stand by me I will go afield and raise the money. . . . What I want you to do is to print the telegrams that I will send each week giving full report of my work and of the money raised." I told him he could have the space and soon the telegrams signed "B. H. Carroll" filled the pages of the Standard.[39]

Norris went on to relate that the Truett-led "opposition to the establishment of the seminary began to pour in arguments, and [Norris] poured every one of them in the wastebasket."[40]

Norris, possessing the single tool that could reach all the Baptists in the state of Texas, immediately began using the front page of the *Baptist Standard* every week to promote the move of the seminary to Fort Worth. Truett and the others who opposed the move became irritated at Norris's constant advocacy, what they considered to be a one-sided, unbalanced approach in the weekly *Standard*.[41] Truett, a member of the board of directors of the *Standard*, convened a secret gathering of other directors in an attempt to remove Norris as editor. However, Norris served as not only the paper's editor but also its majority stockholder, so he preempted Truett and convened a meeting of the stockholders, who subsequently dismissed all the directors.[42] This embarrassing confrontation, coupled with the agitation of losing church members to Norris, signaled the acceleration of the decades-long hostility between these two prominent pastors.

Norris's campaign gained huge momentum and won the hearts of Texas Baptists. Thus in 1909, at the annual state convention meeting held at Truett's own First Baptist Church, young Norris—not Truett—stood beside the tall and stately Carroll at the pulpit to make the final appeal to move the seminary from Waco to Fort Worth. Sitting and watching Norris's ever-growing influence—standing in his own pulpit beside the great and respected Carroll—further contributed to Truett's growing agitation. In unbroken eloquence, Norris invoked, "Not since Peter preached at Pentecost and baptized three thousand converts has there been anything more glorious than the founding, endowing and locating of Southwestern Baptist Theological Seminary."[43] Thus Carroll's seminary, which would later become the largest in the world, found a new home on Seminary Hill in Fort Worth, in no small part because of the efforts and influence of young J. Frank Norris.

A few months later, upon the strong recommendation of B. H. Carroll, the First Baptist Church in Fort Worth called Norris to become its pastor. Once settled in his new city and new church, he began to raise the money to undergird the seminary and build its first building. The *Fort Worth Star-Telegram* reported that Norris met "with members of the church to confer with the committee, which is soliciting subscriptions for the Baptist Theological Seminary."[44] Two days later, the same city newspaper reported:

> At the First Baptist Church Dr. J. Frank Norris . . . preached a strong sermon, presenting to his congregation the great benefit that the proposed big seminary would confer, not only on the church, but on the city and humanity and Christianity in general. He presented a strong case for the seminary and its location here, and his words fell on willing ears.[45]

Norris became instrumental in raising the $100,000 needed to bring the seminary to Fort Worth. In fact, "Norris pledged to raise half that amount from his new church, and he did,"[46] but he did not stop there. Norris helped raise the $200,000 needed to build the seminary's first building—Fort Worth Hall. He led the congregants of First Baptist to give half of that amount as well. Baptist historian Alan Lefever states of Norris, "When the doors of the new school opened, no stronger supporter existed outside Carroll himself."[47] Norris served faithfully and loyally as a founding trustee of Southwestern until after B. H. Carroll's death.

Ironically, after the death of Carroll in 1914, the seminary and its new leader, L. R. Scarborough, found themselves the target of some of Norris's most vocal and vitriolic attacks. A major factor in Norris's new-found opposition to Southwestern and Scarborough was that "Norris saw himself the defender of Carroll's vision"[48] and had hoped, even expected, to be the handpicked successor to his mentor. Upon his death bed, B. H. Carroll issued a final charge to Scarborough. Carroll appealed that if heresy ever came to the seminary, he should take it to the faculty. If they did not give it a fair and honest hearing, then Carroll said to take it to trustees of the seminary. If this failed, then, in Carroll's words, he should take it to "the common people of the churches and they will hear you."[49] Carroll further pleaded with Scarborough to "keep the seminary lashed to the cross."[50] Norris assumed this mantle and spent the rest of his life taking matters he felt were abhorrent to conservative theology to the common people of the churches. Norris convinced himself that Scarborough failed Carroll in honoring his charge and that his continued silence over the evolution controversy in SBC life had disqualified him from being the recipient of his own mentor's death-bed challenge.[51]

Norris sharply disapproved of many of the drastic changes Scarborough made immediately after Carroll's death, primarily in moving away from the English Bible course that Carroll had implemented and to which he was so passionately committed. Later, when Norris founded his own seminary in Fort Worth, the Bible Baptist Seminary, he duplicated almost exactly the English Bible course curriculum developed by B. H. Carroll.[52]

In Scarborough, Truett found a willing accomplice for his future and inevitable conflicts with J. Frank Norris. Scarborough, scrappy and confrontational by nature, became the perfect front man for Truett, who always sought to remain just as Durso said—"serenely above the fray."[53]

As the decades unfolded, Norris's mean-spirited nature increasingly revealed itself. A story has circulated around Southwestern Seminary of how Norris resorted to sending the professors beautifully wrapped Christmas boxes. The appreciative professors eagerly opened them only to find an assortment of rotten fruits. Alan Lefever, director of the Texas Baptist Historical Collection and adjunct professor at Truett Seminary, relates a conversation he had with the now late and legendary longtime SWBTS professor T. B. Maston. Maston related that he well remembered receiving these gifts boxes from Norris at his home, but that they were filled with delicious fruits, none of which were spoiled or rotten. It might well be that this story, like many related to Norris, has, over time, grown into legend instead of reality.[54] As one conflict led to another, Norris continued to draw his circle smaller and smaller until he had shut out much of what might have been his wider influence and lasting legacy among Southern Baptists.

The Baylor Evolution Controversy

The next conflict in which Norris and Truett found themselves embroiled was quite public. The clash began with the revelation that evolutionary teaching was infiltrating Christian institutions of higher learning.

In early 1921, Dr. J. A. Rice, a professor at Southern Methodist University in Dallas, propagated and promoted a pro-Darwinian approach to creation. Norris confronted this perceived heresy, and L. R. Scarborough enthusiastically joined him. Together, their challenges and campaign eventually led to Rice's resignation.[55]

Soon thereafter, Baylor professor Grove Dow published a book titled *Introduction to Sociology*. Within its pages he blatantly argued in favor of the evolutionary process. Norris raised the issue publicly. President S. P. Brooks and Professor Dow quickly denied the charges, and Truett and Scarborough soon jumped to Baylor's defense. But words on the printed page do not lie, and Norris decided to inform the larger Baptist world of the teaching promulgated at Baylor, their flagship college. In his book, Dow openly claimed that prehistoric man "was a squatty, ugly, somewhat stooped, powerful being, half human and half animal, who sought refuge from the wild beasts first in trees and later in caves, and that he was halfway between an anthropoid ape and modern man."[56]

Even the "fellows at the forks of the creek," as Norris liked to call the masses of conservative pastors, could understand exactly what those written words meant. He launched an all-out attack on this heretical teaching at the bastion of Baptist education, expecting that Scarborough would join him in this fight as he had just done at SMU over the exact same issue. But to Norris's utter amazement, Scarborough, along with Truett, remained completely silent on the issue. At the time, they were both leaders in the Convention's 75 Million Campaign to raise millions of dollars for Baptist causes in the 1920s. Their response when questioned about their silence was terse and shocking: "We don't want to have any stir up about this [evolution controversy] . . . you will ruin the 75 Million Campaign."[57]

But Scarborough went further than that. Not only did he refuse to join Norris in challenging the teaching of evolution at Baylor, he actively sought to place his own informers inside Norris's Fort Worth congregation with instructions to report on any questionable activities they might find that would discredit Norris in the eyes of Texas Baptists, believing that "it will not take long until it will not make any difference what he says."[58]

This attitude marked a subtle transition in SBC thought. Southern Baptist historian Thomas Nettles pinpoints this saga as a turning point, blaming Scarborough for diverting the SBC from its deep theological roots by substituting denominational loyalty and fiscal unity as its primary means of cooperation.[59] This call for unity based on a shared fiscal program began to replace theology as the sole unifying principle of the denomination.[60]

Neither Truett nor Scarborough ever criticized or opposed Professor Dow. To the contrary, they actively sought to protect the Baylor establishment from controversy. In the midst of the controversy, Truett, "as was his custom, remained in the background."[61] Baptist Historian W. W. Barnes writes that devotion to the denomination was an "obsession" for Scarborough.[62]

For Scarborough, denominational loyalty preceded all other matters. Conversely, Norris obsessed himself with adherence to biblical and doctrinal truth, and "his spirit of independence came from a conviction that he was fundamentally right on most issues."[63] This perceived hypocrisy on the part of Truett and Scarborough, in lauding denominational loyalty over doctrinal loyalty, contributed to the growing divide between Norris and the leaders in the SBC.

Norris, now in full attack mode, continued to expose the infidelity at his alma mater. In October 1921, Norris announced that he would expose professors by name in his Sunday sermon. This sensational subject drew thousands of people to First Baptist Church: "With a flowing tide of words and violent gestures and the poise of righteous indignation, he proceeded to cry out that compromise, evolution, modernism and infidelity were undermining the fortress of faith at Baylor University."[64] The new coalition of Truett and Scarborough, ever the denominational loyalists, set out on a campaign to defend Baylor University.

At the 1922 annual meeting of the Baptist General Convention of Texas in Dallas, Norris prepared to expose the heresy at Baylor in what promised to be the floor fight of all floor fights. Truett, seeking to preempt Norris and keep the issue from being debated publicly on the floor, held a midnight caucus in hopes of finding some parliamentary procedure that might protect the establishment. In an attempt to cover for the exposed Professor Dow, Truett declared, "We will dehorn him [Norris] now and that will end it."[65] Truett's main layman and chairman of the deacon body—the highly respected, wealthy, and influential businessman M. H. Wolfe—joined the late-night caucus with Truett and the others. As Truett's most ardent and loyal supporter, Wolfe had served on almost every SBC board. But, observing his own pastor seeking to defend such unbiblical positions as were being exposed at Baylor, he stood up in the caucus and confronted the denominational crowd with strong words: "You are doing a most fateful thing, committing the biggest blunder in the history of Texas Baptists."[66] In the end, the convention defused the situation by appointing a committee to look into Norris's charges. This conflict added to Truett's personal and public embarrassment.

Shortly thereafter, Wolfe, disillusioned by the silence of such venerated men as Truett and Scarborough over what he considered blatant areas of biblical infidelity, publicly broke with Truett, left the First
Baptist Church in Dallas, and in the years that followed became a vocal
and loyal supporter of J. Frank Norris. So clear was Wolfe's break with
the SBC leadership that in 1940 he became president of Norris's own
fellowship of independent churches, The World Baptist Missionary
Fellowship.[67] This humiliation propelled the growing rift between Norris
and Truett to greater extremes.

Once again Norris took the issue to the common people of the
churches, and the pressure started to mount on the university to terminate Dow from the Baylor faculty. Norris's tabloid, *The Searchlight*,

> . . . at its peak had a circulation of over 150,000 subscribers,
> [and] began publishing exact, word for word, excerpts from
> Dow's book in 1921. Norris further charged that for fifteen
> years Baylor had been guilty of teaching unsound doctrine while
> charging President S.P. Brooks with a wide spread cover up.[68]

From his pulpit and from his pen, Norris increased the pressure until
his attacks had their desired effect. Dow resigned under pressure from
Baylor University.[69]

J. B. Gambrell's challenge to always remember that "denominational loyalty goes directly to matters doctrinally" continued to motivate
Norris.[70] For him this fight dealt with matters of denominational loyalty,
for true loyalty to the denomination rooted itself in doctrinal fidelity.
The issue that frustrated Norris the most was the stark silence of Truett
and Scarborough during the evolution controversy and their refusal to
acknowledge and apply the truth that, indeed, as Gambrell articulated,
"Denominational loyalty goes directly to matters doctrinally." To the
contrary, they both sought by any means possible to provide cover and
protection for the university's reputation. Norris continued to see himself as the true denominational loyalist, but the widespread, established
influence of Truett eventually positioned the Fort Worth pastor as an
aggressive agitator and angry antagonist.

The 75 Million Campaign

In 1919, Southern Baptists launched the 75 Million Campaign, one of the most aggressive financial undertakings ever attempted by a denomination. The Convention determined to raise $75 million over a five-year period to further the work and expand the SBC's ministries and missions at home and around the world. The SBC elected George Truett as the chairman of the campaign. L. R. Scarborough took a leave of absence from Southwestern Seminary's presidency to be the hands-on director of the massive undertaking.[71] W. W. Barnes noted, "Scarborough was an aggressive money raiser and he often came off as autocratic."[72] His confrontational attitude was a constant source of agitation for Norris. Initially, Norris was fully supportive of the campaign and led his Fort Worth church to make a sizable pledge toward the effort. However, over time Truett and Scarborough continued to marginalize him and sought ultimately to "push him out of the convention."[73] The 75 Million Campaign proved to be the "boiling point" for the relationship between Truett, Norris, and the SBC.[74]

The campaign began to implode when a secretary in Scarborough's office gave sworn testimony that the books of the campaign had been altered and an accountant testified that Scarborough refused to allow anyone to see the books. This revelation only added fuel to the growing fire of controversy.[75] The secretary, Pearl H. Thomas, offered a notarized affidavit:

> This is to testify that I was assistant endowment secretary in Dr. Scarborough's office for eight years. My statement as published in *The Searchlight*, September 29, 1922, saying that the auditor's report was changed after it was made, and before it was read to the convention, is altogether true and correct."[76]

The timing of this bombshell was devastating in light of other major scandals circulating at the same time within the SBC. Norris began demanding an account of where the organizers had distributed the money that had been raised thus far in the national campaign. He was rebuked at every request. Although the serious charge against Scarborough did not deflate the momentum of the campaign, two other events unfolding in SBC life during the 1920s lent credibility to Norris's spoken concerns regarding financial malfeasance.

In 1927, G. N. Sanders, treasurer of the Foreign Mission Board, embezzled $103,000 from mission funds. A year later, Clinton Carnes, treasurer of the Home Mission Board, embezzled more than $900,000 over a ten-year period, covering the entire span of the 75 Million Campaign.[77] Without question, these events embarrassed Southern Baptists and served to sharpen Norris's focus on his growing opposition to Truett and Scarborough and their brand of denominationalism.

The 75 Million Campaign reached its end in dismal failure. As it was drawing to a close, the leaders, in desperation, attempted to assess the churches certain arbitrary dollar amounts. Norris claimed that he was being pressured to accept an "assessment" for $200,000 for First Baptist Church.[78] Norris saw the real issue to be an attempt by a small established group to centralize power in the denomination away from the local churches. When he protested that assessments went against every idea of the long-cherished Baptist conviction of the autonomy of the local church, he claims he was told, "Norris, if you don't cooperate and put on this drive, we will brand you to the end of the earth as an uncooperating Baptist and you will lose out. You won't have any crowd to hear you, your own church will disintegrate."[79] Norris determined such a response as nothing more than an idle threat, and so, once again, he continued to take the matter to "the fellows at the forks of the creek." One of those "fellows," J. Matthew Harder, pastor of a small congregation in Ralls, Texas, chided Truett for "having too much ego and envy" in a letter to the pastor. He continued: "There are some home rats eating up the sacks . . . some of you leaders hurt the cause by being angry with those who don't agree to every thing [sic]. We are losing some of our great laymen's support."[80]

Norris referred to the 75 Million Campaign as "the most disastrous campaign that ever happened to Southern Baptists."[81] The campaign proved easier to pledge than to collect. Initial pledges at the beginning of the campaign soared above the $75 million goal to $92,630,923. However, the campaign ended with actual receipts totaling $58,591,713, almost $12 million below the goal and an astounding $34 million less than was pledged by the churches.[82] Baptist mission boards and institutions planned and spent according to the promised amount pledged rather than the actual receipts. Thus, in the ensuing months and years, these "institutions expecting funds from the campaign fell heavily into debt."[83]

Suspicions continued to linger about whether the money was handled properly.[84] The campaign brought about a bitter ending for Truett, bringing him "one of his first major defeats in fund raising."[85] In Norris's mind, it afforded him the place of rightful heir to Carroll's appeal to take Convention issues to the common people of the churches. Norris resorted to this action by every means possible. When asked why, after initially supporting the campaign, he became so vigorously opposed to it, he asserted, "A fight was on and I knew the physiology of the human mind. I knew when I raised the question about the books . . . that the fellows from the forks of the creeks would line up with me."[86] As always, he took his cause to the common people, those "fellows from the forks of the creeks." They heard him gladly.

Nothing highlights Norris's break with the denomination more than his opposition to the 75 Million Campaign. In the midst of this Convention-wide endeavor, the Baptist General Convention of Texas adopted a resolution in 1924 stating that Norris's Fort Worth church "sows the seed of discord and division . . . and has unjustly criticized, unmercifully misrepresented, and persistently opposed the program, method of work, institutions, causes, and elected and trusted leaders of the SBC."[87] The resolution contained the names of twenty-four of the most prominent Texas Baptist leaders sans George W. Truett. Its glaring omission served as another indication of his constant attempts, after planning and organizing various efforts behind the scenes, to keep himself "serenely above the fray" in the eyes of the public.[88]

As one controversy followed another, frustration continued to mount on all sides. These conflicts led to one of the most dramatic public confrontations in early twentieth-century American ecclesiological life. It would become known as "The Radio Hate Fest" of 1927.

The Radio Hate Fest

The 1920s ushered in the golden age of radio as it dominated the entertainment industry as the first national broadcast medium. The first regularly aired entertainment programs began in 1922, and one million radios graced the homes of America at that time.[89] By the end of the decade, radios were in the homes of millions more. Quiz shows; local, national, and world news; variety shows; situational comedies, such as *Amos and Andy*; sports broadcasts; and many other programs provided evening entertainment in homes that previously engaged in more mundane pastimes, like reading and conversation.

After the embarrassment brought about by J. Frank Norris during the Baylor evolution controversy coupled with the failure of the 75 Million Campaign, the Texas Baptist establishment conceived a plan whereby they would silence Norris once and for all by exposing him to the entire Baptist world via radio. Truett gathered the five most prominent leaders in the state: L. R. Scarborough, president of Southwestern Baptist Theological Seminary; S. P. Brooks, president of Baylor University; F. S. Groner, executive director of the Baptist General Convention of Texas; J. R. Ward, president of Decatur Baptist College; and J. B. Tidwell, dean of the School of Theology at Baylor University. They moved to acquire one-hour time slots for five nights over eight days on the large fifty-thousand-watt radio station KTAT in Fort Worth.

Norris wisely prepared to record each of their tirades on wax cylinders so that their every word would be preserved for posterity.

The battle was engaged on November 28, 1927.[90] The first night featured Scarborough, the next night featured Brooks, then in successive nights Groner, Tidwell, and Ward. The final night was left for Ward's scathing attack, which he concluded by saying, "I expect to look over the parapets of Heaven and see Frank Norris frying in the bottom-less pits of Hell [*sic*]."[91]

Once again, conspicuously absent from the radio microphone during the entire ordeal was George W. Truett. His refusal to join his own coalition on the air is but another example of his using and encouraging others to be out front, executing his plans while seeking to keep himself "serenely above the fray."[92] Norris never had a doubt about who was orchestrating this radio attack from behind the scenes. Over a decade later, in a personal letter to Truett, which Truett never acknowledged with a reply, Norris says:

> When you threw your great weight of influence, and that at the time when you were at the zenith of your power and influence—throwing the weight of the great denominational machine against one man according to all the rules of the game was calculated to destroy that man. I have always known that you were the moving force behind such schemes.[93]

In Truett's defense, those who knew him best said, "There was not a mean bone in his body."[94] Leon McBeth adds, "He was no polemicist who enjoyed attacking others."[95] However, Kelly David Pigott astutely observes that one of the blatant weaknesses in Truett was found in "his implicit trust in the institutions and the people to do the right thing. He was very much a part of the good ol' boy network that defended the status quo, regardless of the glaring problems."[96]

The first night of the radio attacks began with Scarborough delivering a biting, caustic, one-hour diatribe on Norris. He told "the world all the mean things he ever heard, thought or felt about Dr. Norris, and that everybody else ever felt, thought, published, circulated, whispered publicly or privately, and there was no prayer, no scripture, no song."[97] He described him as "malicious, diabolical, [a] falsifier, perjurer, liar, thief, scoundrel, reprobate, despicable, damnable, devilish, infamous, murderer, criminal, dastardly, heinous, wicked, corrupt, and hellish."[98] Scarborough spent the entire hour calling Norris every name he could conjure up and accusing him of everything anyone ever imagined that he did. The presentation was brutal and bombastic.

The denominational loyalists then got the surprise of their lives. Without their knowing it, Norris had acquired the hour immediately following them on each of the nights. On the initial night and immediately after one solid excruciating hour of Scarborough's vicious attacks, Norris signed on the radio with a young girl's quartet singing softly, in perfect harmony, "For you I am praying, For you I am praying."[99] Then, several new converts came to the microphone and gave moving and stirring testimonies of how their lives had been radically transformed through the ministries of the First Baptist Church in Fort Worth. Norris then came on the air with these words, speaking about the Truett-Scarborough coalition:

> These are good men but they are mad. I feel sorry for them and I want you to forgive them. I have been mad myself and I know how bad it makes one feel. They were excited and heated up, and their strong language did not represent their better spirit. You are not interested in what they think of me, or what I think of them, but I want to take this occasion to call this great listening audience to repentance, and after the world is on fire and the heavens have passed away with a great noise out in the eternity of eternities, you will have no concern about a denominational row between one insignificant preacher and a group of denominational leaders.[100]

Norris then proceeded to preach a gospel sermon in the remaining minutes of radio airtime. For the remainder of the Radio Hate Fest, he responded each night in a similar manner.

By the conclusion of the first night, Norris had won the hearts of the people. His soft answers had turned the wrath of his vilest critics against themselves. The Texas Baptists leaders' plan to expose Norris before the public was a huge strategic mistake, and it backfired in the faces of Truett and his five denominational spokesmen. According to Homer Ritchie, "Even George W. Truett, pastor of the First Baptist

Church in Dallas, who usually opposed him, acknowledged that Norris had defeated his antagonists through his psychological response."[101]

Truett immediately called a meeting of his compatriots and strongly suggested calling off the remainder of the broadcasts. He said, "Scarborough fumbled the ball last night. Norris ran rings around him . . . my telephone has been ringing all night. Telegrams are pouring in . . . one week of this will ruin everything."[102] Scarborough was not present, so they called him long distance with the opinion that the Radio Hate Fest needed to be called off immediately. However, Scarborough insisted that it continue, expressing that what they had begun together must be finished. Groner agreed, imploring that they stand together to "the last ditch."[103] Over the next few nights, they continued to excoriate Norris, and he continued to stay, ironically, serenely above the fray following their tirades each night with an hour of kind words in their direction, followed by heartwarming, evangelistic gospel preaching.

The Sunday immediately following the Radio Hate Fest, the First Baptist Church in Fort Worth welcomed 142 happy new members, most coming upon their profession of faith and for believer's baptism.[104] Many of the new converts testified of having come to Christ the preceding week listening to the radio broadcasts. Testimonies abounded, such as that of socialite Alice Ellie. She had gathered a group of friends and, imbibing on the liquor she made available, they were around the radio "wringing their hands with glee at the cussing and abuse that was heaped upon the head of J. Frank Norris."[105] Norris then began to preach Christ, and her hardened heart was melted. She ended the party and gave her heart to the Lord. Standing before the vast congregation at First Baptist, she was among those who testified of her newfound faith in Christ, followed him in baptism, and became an active church member for years to come.

In the days immediately following the radio broadcasts, Norris wrote personal letters to several of the men involved. Feeling the momentum he had achieved, Norris wrote to L. R. Scarborough, offering him

> . . . the free and unconditional use of Radio KFQB on the time controlled by the First Baptist Church. . . . You will have

unconditional use, and by that I mean to discuss any matter, about me or anything connected with me. You can make any attack on me and my work; you can give out any documents or have any witnesses to testify that you wish, and this means to include any former members of the First Baptist Church and particularly any former employees who have been in my closest confidence. You will no way be interfered with, nor will I answer any address that you and your associates might make by going on the air immediately after you. I repeat this will not cost you one cent. You will kindly bear this information to Dr. S. P. Brooks, Dr. F. S. Groner, and the other brethren who have been discussing me.[106]

No record exists in any archives that Scarborough ever answered his offer.

Exactly two weeks after dispatching the letter to Scarborough, Norris wrote to Frank Groner on December 15, 1927. This particular epistle added an additional layer of intrigue to the drama. Norris began, "This is to thank you and others for your recent hate fest over the radio." He then offered the Texas Baptist leader free use of his radio time as he had done to Scarborough. However, in the last paragraph he referred to various telegrams he had received from radio listeners in Waco and Stamford, locations where Groner had previously served as pastor. These related to "the testimony of your separating a man and his wife."

He concludes by saying, "Of course, you are thoroughly familiar with these matters. I shall be glad to turn the whole matter over to you or publish it or put it on the air just as you wish. Yours for peace, prosperity, fair play and good will. J. Frank Norris."[107] A few weeks later Groner resigned his position as executive director of BGCT and moved to East Texas to assume the presidency of Marshall Baptist College, known today as East Texas Baptist University. Subsequently, he broke with Truett, and in the ensuing years developed an ongoing personal relationship with Norris, as evidenced by several letters exchanged between the two men.[108]

Conclusion

J. Frank Norris lived a life embedded with conflict and controversy. He watched others condone unbiblical beliefs and behaviors, capitulate, and compromise on important doctrinal issues. He chose the path of confrontation. In so doing, across the decades his strident fundamentalism and his proclivity for conflict overshadowed many of his arguments for truth as he continued to draw his circle of influence smaller and smaller. He never doubted that he was the true recipient of the mantle of B. H. Carroll. Scarborough continued to insist that "Norrisism misrepresents the facts and brings false accusations against such causes and men, masquerading under the cloak of orthodoxy and fundamentalism."[109] Through it all, Norris's ability to endear or alienate people soon became the normal experience of those who interacted with him. Norris's popular appeal aimed at the hearts of the "fellows from the forks of the creek" gained him a large and loyal following among the common people sitting in the Baptist pews. But the denominational hierarchy continued to view him as a threat and a nuisance. Norris wore this conviction as a badge of courage.

5

The Influence of J. Frank Norris on Modern Southern Baptist Theology, Church Growth, Evangelism, and Practice

When J. Frank Norris arrived on the scene of broad public ministry in the first decade of the twentieth century, Baptists widely viewed him as the consummate denominational loyalist. His educational pedigree and academic prowess from his studies at Baylor University and the Southern Baptist Theological Seminary far exceeded the typical Baptist preacher of his day. The years he invested in receiving the best education possible for any minister in his time were "extremely formative and incredibly successful."[1] Although mentored by notables in Southern Baptist history such as J. B. Gambrell, S.P. Brooks, A. T. Robertson, and E. Y. Mullins, Norris revered the mentorship of B. H. Carroll most. Norris's editorship of the popular *Baptist Standard*, his advocacy and partnership with the venerated Carroll in the establishment of Southwestern Baptist Theological Seminary, and his call to the wealthy and prestigious First Baptist Church in Fort Worth in his early thirties thrust him into growing popularity.

After Carroll's death, Norris contended that leaders like George W. Truett and L. R. Scarborough were assigning higher importance to denominational loyalty than doctrinal fidelity. This accusation was initially evidenced in the evolution controversy at Baylor and served to transform Norris into Southern Baptists' most outspoken antagonist. Baptists of the day either loved him and followed him with near blind allegiance, or they feared him, some despising the very mention of his name.[2]

Through decades of conflicts and controversies, Norris viewed himself as the true and loyal Baptist protecting the high view of Scripture and the autonomy of the local church above all. In his later years, when at odds on many points with Southern Baptists, "he never wished to be seen as anti-convention, but rather as a true Southern Baptist who revealed and opposed outside encroachments of modernism and unscriptural practices."[3]

Baptist historian Leon McBeth contends that J. Frank Norris "had no constructive part in Southern Baptist ministries in this [twentieth] century."[4] Nevertheless, while Norris may have been unable to influence Southern Baptist theology and practice in his lifetime, years after his death, he accomplished such influence in contemporary Southern Baptist theology, church growth, evangelism, and practice. In matters of theology, particularly related to inerrancy and eschatology, Southern Baptist leadership since 1979 has aligned with Norris's positions more than Truett's. Southern Baptists' evangelism and church growth ideology, with its emphasis on direct evangelism, multisite campuses, and use of social media, mimics Norris's faith and practice at First Baptist Church in Fort Worth. Southern Baptists' ministries during and since the Conservative Resurgence reveal that Truett's "leadership style is shown to align more with moderates today," and "what he [Norris] failed to do in the 1920s—take control of a denomination—he accomplished in the 1980s."[5]

Beginning in the 1920s, three decades of constant conflict ensued between Norris and the SBC as the denomination continued to distance itself from him. Norris thought he could change the trajectory of the Convention by attacking it from without, correcting what he viewed as its biblically deviant ways. His failure to do so served as a pattern later for the early leaders of the Conservative Resurgence in the 1970s and 1980s, revealing that the only way to truly transform a denomination was from within.[6]

Norris failed in his attempts to influence the SBC to be more conservative during his lifetime. A quarter of a century after his death, however, his tireless efforts began to yield results. A close examination of the SBC in the contemporary era finds a theologically strong Convention holding to conservative values and adherent to its confessional statement.[7] The expository, text-driven approach to preaching that is taught in all six SBC seminaries, as well as their decidedly conservative course correction, resembles J. Frank Norris far more than it does George W. Truett. The observance of several significant markers propelled the growth of the SBC and its churches in the late twentieth century into the twenty-first century. While J. Frank Norris built his own evangelistic empire, the SBC entered its most expansive years of numerical and spiritual growth. Among the most significant of these markers is the massive Sunday School Movement that propelled virtually every church in SBC life in the twentieth century.

The Sunday School Movement

The Sunday School Movement among Southern Baptists exploded onto the scene in 1922 with the publication of Arthur Flake's book *Building a Standard Sunday School*,[8] geared to growing New Testament churches by establishing Sunday schools on church campuses. The model was to provide small, age-graded Bible studies before worship services. Flake believed that the Sunday school should become the primary evangelistic mechanism to empower church growth.

In 1921, Arthur Flake joined the Sunday School Board of the SBC and soon became the nationally recognized authority on church growth. "Flake's Formula" for Sunday school and church growth became the standard in virtually every SBC church for decades. *Building a Standard Sunday School* provided a simple pattern for churches to follow. Flake proposed that churches structure Sunday schools according to age, teach the Bible for discipleship, and become the outreach arm for the church as a tool for evangelism. His "formula" consisted of five principles: discover the prospects, expand the organization, train the workers, provide the space, and go get the people.[9]

Charles Kelley, former president of New Orleans Baptist Theological Seminary, observes that "Flake's formula was no fluke."[10] This approach made Sunday school the primary engine for SBC growth in the twentieth century. When unbelievers visit a Sunday school class, two important things occur: they hear "more and more of the Bible explained and they have natural opportunities to form relationships with Christians in the class and in the church."[11]

Flake failed to mention one important piece of information in all his books and promotions through the Convention. Before coming to serve at the SBC Sunday School Board in Nashville in 1921, Flake served the preceding three years on the church staff of the First Baptist Church in Fort Worth under the pastoral tutelage of J. Frank Norris. "Flake's Formula" for Sunday school growth comprised the very principles that Norris incorporated at the Fort Worth church since his arrival as pastor in 1909. According to Homer Ritchie:

> Norris was the first one to ever "age grade" the Sunday School resulting in the church becoming the family place to be on Sunday mornings. During the early years at First Baptist, Norris had fashioned his Sunday School to be the evangelistic arm of the church when most other churches were seeing it as something for children only.[12]

Flake arrived in Fort Worth with the title of "church manager" but became better known in the church as the "paid Sunday school superintendent."[13] Norris thought so highly of him that he put him in charge of all church ministries and activities "at the same salary as the pastor."[14] Norris's ability to attract crowds coupled with Flake's organizational expertise produced exploding numbers in First Baptist's Sunday school. An advertisement in the *Fort Worth Star-Telegram* on Saturday,

March 22, 1919, featured a large picture of Arthur Flake accompanied by the announcement that the following morning, "People who want to know how the First Baptist Church built the greatest Sunday school in America can see the inside workings of the machinery at the 11 o'clock hour. We will give diplomas to three hundred who have finished the training school."[15]

The Fort Worth church served as the testing ground for "Flake's Formula," which he learned directly from J. Frank Norris. Norris assigned high priority to the Sunday school, organized its classes by age groups, had midweek teacher trainings, and bused people to church. Flake ensured that "The Sunday School Board at Nashville adopted many of the plans and methods of the First Baptist Church, which originally pioneered them."[16] Church historian Leon McBeth contradicts his own statement that Norris "had no constructive part in Southern Baptist ministries,"[17] admitting that "much of Southern Baptist organization and methods of Sunday school work, so important in Baptist growth in this century [twentieth century], were created and tested in the unlikely locale of First Baptist Church of Fort Worth, under the pastorate of J. Frank Norris."[18]

Surprisingly, Southern Baptist churches incorporated Flake's growth principles in their ministries during the same decades in which they were in bitter conflict with Norris. Few, if any, of these churches recognized that the ideas and methodologies they incorporated in their churches found their genesis in the First Baptist Church in Fort Worth years before Flake ever joined the Sunday School Board in Nashville. The ongoing success of SBC Sunday School growth provides an example of Norris's contribution, directly challenging Leon McBeth's premise that Norris "had no constructive part in Southern Baptist ministries in this century."[19]

The Cooperative Program

The adoption of the Cooperative Program (CP) in 1925 is another factor in the rise of the SBC in the twentieth century. The CP enables every

Southern Baptist Church, regardless of size or location, to participate in cooperative giving to all the ministry and missionary enterprises of the SBC. Launched in 1925, the CP called for churches to "send their offerings for denominational ministries to their state conventions."[20] The state conventions forwarded a percentage of these offerings to the national SBC, which then dispersed them to the various mission boards, seminaries, and other SBC entities. This funding mechanism enabled a multitude of helpful and efficient means of preparing men and women for worldwide ministry and supporting them once they were on the field. Seminaries used these CP funds to provide discounted tuition for students from SBC churches, enabling many of them to graduate and enter vocational ministry without the burden of student debt. The funds also provided international missionaries with support for housing and automobiles, as well as other expenses, enabling them to focus entirely on their work and calling instead of the constant pressure of raising funds. This voluntary program provides both balance and perspective to Southern Baptist entities and fuels a multiplicity of worldwide ministries.

The Cooperative Program's origin in 1925 immediately followed the failed 75 Million Campaign, led by George W. Truett, which Baptist historian Barry Hankins describes as an "inglorious flop."[21] Southern Baptist leaders felt compelled to blame J. Frank Norris.

Throughout the early 1920s, Norris fueled the flames against the campaign with weekly front-page articles in his tabloid, *The Searchlight*.[22] Every Truett setback seemed to coincide with a Norris success. The growing failure of the 75 Million Campaign, coupled with the ongoing controversy over evolution at Baylor, Texas Baptists' flagship university, created a climate of distrust among more than a few Texas and Southern Baptists.

Keith Durso writes, "Blaming one person for the dissension Southern and Texas Baptists experienced would be unfair. Nevertheless, one man did his best to sink the Seventy-Five Million Campaign and to destroy the reputations and careers of people who did not believe the Bible the way he believed it."[23] J. Frank Norris was that one man.

Baptist historian W. W. Barnes blames the failure of the 75 Million Campaign squarely on J. Frank Norris.[24] Norris believed the headquarters of the Southern Baptist Convention existed in neither Nashville nor Dallas, nor in the hands of a few elite leaders; rather, it resided in the local churches. The fact that Truett, as the leader of the campaign, had resorted to assessing churches an arbitrary amount of money to give to the campaign was in Norris's view a direct assault on the autonomy of every local SBC church.

Durso states, "SBC leaders should have known that the denomination's assigning quotas for churches, rather than letting churches themselves determine how much they wanted to pledge, violated the Baptist autonomy of the local church and that such a violation would cause resentment among pastors and churches."[25] This failure was a fatal blunder on Truett's part and led, more than anything else, to the campaign's failure.

In Truett's mind also the blame could be placed solely with Norris. In a paper Truett presented on Christian education at the 1926 SBC meeting—and without mentioning Norris's name, as was his custom—Truett seemed to envision Norris when he declared:

That word "cooperation" is a challenging word for our Baptist people. . . . Their poise and self-restraint and patient continuance in well-doing, in the face, sometimes, of self-appointed, noisy, self-advertised, and sometimes reckless agitators is a chapter clothed with the most significant meaning. . . . At no time have half-baked and reckless disturbers succeeded in misleading many of our people and diverting them from the common and glorious work fostered by our churches. Nor will they succeed.[26]

The perfect storm of defeat and failure came together in 1924 when the 75 Million Campaign limped to a close. Although the denominational loyalists led by Truett intimated the blame belonged to Norris, the reality was that even under Truett and Scarborough's leadership Texas Baptists raised only half of their $16 million goal. Furthermore, Truett's own church "never came close to reaching the six million dollars it had pledged."[27] The assessments Truett placed on the churches, coupled with their excessive pledges, "produced visions of grandeur as Southern Baptists secured loans to fund building projects, mission programs, and educational institutions with money they did not have. . . . Debt would plague the Convention for many years."[28]

Following the failure of the massive financial campaign and in the throes of a denominationally charged doctrinal battle, Southern Baptists required a cause around which they could all rally. They found the Cooperative Program to be this cause. The very word *cooperative* points to Norris's efforts to undermine the cooperative spirit of the 75 Million Campaign. His uncooperative spirit, his insistence on local church autonomy, and his growing influence in moving people to question their leadership were the catalysts that would ultimately lead Southern Baptists to regroup and design another ongoing giving initiative to call the SBC to truly local church-centered cooperative giving. In a uniquely inadvertent way, Frank Norris played a reluctant part in the establishment of the incredible funding mechanism that has supported the vast and growing ministries and missions of the SBC for the past century. Norris's indirect contribution to the Cooperative Program challenges Leon McBeth's claim that Norris offered no constructive part in Southern Baptist ministries."[29] What Norris may have meant for evil resulted in good.

The Baptist Faith and Message

In 1925, the SBC messengers who met in Memphis, Tennessee, adopted a confessional statement of faith titled the Baptist Faith and Message. Those who led, served, or taught in CP institutions were required to endorse this statement of faith. The Baptist Faith and Message, enacted in 1925 and revised in 1963 and 2000 to reflect more contemporary issues, assures the doctrinal fidelity of those who are a part of CP-related institutions. The Baptist Faith and Message attests to the belief and doctrinal adherence of such fundamentals of the Christian faith as "the nature and purpose of the Bible, God, 'the fall of man,' salvation, the church, and eschatology, as well as other topics such as religious liberty, some social issues, evangelism, and cooperation with other denominations."[30]

Baylor University had adopted intellectual modernism in the form of the theory of evolution. Norris's assault exposed what he considered to be unbiblical excesses in the classrooms of Baptist schools, resulting in the termination of a number of faculty members at Baylor. Norris's charges included not just what was being taught in the classroom and written in the textbooks, but also the alleged cover-up perpetrated by Baylor president S. P. Brooks, George W. Truett, and L. R. Scarborough. For example, Norris exposed and questioned why Scarborough had known for more than a year about the advocacy of evolution in Baylor professor Grove Samuel Dow's book, *Introduction to the Principles of Sociology*, yet made no move to reveal it.[31]

Such Southern Baptist loyalists as J. B. Cranfill, former editor of *The Baptist Standard*, had learned of what Dow was advocating in the Baylor classroom as early as 1921 and issued warnings early on that "if something was not done to eliminate all just cause of such heresy, the reputation of Baylor as being orthodox in its Baptist beliefs would be in dire jeopardy."[32] James Thompson adds, "With the fundamentalist-modernist controversy still perking along in northern denominations, creedal fundamentalists in the SBC were clamoring for an official state-ment that would put Southern Baptists on record as anti-evolution."[33] Southern Baptist leaders in the middle part of the decade realized their need for a vehicle that would serve to assure the churches of their adher-ence to biblical truth and Baptist traditions. The adoption of the Baptist Faith and Message statement in the midst of the widely reported evolu-tion controversy likely resulted from Norris's continual public criticism. In fact, Durso claims that Norris's lead in the debate over evolution "played an instrumental role in Southern Baptists adopting in 1925 the first confession of faith in their eighty year history."[34]

E. Y. Mullins, president of the Southern Baptist Theological Seminary, chaired the committee that formulated the doctrinal statement. Baylor historian Barry Hankins indirectly credits Norris's role in the formulation of the Baptist Faith and Message, acknowledging that "Mullins and his allies were able to steal the fundamentalists' thunder by adopting the idea of a confession," thereby heading off a growing denominational controversy.[35] Dr. Bob Schuller, the well-known Methodist minister and editor of *The Methodist Challenger* weekly periodical, observed that "Frank Norris really saved the Southern Baptist Convention from modernism. . . . Dr. Truett, the celebrated pastor of First Baptist Church, Dallas, who was far from being an admirer of Frank Norris, acknowledged to me that Norris had rendered an invaluable service at this point."[36]

To claim that Norris had no influence on Southern Baptist ministries, as Leon McBeth has attested, belies the reality that Norris was the prominent architect behind the Sunday School Movement, had a part in bringing about the convention's adoption of the Cooperative Program, and also played a significant role in forcing the denomination to adopt their doctrinal statement, now adhered to for a century.

The Conservative Resurgence

A fourth major event that shaped the direction of SBC life in the twentieth century is the so-called "Conservative Resurgence" (1979–2000).[37] In the 1970s, conservative leaders in the SBC became increasingly concerned with what they perceived to be an ever-encroaching liberalism in their seminaries.[38] Continued support to such seminaries with Cooperative Program dollars became an affront to them. The two recognized architects of this growing effort to return the SBC to its more conservative roots were Paige Patterson, president of Criswell College, and Judge Paul Pressler, a Texas state appeals court judge from Houston. They saw the need for change due to "a decline they attribute to the failure to resist encroaching theological liberalism."[39]

Patterson and Pressler met for the first time in New Orleans in early March 1967. Pressler had been concerned about the theological drift in the SBC and had heard from mutual friends of Patterson, a young PhD student at New Orleans Baptist Theological Seminary. They met for coffee and beignets, along with their wives, at the Café du Monde until past midnight on a spring evening.

Pressler recalls:

> Others have reported that the Café du Monde that night was the scene of scheming and plotting to take over the Southern Baptist Convention. This simply is not true. The conversation was between four individuals who had a mutual interest in reaching people for the Lord Jesus Christ. We shared our hearts with each other. It was also a time for ones who had experienced liberalism in the Southern Baptist Convention to share their mutual concerns about the effect this was having on the proclamation of the gospel. It was a time when two young couples enjoyed being with each other—fellowshipping and getting acquainted. I was greatly encouraged that Dorothy and Paige had the same concerns we did.[40]

In the ensuing months what would later become known as "The Patterson-Pressler Coalition" gained momentum and broadened its base of sympathetic Southern Baptists throughout the 1970s.

Two well-known pastors served to bridge the generational gap as the titular heads of the movement. W. A. Criswell, George W. Truett's successor, was the well-established pastor of the First Baptist Church in Dallas, where he had served since 1944. Adrian Rogers served as pastor of the Bellevue Baptist Church in Memphis, Tennessee. For Rogers, the issue at hand was far more widespread than just the inner workings of the SBC. In an interview with the *Indiana Baptist,* he admitted:

> This is going to sound melodramatic, but I believe the hope of the world lies in the West. I believe the hope of the West lies in America. I believe the hope of America is in Judeo-Christian ethics. I believe that the backbone of the Judeo-Christian ethic is evangelical Christianity. I believe that the bell weather of evangelical Christianity is the Southern Baptist Convention. So

I believe, in a sense, as the Southern Baptist Convention goes, so goes the world.[41]

Motivated by this worldview, the movement grew until it burst into the open with Rogers' election as president of the Southern Baptist Convention during their annual meeting in Houston in 1979.

The need for a resurgence back to biblical fidelity had been brewing for decades. While no single, isolated event triggered the emergence of the Conservative Resurgence, the 1961 Broadman Press release of *The Message of Genesis*, a book by Midwestern Baptist Theological Seminary professor Ralph Elliot, kindled the fire.[42] This volume, utilizing a higher critical approach to biblical interpretation, questioned the historicity of the first eleven chapters of Genesis.[43] Elliot rejected the biblical account of the historicity of the persons of Adam and Eve, Noah's flood, and God's command to Abraham to sacrifice his son Isaac. At the next annual meeting of the Southern Baptist Convention, SBC president K. Owen White delivered a public and prominent criticism of Elliot, as well as the denominational press, ultimately resulting in the book's immediate withdrawal from publication and Elliott's dismissal from Midwestern Seminary for teaching outside the Baptist Faith and Message (and for insubordination as well). James Smith later reported that Elliott tragically "moved on to reject the deity of Christ and accepted the heresy of universalism."[44]

In the late 1960s, the Sunday School Board of the SBC announced a projected twelve-volume Broadman Bible Commentary. They published the first volume covering Genesis and Exodus in 1969. Broadman Press repeated the error that occurred when it published Elliot's volume. This new commentary repeatedly questioned the reliability of stated biblical episodes, including Abraham's sacrifice of Isaac, ultimately forcing this volume to be recalled as well.

Soon, numerous publications from Southern Baptist seminary presidents and professors hit the shelves, and many viewed them as abhorrently problematic to traditional conservative Southern Baptist doctrinal convictions. Roy Honeycutt, president of Southern Baptist

Theological Seminary, openly discounted many of the miracles of the Bible in his Broadman commentaries. Editing the Exodus commentary, he alludes to the fact that the burning bush in Exodus 3, from which God spoke to Moses, was most likely different-colored leaves blowing in the wind. In his commentary on 2 Kings, while discounting the miracle of the axe head floating, he allows, "Elisha secured the axe head with a long pole. Therefore, the 'iron' did not really float to the surface as the story indicates. It is . . . an example of the manner in which historical events were elaborated across successive generations until the narrative becomes a combination of saga and legend, inextricably woven together."[45]

One after another, Southern Baptist seminary professors wrote books revealing and uncovering views that conservatives considered heretical. Fisher Humphreys, a professor at the New Orleans Baptist Theological Seminary, questioned the efficacy of the blood of Christ, particularly at the point of his substitutionary death and atonement. To Humphreys, "it always seems morally outrageous that any judge would require a substitute. However noble the substitute's act might be, the judge's act seems despicable."[46] Other books blatantly questioned the long-held high view of Scripture by Southern Baptists, and they stood in diametric opposition to the Baptist Faith and Message. This list includes works from the pens of such prominent SBC professors as Glenn Hinson, Temp Sparkman, Frank Stagg, and William Hull. The fact that Cooperative Program funds from the churches were paying the salaries of these professors caused a growing agitation to a silent majority of Southern Baptists. An increasing number of Southern Baptists awakened to the need for a resurgence of traditional conservative beliefs and values in the denomination.

The issue reached a public boiling point in 1976 when Noel Wesley Hollyfield, a student at Southern Seminary, wrote a ThM thesis related to a survey he conducted of fellow Southern students. The survey revealed a striking inverse relationship in the amount of time a student spent in classes at Southern Seminary and his or her belief in Christian orthodoxy. According to Hollyfield's findings, 87 percent of first-year students had no doubts that Jesus was the divine Son of God. By their final year, the number had fallen to 63 percent. The study also revealed that 85 percent of first-year students insisted that belief in Christ was absolutely necessary for salvation; by their final year in seminary, only 60 percent held that view.[47]

Danny Akin wrote a booklet to show the contrast of SBC moderate and liberal beliefs during the 1970s and 1980s with more conservative ones. Among the most obvious contrasts is that conservatives affirmed the "inerrancy of Scripture," while moderates affirmed the "authority of Scripture in matters of salvation." Conservatives affirmed that the "Bible is the Word of God," while moderates believed the "Bible contains the Word of God." Conservatives held to "soteriological exclusivism (people are saved only through Christ)," while many moderates affirmed "soteriological inclusivism (some in other religions may be saved)." Conservatives "see the priesthood of all believers as guaranteeing direct access to God for all believers and as a doctrine of responsibility," while moderates "see the priesthood of all believers as a doctrine which gives to each the right to believe anything he/she wishes."[48]

The 1960s and 1970s signaled a repeat of the issues facing the SBC in the 1920s. Not unlike George Truett and L. R. Scarborough during the SBC's evolution controversy a half century earlier, moderates of the SBC in the 1970s could not bring themselves to acknowledge, much less address, the growing liberalism infiltrating their institutions of higher education. The inability brought about the biggest transformation in Southern Baptist history.

Although the Conservative Resurgence in the SBC did not begin until almost a quarter of a century after the death of J. Frank Norris, Paige Patterson identifies Norris as one of the models by which the Conservative Resurgence emerged. Patterson observed two distinct elements from J. Frank Norris's legacy. From Norris's example, Patterson learned what to do and not to do. Patterson admits he averted the example of Norris, who sought to change the establishment from outside.[49] Norris stood up against the encroaching liberalism of his day by exposing and attacking it from without, often in caustic and overly confrontational ways. Patterson, a student of Baptist history, had decided this approach was flawed and ultimately futile. Learning from Norris's failures a half century earlier, Patterson sought to bring theological change, not from without, but from within the very structure of Southern Baptist policy and polity. He also learned another valuable lesson from Norris. He took the fight to what B. H. Carroll had earlier called the "common people of the churches"[50] and what Norris referred to as the "fellows from the forks of the creeks."[51] In so doing, Patterson and the leaders of the Resurgence mobilized an army of smaller church pastors, organizing them by counties and states across the breadth of the Southern Baptist Convention.[52] These pastors traveled to future SBC annual meetings by multiplied thousands, often sleeping in their automobiles due to lack of funds, to vote for their conservative, biblical values and to support SBC presidential candidates who would boldly take their stand on what became their by-words: "the inerrant and infallible Word of God."

William Powell, at the time an employee of the Home Mission Board of the SBC, joined Patterson and Pressler in this endeavor. They developed a simple and workable plan to take control of the SBC within ten years. This plan involved making sure a sympathetic SBC president was elected each year to head the denomination. The president then would be empowered to appoint the all-important Committee on Committees, which, in turn, would appoint two like-minded people from each state to serve on the Committee on Nominations. This important committee then presented to the convention a slate of new trustees for all SBC entities, including the six seminaries. Since all the boards had a rotating system for trustees, occupying the presidency of the SBC for a period of ten successive years would assure majorities of conservatives on every board.

The presidential election of Adrian Rogers in 1979 began the public battle for the Bible in SBC life. In the following years, a succession of events unfolded that ultimately resulted in the firings or resignations of most of the moderate seminary presidents and entity heads over the next several years.[53] The culmination of the confrontation occurred when the SBC met for its annual meeting in Dallas in 1985. A record forty-five thousand messengers were present and registered for the convention. The point at which the pendulum swung once for all in favor of the conservatives was the sermon preached by W. A. Criswell, titled "Whether We Live or Die." Criswell, then seventy-six years of age, delivered the death knell to the moderate cause.

Interrupted dozens of times by cheers and applause, he related the damaging effects of liberal theology on individuals, churches, and denominations. He delineated how several Baptist institutions of higher learning, one after another, were destroyed by the infiltration of the liberal tenets of German higher criticism, revealing how the "curse, the rot, the virus, the corruption of a higher critical approach to the gospel began to work."[54] He continued:

> If neo-orthodoxy were a separate movement in itself, built its own churches, launched its own institutions, projected its own denomination, then we could look at it as just another of the many sects that appear on the surface of history. But, neo-orthodoxy, in itself, builds nothing. It is a parasite that grows on institutions already built. . . . No minister who has embraced a higher critical approach to the gospel has ever built a great church, held a mighty revival, or won a city to the Lord. They live off the labor and sacrifice of those who paid the price of devoted service before them. Their message, which they think is new and modern, is as old as the first lie, "Yea, hath God said?"[55]

Through his tears, Criswell concluded his message by saying, "No battle was ever won by retreat, or submission, or surrender. When Alexander the Great lay dying, they asked him, 'Whose is the kingdom?' And he replied, 'It is for him who can take it. It will be we, or somebody else.'"[56] From that moment there was no stopping the Resurgence, which continued to gain momentum and spread through Southern Baptist life, transforming the theological climate of an entire denomination.[57]

The processes involved in the Conservative Resurgence took incredible behind-the-scenes organization and long-term patience to accomplish but, in the end, assured the future conservative trajectory of SBC ministries and missions. In an indirect way, Southern Baptists owe a debt to J. Frank Norris, who taught the leaders of the movement not only how *not* to accomplish their task, but also *to* accomplish it by motivating and mobilizing the masses of "fellows from the forks of the creeks" to see the task to its completion.

The Conservative Resurgence was not simply the extension of the methodology of J. Frank Norris but also of his ministerial vision. Norris led the way against those who sought the middle ground in the struggle over creationism and evolution. He spoke out boldly against colleges, universities, and seminaries when he sensed liberalism and modernism had gained a foothold. He rallied the common people against denominational leaders who, by their actions and inactions, elevated denominational loyalty over doctrinal loyalty. These were the very issues facing the SBC a quarter of a century after Norris's death, leading to the resurgence of conservative values and beliefs.

Baptist historian James C. Hefley calls the Conservative Resurgence a "coming home" and points to Norris as a major catalyst that incited the movement. In fact, in his book *The Conservative Resurgence in the Southern Baptist Convention*, Hefley begins his treatise with a detailed review of the charges of liberalism at Baylor University, led by J. Frank Norris.[58] Speaking of Norris, Southern Seminary professor Thomas Nettles observes:

> [B]ehind the militancy and the apparent self-serving sensationalism lurked an academic and philosophical brilliancy that comprehended the destructive nature of a loss of theological coherence. His fear for the culture was a secondary manifestation of his alarm at the tendency of higher criticism and evolutionary thought to pare away necessary biblical ideas in a holistic presentation of the gospel. The irascible style and pugilistic proclivities of Norris, however, so overshadowed the argument for truth that soon the coalition of doctrinal criticism broke apart. Every voice that sounded the doctrinal concern seemed to manifest the timbre of Norris and so could be discounted as an obstruction to denominational progress.[59]

Nettles correctly identifies that, over time, the substance of what Norris was saying became lost in the sensational and bombastic style with which he approached the issues. A quarter of a century after his death, Norris resurfaced in Southern Baptist life, with little to no attribution, in the very mood, methods, and manners of those who led the Conservative Resurgence. While historians have been reluctant to acknowledge his contribution, advocates for theological change in the last half of the twentieth century adopted his role.[60]

The theological stance of today's SBC aligns with Norris's in the early twentieth century. In contrast, Truett's pastoral successor, W. A. Criswell, believed that Truett would have been "solidly in the camp of the moderates and not in sympathy with the conservatives."[61] Kelly David Pigott agrees, noting, "Southern Baptist ministries during and since the Conservative Resurgence reveal that, in the end, Truett's leadership style is shown to align more with moderates today."[62] To say that "Norris had no constructive part in Southern Baptist ministries in this century,"[63] as Leon McBeth asserts, ignores Norris's influence on those who crafted and carried out the Conservative Resurgence in SBC life in the 1970s and 1980s. The Conservative Resurgence provides the proof of Gwin Morris's prophetic prognostication that "what he [Norris] failed to do in the 1920s—take control of a denomination—he accomplished in the 1980s."[64] Ample evidence suggests that "the transformation of the Southern Baptist Convention beginning publicly in 1979 is in a measure an extension of the ministerial vision and methods of J. Frank Norris."[65]

Preaching in Southern Baptist Life

Southern Baptists of today are best known for their preaching of the Word of God.

Southern Baptists place their pulpits in the middle of their worship centers and sanctuaries for good reason: preaching is at the very center of the Baptist worship experience. There is a popular by-line for Baptist preaching today—"text-driven." This concept was made popular by the 2010 book *Text-Driven Preaching* and is defined as "a sermon that develops a text by explaining, illustrating, and applying its meaning . . . staying true to the substance of the text, the structure of the text, and the spirit of the text."[66] Although different in style and delivery, both Truett and Norris preached powerfully in the pulpit. Both had no question concerning the authority and trustworthiness of the Scriptures they expounded. Both possessed the God-given gift of exhortation and the ability to move their hearers with passionate words of persuasion.

However, in their hermeneutics, sermon preparation, and sermon delivery, Truett and Norris differed. One example of the contrast in their preaching style relates to their use of personal pronouns in their sermons. Norris called upon his hearers to take personal responsibility for the death of Christ. His repeated use of the second-person singular pronoun *you* served to reprove people in and of their sin. Consider how Norris reproved his hearers in one sermon:

> *You* can talk all you want to about *your* activities, *your* organizations, *your* machinery—what God wants is for *you* to die (to self). When *you* see that, *you* will see the world coming to Christ. Oh wife, mother, *you* have a prodigal . . . when he sees *you* die, when he sees the cross in *your* life; when he sees the Gethsemane in *your* face; when he hears, "My God, My God" is when he will be won.[67]

Truett, in contrast, avoided the use of second-person singular pronouns and even second-person plural pronouns, opting for the more positive and less confrontational approach of *we* and *they*; first- and third-person plural were his preferred pronouns. He speaks of how "we all have sinned," and how "one may be saved," and how "Christ died for us."[68] Dewitt Talmadge Holland specifically observes that Truett was "opposed to second-person pronouns in his preaching in favor of a more gracious approach."[69] Norris, like the recorded sermons of Peter and Paul, was fearless in calling people to take personal responsibility: "You have sinned . . . you may be saved . . . Christ died for you."[70]

Another glaring difference in the content of their messages was in the way they illustrated biblical truth. Truett, on the other hand, was fond of illustrating his points with secular literature. He called upon the people to "look at the great dramatists and novelists, like Shakespeare and George Eliot, and see how their writings live on because they recognize the vitality and power of conscience."[71] Norris primarily illustrated his sermons with correlating Scripture narratives or personal encounters with people he met in the normal patterns of life.

Both Norris and Truett learned preaching and received personal mentoring from B. H. Carroll during their Baylor years. Although they both learned the same versions of Carroll's pastoral theology and homiletics, Norris applied his mentor's advice to his sermon preparation much more than Truett. Carroll taught that the pastor's message was "not the world's great literature . . . not history . . . not philosophy . . . not theology as a system . . . but the preacher's message is the Bible, nothing but the Bible and all the Bible."[72] Carroll emphasized that in order to preach the cross, a preacher had to "preach sin and God's wrath."[73]

Norris and Truett also took distinctly different approaches in the hermeneutic interpretation and explanation of the sermon. Truett preached topically. He did not utilize exposition in his approach to preaching. His sermons reveal he "did little exegesis" of the text at hand.[74] He never preached through a book of the Bible or verse by verse through a chapter in his entire pulpit ministry at First Baptist Church in Dallas.[75] Although W. A. Criswell publicly honored his Dallas predecessor every year on the anniversary of Truett's death, he privately lamented the fact that "he never preached an expository sermon, not one, in his entire life."[76] Criswell relates the challenges he faced as Truett's successor in exegeting the text and preaching the Bible verse by verse:

> You never heard such lugubrious proliferation in your life. Even the finest deacon I had said, "You will clear the church. Nobody is coming here to listen to a sermon on Haggai, Zechariah, or Malachi. I don't even know where they are found in the Bible." They were correct in one instance. The people never heard such sermons.[77]

After several months of what Criswell called "preaching to wood," the people started coming to hear the Word of God such that the church auditorium could not contain the crowds and additional services were added to accommodate the overflows.[78]

Truett kept his library at his home and was a voluminous reader, especially in the evening hours. Leon McBeth reports that he was in such high demand for speaking assignments at civic clubs, schools, churches, and the like, that "he averaged speaking once a day for over forty years."[79] McBeth further reveals:

> The Truett files in Robert's Library include a twenty-six page list of Truett's book purchases between 1919–1921, with hundreds of entries. This list shows that Truett's reading interests were wide ranging, with a preference for history, biography, and inspirational volumes. Notably underrepresented are the more technical biblical studies, commentaries and heavy theological treatises.[80]

This apparent lack of theological, biblical, and exegetical curiosity may account for his topical approach to preaching and his total avoidance of text-driven exposition. This, coupled with the fact that he "averaged speaking once a day for over forty years," indicates that the exegetical study time involved in the preaching of text-driven sermons was not a high priority. Furthermore, Truett did not write a single Bible commentary or any volumes, for that matter, that actually emerged from his own hand. While there are fourteen volumes of Truett's published sermons, they were all stenographically copied, the majority of them published after his death.

Truett's son-in-law, Powhatan James, heavily edited the volumes, leading Clyde Fant and William Pinson to observe that "Truett was one of the most exciting preachers to hear and one of the most disappointing to read."[81]

In sharp contrast, Norris prolifically wrote and preached. He left much of his verse-by-verse commentaries on the Bible in print from his own hand for those who would come after him. He wrote a text-driven, two-volume, 644-page Genesis commentary; a 489-page commentary on the Revelation; a 339-page commentary on Isaiah; a 195-page work on the Roman epistle—and many more.[82] Norris used the printed page to multiply his message far beyond his Fort Worth pulpit. J. B. Leavell once said of Norris:

> Few, if any, living preachers have so mastered the Book. Surely, no living preacher is so zealous in its defense. The preacher not only unfolded the Word in a most masterful fashion in every service, but flayed error and the enemies of the truth in the most fierce and fearless fashion, that the mind could imagine."[83]

In relation to their pulpit presence, Truett and Norris were extreme opposites. Although not an expository preacher, Truett always preached "the thought of the text."[84] He is remembered as a great orator, powerful exhorter, and highly accomplished and skilled pulpiteer. By any measure, he was among the most popular and revered preachers of the first half of the twentieth century. His stately presence carried with it an aura of authority, and his voice was among his greatest assets. He stood stoic behind the pulpit and seldom gestured. McBeth relates that he seldom ever wrote out a sermon in manuscript, deferring to simply writing out a few notes, usually on the back of an envelope.[85] He placed a high value on dignity and decorum in the worship service: "Truett frankly admitted his deep indebtedness to B. H. Carroll, but he deliberately avoided absorbing Carroll's scrappy, polemical style."[86]

If Truett avoided Carroll's polemic approach to preaching, Norris embraced it with abandon: "Norris was overly expressive in body language, he waved his arms and kicked his feet and he often wept in his sermons and his people wept with him."[87] Unlike the much more formal Truett, Norris never confined himself behind his pulpit. James O. Combs relates, "He stood tall and poised often beginning with his hands in his side coat pockets, beginning with a soft voice and later rising to a cascading crescendo. Quick hand gestures punctuated his sentences. He held us spellbound for well over an hour."[88]

W. A. Criswell recounts his visit to Norris's church in Fort Worth during his high school days while on a visit to the city on a band tour:

> The First Baptist Church of Fort Worth was packed with people, young and old, rich and poor. The excitement was electric,

filling the room. I had to sit near the back and I can still remember the pipe organ playing the prelude and the great choir singing a call to worship. As the anthem's amen echoed through the church, Norris walked dramatically onto the platform and stood silently beside his pulpit . . . he commanded attention and immediately upon his entrance the people grew silent. No one moved. Norris spoke softly at first. . . .

Sixty-three years later I can still remember that sermon. Norris was preaching on the evils of sin. Before the message ended, I could smell the acrid smoke and feel the burning coals of hell. . . . When Norris gave the invitation, the aisles filled instantly with men and women, boys and girls, all weeping, all moving forward to pledge their lives to Christ. . . . I was sixteen. I didn't cry in public in those days, at least not very often, but after J. Frank Norris preached, I stood there and cried like a baby."[89]

Today's emphasis on "text-driven" preaching in Southern Baptist life can trace its roots to preachers in the vein of J. Frank Norris.[90] While not always technically expository in his sermons, he remained driven by and from the text at hand. His sermons leaned far more to the polemical than the positive as he never shied away from calling his hearers to take personal responsibility for their sin. Ritchie explains:

Norris was endowed with innate powers of persuasion and imagination, which enabled him to move thousands with his eloquence and oratory. . . . He was an ardent student of the Bible and of human nature. As a result of this accumulated knowledge, he became a master pulpiteer.[91]

The modern "purpose-driven" approach to preaching made popular by Rick Warren,[92] in contrast to the text-driven approach, can trace its roots back to the preaching pattern and style of George W. Truett. Purpose-driven preaching is characterized by its avoidance of biblical context and, in many cases, its aversion to confrontation and controversy. Truett and Warren's approach, more human-centered, appeals to the positive rather than the polemical. Even though Truett was persuasive in his exhortations and appeals, since his messages were virtually void of any exegesis of the text, they were not driven by the text. In contrast, Josh Smith notes that true "exhortation is not merely persuasion. Exhortation is text-driven persuasion."[93]

George W. Truett and J. Frank Norris live on in history as classic examples of evangelistic preachers. They both witnessed a multitude of converts to the faith and added to the kingdom of God across the decades of their respective ministries. Truett, at best, can be characterized as a "textual/argumentative preacher applying the principles of rhetoric to his preaching."[94] While both may be known as examples of evangelistic preaching, Norris stands apart as a model of the text-driven preaching style that explains, illustrates, and applies the text at hand. He was true to the substance, structure, and spirit of the text while implementing doctrine, reproof, correction, and instruction into his sermons. The influence and example of Norris's text-driven approach to preaching is evidenced in Southern Baptist pulpits today, while Truett's more positive, purpose-driven approach, void of exegesis, is out of favor among the professors of preaching and pastors in the SBC pulpits today.

Southern Baptist Eschatology Today

Eschatology, the study of last events, played an important part in the formational theory of the approach to the preaching event for both Truett and Norris. Like many before the days of the First World War, Truett was a postmillennialist. Postmillennialists believe that Christ will return to the earth after a thousand years of peace has been accomplished by the spreading of Christian principles throughout the earth.[95] Truett was among those who were "fueled by the faith that God was now working through the church to create the millennium on earth. Postmillennialism appealed to Truett because he was an optimist."[96] Truett believed that the power of the gospel would eventually triumph over evil and, through divine intervention, the kingdom of God would transform the world into a glorious age, called the millennial kingdom. This predetermined attitude toward the future brought a positivity to Truett's preaching that lent itself to his limited use of reproof and his optimistic flair that the world was coming to Christ.

Norris, on the other hand, serves as a chief proponent in the twentieth century of a dispensational premillennial hermeneutic, believing that Christ would come and rapture his church out of this world. Then, following a seven-year period of tribulation on earth, he would return to set up his earthly kingdom, reigning and ruling for a thousand years of peace from the throne of David in Jerusalem.[97] This belief contributes, in part, to the repeated use of reproof and correction in his messages, a more polemic approach than Truett's positive approach. This theme became so central to Norris's message that between 1917 and 1952 he printed and widely released 111 sermons on the Second Coming of Christ.[98]

Premillennial eschatology brought to Norris an urgency in his message and an adherence to the text not commonly found in proponents of postmillennialism. From Truett's eschatological perspective, the world was going to get better and better until Christ's coming. Norris held to the worldview that instead of getting better and better, the world was constantly declining in lostness, morality, and global conflict.

In fact, when President Harry Truman, a Southern Baptist himself, faced the decision of whether to recognize the new state of Israel, he turned to Norris, not Truett, for counsel. Israel plays a prominent role and is at the very heart of premillennial thought and practice. Late in 1947, Norris wrote to President Truman laying out the scriptural, ethical, and moral grounds for the legitimacy of a Jewish state. In the letter, he bases his argument on biblical texts such as Deuteronomy 30:3–5, which shows that God was in covenant relationship with the Jews.[99] A few months later Truman invited Norris to Washington to participate in a conference on Israel and the conflict in the Middle East. Norris followed this invitation with a letter to the President encouraging the shipment of arms to Israel to aid in their coming conflict with the surrounding Arab states over their statehood.[100] Following a vast exchange of correspondence between these two men, Norris wrote a congratulatory letter thanking the President for siding with "the covenant people" and their "God given inheritance."[101] On May 14, 1948, the new state of Israel proclaimed its independence. Within minutes of this proclamation, President Harry S. Truman extended de facto recognition, making the United States the first nation to recognize the new and independent State of Israel.[102]

While conservative premillennial Christians welcomed this event with enthusiasm, deep division grew among Christians in America. Just five days after Truman's recognition of Israel, the 1948 Southern Baptist Convention annual meeting in Memphis, Tennessee, strongly defeated all motions to recognize the Jewish state. In a standing vote of eight thousand messengers, *The New York Times* reports, "Less than 100 delegates rose to signify their favor of the motion to recognize the establishment of the Jewish State."[103] Louie Newton, the Convention president, managed to lead the Convention in opposing Truman's action. Newton, a postmillennialist, was adamantly against a Jewish state. While Truett had been dead for almost four years by that time, there is no record of his support of Israel. Newton had been Truett's closest confidant as well as the man Truett chose to preach his own funeral message, and Newton shared the same eschatological perspectives as Truett.

Since 1979, the SBC has shown almost universal support and advocacy for the modern State of Israel. There is also a common thread woven through the lives and eschatological persuasions of each president of the Southern Baptist Convention since the election of Adrian Rogers more than forty years ago. Every one of them has believed in and passionately proclaimed a premillennial hermeneutic coupled with an urgency to win the world to Christ before his promised return. From most every perspective, especially eschatologically, the SBC resembles J. Frank Norris while outright rejecting the postmillennialism of George Truett.

On May 14, 2018, seventy years to the day after the establishment of the modern State of Israel, President Donald Trump ordered the United States embassy to be moved from Tel Aviv to Jerusalem as a statement that Jerusalem was, and forever will be, the eternal and undivided capital of Israel. In a twist of historical irony, Robert Jeffress, pastor of Truett's First Baptist Church in Dallas, prayed the dedicatory prayer at the ceremony acknowledging that Israel had blessed the entire world "by pointing us to You, the one, true God, through the message of the prophets, the scriptures, and the Messiah."[104]

Anecdotally, not long after Criswell arrived at First Baptist Church, he set out to rewrite the church's long held Articles of Faith. He inserted into them a strong paragraph regarding adherence to a more premillennial, dispensational view of eschatology. When these revisions were presented to the deacon body for official approval, one of the older deacons stood to say that the great pastor George W. Truett would not sign that statement of faith because he was an ardent postmillennialist. Young Criswell immediately responded, "You, sir, are absolutely correct in that. The late, great Dr. Truett would not have signed this statement when he was here . . . but he would now!"

History reveals that behind the scenes of America's recognition of and aid to the Jewish State of Israel was none other than J. Frank Norris, whose persuasive and persistent communication with the leader of the free world found fruit in the establishment of Israel, the only true democracy in the Middle East to this day. In terms of eschatology, biblical prophecy, and the urgency of evangelism, the present SBC aligns far more with J. Frank Norris than with George W. Truett.

Evangelism and Church Growth

Through their history, Southern Baptists have emphasized personal evangelism and church growth. Well-known SBC megachurches have made widespread use of media to promote and propagate their ministries alongside their multisite approach to church expansion. Norris, not Truett, served as a prototype to each of these approaches decades before they came into vogue in Southern Baptist life.

Megachurches and Church Growth

Norris preceded the contemporary megachurch pastor. In the 1920s, the First Baptist Church in Fort Worth gathered multiplied thousands each

Sunday to both Sunday school and worship services. At the dedication of the new auditorium, ten years into Norris's pastorate, *The Fort Worth Record* reported, "Total attendance for the day was more than twelve thousand with at least two thousand turned away and two hundred new converts were added to the church."[105] By 1924, the First Baptist Church in Fort Worth was recognized as "the largest Protestant church in America."[106] The more modern phenomenon of megachurches in almost every city of America today has its origin in the life and ministry of J. Frank Norris, whose influence, whether intended or inadvertent, continues to live on in today's church growth methodology.

Multisite Campuses

Norris originated the use of multisite campuses in the practice of church evangelism and growth. He used local theaters to reach people who would not come to church, a practice now used widely by church planters.[107] He built wooden tabernacles across the city of Fort Worth to take the church to the outlying neighborhoods. In 1935, he assumed the pastorate of the Temple Baptist Church in Detroit, Michigan, while simultaneously maintaining his pastorate in Fort Worth, thirteen hundred miles away. The Detroit congregation quickly grew to enormous size. On June 5, 1938, a crowd of more than thirty thousand people gathered on the banks of the Detroit River for a baptism service, then Norris returned to Fort Worth and preached to a crowd of twenty thousand gathered in Trinity Park for a special preaching service.[108] For the next decade both congregations grew in number, enjoying unparalleled success as their pastor, by train or plane, alternated between both pulpits, proving the fallacy of Leon McBeth's extreme claim that Norris "destroyed a great church" when he came to the Fort Worth pastorate in 1909.[109]

The modern craze of establishing multisite locations of one church is high on the popularity scale in the SBC today. Multitudes of local congregations now meet in myriad locations across metropolitan areas and beyond. Eight full decades earlier, J. Frank Norris originated the idea.

Media and the Gospel

Another important venue for evangelism in the modern church growth movement is the effective use of various forms of media to translate the gospel message. Radio, television, podcasts, the internet, blogs, Facebook, and various other highly effective forms of social media are the church's tools to promote and publicize her message. Although Truett is not known to have taken advantage of multiplying his church's ministries through media other than local radio, Norris effectively used national and local media as a tool for church growth and evangelism. Of Norris, Samuel Tullock states, "No one in his day utilized the radio and print media better than J. Frank Norris."[110] He was the first major Christian media personality. He pioneered religious broadcasting, and he "helped set the pace for the modern 'electric' church movement."[111] Long before the invention of the television set, Norris was broadcasting "nationwide on more than two dozen major radio stations,"[112] reaching the great metropolitan regions of the country. While various forms of social media reach the masses today, Norris maximized the same idea decades before the invention of electronic media. Since he did not have the internet by which to express his thoughts, promote his church, and advocate for the issues near and dear to him, he instead did so weekly in his widely circulated tabloids. *The Searchlight* and *The Fundamentalist* found their ways into the mailboxes and minds of hundreds of thousands of people across the country every week.

Leaders and supporters of the Conservative Resurgence rallied around the theme of evangelism. While theology managed to rise as a major theme in Southern Baptists' "Battle for the Bible," evangelism served as its impetus because a weakened denomination doctrinally results in a loss of passion for a lost world and a waning commitment to the exclusivity of the gospel. In *A Hill on Which to Die*, Paul Pressler expresses this truth, saying, "We believed that many people who could have been won to Jesus Christ would be eternally lost if liberal theology destroyed the Southern Baptist Convention as a force for evangelism and missions. This conviction made the cause truly 'a hill on which to die.'"[113]

Many ministry similarities existed between Truett and Norris. They both were strong, charismatic leaders as well as powerful orators who built two of the nation's largest churches in their day. They both stayed where God planted them, spending the bulk of their lives in their respective pulpits serving their people until their deaths: Truett in Dallas for forty-seven years and Norris in Fort Worth for forty-three years. Their respective families were a source of constant strength to them, a testimony to their love and nurture. Both men led lives of moral impeccability, in the sense that they both stayed free from the slightest hint of scandal in the realms of money or morals. However, their similarities end in the ways they led their churches.

Norris believed in a pastor-led church. Truett believed in a deacon-led church. Norris led with deep biblical convictions about the authority of the office of the pastor and that evangelism and church growth were best served when the pastor was free to lead without restraint. Truett, on the other hand, felt that pastors must earn authority by placing trust and confidence in a board of deacons and leaving major decisions to their care. This leadership philosophy likely stemmed from his nonconfrontational personality and his proclivity to avoid controversy and conflict when at all possible. As the First Baptist Church in Dallas continued its numerical decline the last twenty years of Truett's pastorate, Pigott points out that "rather than respond to the church's inability to attract younger couples, Truett merely resigned himself to maintaining the status quo and ministering to his own aging congregation."[114]

Almost all the growing SBC congregations during and since the Conservative Resurgence share a common feature. Each of them utilizes a pastor-led leadership style, in the Norris tradition, seeing the diaconate as a servant ministry. SBC leaders throughout the past four decades have been strong believers in the authority of the spiritual office of the pastor, and virtually all have the common denominator of strong, servant-hearted pastoral leadership. As SBC churches today seek to evangelize and grow their churches, they stand much more in line with the pattern set by Frank Norris than that of George Truett.

J. Frank Norris indirectly contributed to dominant features within today's SBC. These features include the elevation of doctrinal loyalty over denominational loyalty; biblical and doctrinal fidelity; text-driven preaching; an ever-broadening use of public, print, and social media to spread the gospel; and a heightened focus on evangelism and church growth. Norris pioneered these factors in the early part of the twentieth century. Leon McBeth's claim that Norris made "no contribution to Southern Baptist ministries in this [twentieth] century"[115] fails to consider the indirect and contemporary evidence. The contributions that Norris "failed to do in the 1920s . . . he accomplished in the 1980s" and beyond.[116]

6

Conclusion

"Two Baptists" Revisited

In his description of "two Baptists"—Truett and Norris—Leon McBeth claims, "Truett became, by all odds, the most famous Southern Baptist pastor."[1] Today, over three-quarters of a century after his death, his works still follow him. Truett and Norris were both incredible visionaries. They knew where they were going and both attracted large followings. They were both moved and motivated by a driving purpose. They both were blessed with loyal and supporting wives from the moment they left their respective wedding altars until the day each man died. Josephine Truett spent her life making it her ministry to protect her husband in life and preserve his legacy after his death. She was fiercely loyal, his place of refuge, and a source of wise counsel that he valued. Few women have so loyally stood beside their husbands through as much adversity as Lillian Norris. She witnessed two of her homes burn, saw their church burn twice, and went to court with her husband as he was indicted for crimes on more than one occasion. According to Morris, "She seldom disputed his word though she must have disagreed with him on occasion. When all others forsook him, she was there, and there is no reason to suspect that Norris didn't love her tenderly, a feeling that grew increasingly through the years."[2]

Although Norris and Truett shared a few things in common, they possessed far more differences than similarities. While Truett's name was synonymous with integrity, Norris was better known for his intensity.

Revered and Reviled

Through the decades, Truett has been almost universally revered, while Norris, for the most part, has been reviled. J. Frank Norris and George W. Truett are among other popular historical figures who have been written about with bias—hidden or intended. This bias on Truett's behalf appeared early on in 1939 with the publication of his authorized biography, written by his own son-in-law, Powhatan James. This volume, *George W. Truett: A Biography*, is a classic case of hagiography without the slightest hint of criticism within its 311 pages. Leon McBeth made little attempt to cloak his personal bias for George W. Truett over and against W. A. Criswell, Truett's successor at the First Baptist Church. Having been hired by the church to write its centennial history from 1868 to 1968, he relates a conversation with Criswell in the middle of his research. Criswell, who had built the church to its greatest heights over a quarter of a century, asked McBeth how his work was going and if he had thought about how he intended to write the history of the great church. McBeth replied, "Yes, pastor, I have. . . . The years before Truett, the Truett years, and the years after Truett."[3]

Historians Leon McBeth and Mark Toulouse both illustrate obvious personal bias against J. Frank Norris. Their treatment of Norris's shooting of D. E. Chipps serves as an example. McBeth's account begins by casually mentioning that Chipps paid a visit to Norris's office and "the two men exchanged angry words," whereupon "Norris took a gun from his desk and shot Chipps three times."[4] McBeth fails to mention several key facts that eventually led to Norris's complete vindication.

Completely absent in the McBeth account of this tragedy are the numerous sworn testimonies of Chipps's repeated threats to kill Norris. Among these testimonies, recounted in more detail in chapter two, were those of Fort Worth police officers Harry Conner and Fred Hollond, who testified under oath as having visited Norris in his office on July 16, 1926, to warn him of the threats, specifically that Chipps was overheard saying the night before, "I am going to kill J. Frank Norris."[5] The following afternoon at 3:30, Chipps telephoned Norris at his office from his room in the Westbrook Hotel, where he lived. The hotel switchboard operator, Fannie Tom Greer, placed the call through the PBX switchboard at the hotel and listened in on the call. She later testified, under oath and subject to perjury, that Chipps was angry and abusive and everyone who worked at the Westbrook Hotel was afraid of him. In a sworn affidavit, she stated under oath that she heard Chipps call Dr. Norris many vile names with repeated profanity. She said, "I heard him repeat several times, 'You blankety-blank-blank, I am coming over there and kill you.'"[6] L. H. Nutt, an officer at a local bank and a respected deacon at the First Baptist Church, was the only eyewitness to the shooting. He was seated in Norris's office when Chipps burst through the office door unannounced, startling the two men. Nutt became the defense's star witness at the murder trial as he emotionally reenacted Chipps's last act of rushing toward the pastor while reaching toward his back pocket as if for a gun. He continued by telling how Norris, in fear for his life and in self-defense, fired four shots, three of which hit and killed D. E. Chipps.[7] McBeth's account in "Two Ways to Be a Baptist" omits these testimonies. His bias leaves the impression that this was simply an impulsive act of murder on Norris's part following a heated argument.

Mark Toulouse addresses the same encounter of Norris and Chipps in his paper, "A Case Study of Schism: J. Frank Norris and the Southern Baptist Convention." While Toulouse allows that Chipps "allegedly"[8] told Norris he was coming to kill him, like McBeth, he finds it unnecessary to mention any of the many on-the-record-testimonies about Chipps's intention to kill Norris. By using the word *allegedly*, Toulouse does not simply question the veracity of sworn testimonies—he ignores them altogether.

A Paradoxical Irony

Much of what Norris fought so feverishly ended up flourishing. The First Baptist Church in Dallas currently witnesses some of its greatest days of spiritual impact. Baylor University serves as a world-class center of learning, recognized as one of the outstanding colleges in the Southwest. Southwestern Seminary thrived after Norris's death, becoming indisputably the largest seminary in the world with nearly five thousand students at its peak. The Southern Baptist Convention grew to more than fifty thousand cooperating churches, training thousands in her seminaries and sending out the greatest force of missionaries the world has ever seen.

In the end, much of what Norris stood for diminished. His network of churches has repeatedly divided across the decades and is virtually unnoticeable today. His church and his school are but shells of what they once were. So many of the right things for which he advocated and the right stands for which he stood were wrapped so tightly in the chords of strident, narrow fundamentalism that his circle grew smaller and smaller in life, and his observable influence became even smaller in death. However, the unvarnished truth of his bold stand on doctrinal fidelity remains, and his influence, even if inadvertent, is behind many of the mechanisms that have propelled the Southern Baptist Convention for the past half of a century, including but not limited to the Sunday School Movement, the Baptist Faith and Message (1925), and the Conservative Resurgence.

During their lifetimes, most Southern Baptists followed Truett rather than Norris. However, in the decades since their deaths, the course has reversed as their works continue to follow them.[9] Norris never wavered from considering himself to be "the defender of Baptist orthodoxy in America."[10] In truth, Texas Baptists and Southern Baptists could well have drifted into modernism, as did their Northern Baptist cohorts, had it not been for the tireless efforts of J. Frank Norris.[11] The same might well have been said of more modern Southern Baptists had the Conservative Resurgence not been successful in turning the tide of liberalism that was beginning to manifest itself in SBC seminaries in the 1960s and 1970s. Norris may have been a constant boil festering on the flesh of many Southern Baptist leaders, but he was never allowed to become a cancer. When the First Baptist Church in Fort Worth was welcomed back into a more Norris-like Southern Baptist Convention of Texas in the early 1990s, many felt Norris had won at last.[12]

Southern Baptists Today

Are Southern Baptists more like Truett or Norris today? Truett and his style of leadership is "shown to align more with moderates today."[13] In 1991, when the leadership at Baylor University, unwilling to adopt the principles and premises of the Baptist Faith and Message doctrinal statement, inaugurated their new seminary to accommodate more moderate persuasions, it was fitting that they chose the good name of George W. Truett. For three decades, the George W. Truett Seminary has educated and prepared a new generation of ministers in the moderate lineage of the man whose name graces their school. In a twist of irony, Joel Gregory, a former leader in the Conservative Resurgence and the immediate pastoral successor to W. A. Criswell at the First Baptist Church in Dallas, serves as Truett Seminary's popular and distinguished professor of preaching.

The SBC's more recent strict adherence to biblical inerrancy, its text-driven preaching approach, its practice of strong pastoral leadership, its insistence that the scriptural role of the pastor is restricted to men, and its emphasis on doctrinal loyalty above denominational loyalty all carry the brand of J. Frank Norris. And, as Gwin Morris articulates, the irony of ironies is that "what he [Norris] failed to do in the 1920s—take control of a denomination—he accomplished in the 1980s."[14]

Frank Norris was Southern Baptists' greatest adversary and antagonist during the first half of the twentieth century. His emphasis on doctrinal fidelity served (perhaps inadvertently) to fuel the SBC's greatest years of evangelism and church growth—not to mention its conservative theological trajectory in the last half of the century. His evangelistically charged Sunday school outreach program, repackaged and marketed by Arthur Flake through the SBC's Sunday School Board, propelled thousands of Southern Baptist churches to reach millions of people through Sunday school. His onslaught against the assessments of the 75 Million Campaign, which contributed to its failure, ignited a new and completely voluntary Cooperative Program in response. This ingenious program of cooperative giving, respecting Norris's strong convictions regarding local church autonomy and void of any type of assessments or pressure, has fueled the massive ministries and missions of the SBC for a century. Norris's relentless attacks on the theological drift at his alma mater, Baylor University, brought about the necessity of the Baptist Faith and Message (1925), designed to set the doctrinal parameters for workers in SBC entities and to assure the rank and file of adherence to biblical fidelity in high places. Finally, Norris might be most proud of the contribution he unknowingly made in showing the leaders of the Conservative Resurgence the futility of his approach to attack from the outside, thereby providing the basis for the conservative roadmap that ultimately made lasting change from inside the SBC. His imperative to take the denominational concerns to the "fellows at the forks of the creeks"[15] mobilized an army of thousands of pastors who rose up in the 1980s demanding change within the SBC. In a way that those who opposed him at the time could never have understood, Southern Baptists owe Norris, the "Texas Tornado," a convoluted debt of gratitude.

In studying his methods and manners—and by showing the resurgence leadership how not to do things—they learned how to do them.

Leon McBeth asserts that J. Frank Norris "destroyed a great church," alluding to the mass exodus in 1911 when—after Norris's return from Kentucky with his new sensational, more confrontational style of ministry—the more dignified, upper-crust parishioners rose up in rebellion, demanding their church back.[16] However, masses of common men and women were converting and quickly becoming the majority, filling the church Sunday by Sunday. The pastor took the fight to the entire church, and the masses of new converts, totally loyal to him, gave him an overwhelming vote of confidence over the disgruntled longtime congregants. Hundreds of longtime members left the church and dispersed to other Baptist churches in the city. Rather than destroying a great church, Norris did just the opposite. He built a church that ten years later saw more than twelve thousand in attendance.[17] Over the following decades, the church saw multiplied thousands of new converts, trained hundreds of pastors and missionaries, and, by the late 1940s, was enjoying unparalleled success, reaching a membership of twenty-two thousand and an average Sunday school attendance of more than eight thousand.[18] Under Frank Norris's leadership, the First Baptist Church in Fort Worth was the "largest church membership in the world under one pastorate."[19]

Kelly David Pigott acknowledges, "His ministry in Fort Worth resulted in a church that fragmented after he passed away."[20] This is an uncontested truth. However, the fact that the First Baptist Church in Fort Worth fragmented after the death of Norris meant that many of the churches in the city prospered from the passionate evangelistic hearts, the deep knowledge of the Scriptures, and the commitment to the local church that characterized the lives of thousands of "Norrisites" who immersed themselves in the lives and ministries of other local churches.

A classic example is the Sagamore Hill Baptist Church in Fort Worth. This local congregation received a multitude of loyal church members after the fragmentation. Pastored by W. Fred Swank for more than forty-three years (1933–1977), Sagamore Hill was known for its evangelistic fervor and deep commitment to the Tarrant Baptist Association, the Baptist General Convention of Texas, and the SBC. This church was filled with men and women who were formerly Norris loyalists, like Elizabeth McClure Swank, who taught the teacher training classes at Sagamore Hill using Norris's curriculum, training an army of Bible teachers through the years. Kathryn Jackson, who had been Norris's longtime children's minister, led all the growing children's ministries. Francis McGee, Norris's favorite soloist, had sung hundreds of times immediately before he entered the pulpit and now blessed her new church home with the music of heaven on a regular basis. Fred and Margaret Davis, both graduates of Norris's seminary, were impactful teachers in the youth department. Fred's big black Bible had every page filled with notes from Norris's sermons. The Cains, the Scarboroughs, the Tuckers, and so many more former First Baptist in Fort Worth faithful filled the pews and Sunday school lecterns of this church every week.

The abiding fruit of Norris's life and ministry manifested itself through each of their lives as they had sat at his feet as he expounded God's Word Sunday by Sunday. They loved the Word of God, memorized it, understood the great doctrinal truths of Scripture, were consistent and passionate in sharing their faith with their lost friends and neighbors, and had a deep commitment to the local church.[21] The statement that Norris "destroyed a great church" could not be further from the truth. The fact that the church did, indeed, fragment after his death proved to be a blessing to many sister churches as Bible-believing men and women dispersed to find their places in the local churches of their city, thereby multiplying the ministry and lasting influence of J. Frank Norris many times over.

Making Matters Right

When the end of life approaches, great men and women want to make ready to meet their Maker. For both Truett and Norris, trivial earthly skirmishes faded into insignificance in light of seeing face to face the Christ whom they had preached for a lifetime. As Truett faced this reality, he related his dying wish to his longtime associate, Bob Coleman, and shared with him a deep burden of his heart. The pastor said, "Bob, I am soon to cross over, and I don't want any bitterness on my lips and I don't want any man to have bitterness against me. Call Frank Norris and tell him I want to see him."[22] Coleman never made the call to Norris.

Louis Entzminger, a close personal friend of Coleman, says, "It would be too indelicate to tell why and who interfered and persuaded Bob Coleman not to make this call. This would not be published if it were not well known."[23] This is a more than subtle insinuation that the only person alive who could have persuaded the faithful Coleman, who had served every wish of George Truett for decades, from following the dying wish of his pastor was Josephine Truett, her husband's constant and abiding protector and defender. Thus, for whatever reason, one of the most potentially humbling and God-honoring reconciliations ever recorded in Baptist annals was prevented.

Like Truett, Norris in his later years desired to seek forgiveness and make things right with those with whom he battled through the years. His most public confrontations and his most vicious accusations through the decades were directed at the scrappy and hard-hitting L. R. Scarborough. Scarborough, for his own part, was equally as confrontational and accusative toward Norris. As Scarborough lay dying in a hospital in Amarillo in 1944 under the watchful care of his daughter, Euna Lee Foreman, Norris took pen in hand and wrote to him:

> You are a heroic soul and a long, long time ago you settled the whole question of the great crossing. Naturally, I too have thought a great deal of it though it may be years for both of us, and yet it may come at any hour. To me one of the greatest scriptures is "To die is gain."
>
> . . . I am giving lectures in the Bible Institute on the Life of Paul, and only yesterday I came to that experience where they had a sharp difference over a third preacher, young John Mark. The Lord, in this case, overruled this difference and there were two great missionary journeys instead of one. How beautiful and tender Paul wrote, "Take Mark, and bring him with thee; for he is profitable to me for the ministry." But all of them are in glory. You will have a multitude of souls to meet you that were saved through your preaching of the gospel of Blood Redemption. If you get there first—and I may get there first—but if you get there first I envy you the joys that await you. I am certain as I am

a living man of the realities of the glories in the Father's home, that awaits all the redeemed.[24]

And then, in a compassionate yet sincere tone, he includes, "Yours tenderly, J. Frank Norris."[25]

So sick he was unable to reply, Scarborough had his daughter respond to Norris:

> Your letter to Daddy was so much appreciated by us all. It was so kind of you to write and the nice things you said about him will linger long in our hearts. He is still in the hospital and very seriously ill, but we are finding God's grace sufficient for our needs. . . . Thank you again for your thoughtfulness and continue to remember us all in your prayers.[26]

The letter is signed Euna Lee Foreman.

L.R. Scarborough died on April 10, 1945, at the home of his daughter. His body was brought back to Fort Worth and buried in a cemetery a few miles from the seminary where he had poured out so much of his life for decades. Raymond Barber, founder of the Worth Baptist Temple in Fort Worth and a graduate of Norris's Bible Baptist Seminary (BBS), relates the story of a strange request received by his brother, Bob, also a student at BBS, in 1947. On a given day, Norris sent for young Barber, who possessed in those days one of the few automobiles on the campus. Norris asked Barber to drive him to an appointment.

At the appointed time Norris emerged from his office with a large and beautiful bouquet of flowers in his hand. Upon getting into the car, he then instructed Barber to begin to drive out west of town. They came to a windblown cemetery.[27] The pastor told the seminarian to remain in the car as he had some business to which he needed to attend. He walked across the endless sea of tombstones until he went over a small hill out of sight. After about twenty minutes, he returned to the car without the bouquet of flowers and with the command to take him back to the office and to get back in his seminary classes as soon as possible. Upon their return and Norris's disappearance back into the buildings of the First Baptist Church, Barber, now filled with suspense and interest, rushed back to the cemetery and scoured the graves until he came to the one upon which the flowers had been placed. Looking down, he read the following words on the tombstone—Lee Rutland Scarborough, 1870–1945.[28]

During the intensity of one of their many previous skirmishes, Norris had written to Scarborough with the assurance that one day all would be well. "When you and I get to heaven," he wrote, "we will have many good times sitting down and talking all these matters over."[29] The two of them rest today only a few hundred yards from each other at Greenwood Cemetery in Fort Worth. "Their conflict is left to historians."[30]

Conclusion

"In retrospect, there have always been two Frank Norris's [sic]—the historical and the mythical—the rascal and the reformer. Both have taken on lives of their own."[31] In seeking to understand his mission and motivation, the question asked by Leon McBeth is still pertinent: "Which Norris?"[32] That is, a distinction must be made between the constructive one who built a great church and the controversial one who sought to fight a great denomination. He might well have been, as is the opinion of his successor Homer Ritchie, "a classic example of a schizophrenic who could be the kindest, most loving person, but if ever crossed could be as mean as the devil himself."[33] It is tragic that someone so brilliant, possessing so many positive gifts, can also be forever associated with that which is considered destructive, demeaning, and divisive.

Despite his self-promotion, questionable methodologies, and sometimes suspect motives, J. Frank Norris must be listed among of the major figures of religious, societal, and cultural discussions of his time. He was the quintessential Texas Tornado who, often unexpectedly, swooped down out of his own dark cloud and struck with dastardly force, leaving in his wake the ruin of lives and even legacies of those unfortunate enough to be found in his path. Yet at the same time, contrary to Leon McBeth's contention that he "had no constructive part in

Southern Baptist ministries"[34] in the twentieth century, Norris served as the role model for the transformation of an entire denomination a quarter of a century after his death.

Upon Norris's death in 1952, his son George observed that of all the things that could have been said about his father, the one thing that came to mind was that "he changed things."[35] Today, no one studying or researching his life or legacy seems to disagree, though whether he changed things for good or bad is debatable. A new breed of Southern Baptists, a generation after his death, realized his legacy and learned from his methods and his mistakes. But they too have changed things. George W. Truett and J. Frank Norris live on in heaven and in history, and one thing is certain three-quarters of a century after their deaths: they each left us a legacy that in their own respective minds was all carried out . . . IN THE NAME OF GOD.

NOTES

Chapter 1

1. Leon McBeth, *The First Baptist Church of Dallas: Centennial History* (Grand Rapids, MI: Zondervan, 1968), 18.

2. Tommy Stringer, "How Did Dallas Get Its Name?" *Corsicana Daily Sun,* April 12, 2008, https://www.corsicanadailysun.com/news/local_news/stringer---how-did-dallas-get-its-name/article_10df5bb3-45e1-5e6d-abf4-cc5b233cab15.html.

3. "Dallas History," Dallas Historical Society, https://web.archive.org/web/20060422183559/http://www.dallashistory.org/history/dallas/dallas_history.htm.

4. "Dallas History."

5. "Dallas History."

6. "Dallas History."

7. Jackie McElhaney and Michael V. Hazel, "Dallas, TX," Texas State Historical Association, November 3, 2015, https://tshaonline.org/handbook/online/articles/hdd01.

8. Julia Kathryn Garrett, *Fort Worth: A Frontier Triumph* (Austin, TX: Encino Press, 1972), 75.

9. Garnett, 67.

10. Leonard Sanders, *How Fort Worth Became the Texasmost City 1849-1920* (Fort Worth, TX: Texas Christian University Press, 1973), 40.

11. Sanders, 56.

12. Garrett, *Fort Worth,* 339–40.

13. Judy Alter and James Ward Lee, *Literary Fort Worth* (Fort Worth, TX: Texas Christian University Press, 2002), 301.

14. *The Fort Worth Register,* October 8, 1901, 1.

15. Richard F. Seller, *Hell's Half Acre* (Fort Worth, TX: Texas Christian University Press, 1991), 271.

16. Seller, 8.

17. Oliver Knight, *Fort Worth: Outpost on the Trinity* (Fort Worth, TX: Texas Christian University Press, 1990), 91.

18. Seller, *Hell's Half Acre,* 25.

19. Charles Scudder, "Why Is Fort Worth Called a Panther City?" *The Dallas Morning News,* June 6, 2018, https://www.dallasnews.com/news /curious-texas/2018/06/06/why-is-fort-worth-called-panther-city-curious -texas-investigates-a-regional-rivalry.

20. Scudder, 3.

21. Scudder, 3.

22. Jerry Flemmons, *Amon: The Life of Amon Carter, Sr. of Texas* (Austin, TX: Jenkins Publishing Company, 1978), 350.

23. Dave Lieber, "Amon Carter's Old Fort Worth Rivalry with Dallas Still Haunts Us," *The Dallas Morning News,* September 15, 2019, https:// www .dallasnews.com/opinion/commentary/2019/09/15/amon -carter -s-old -fort-worth-rivalry-with-dallas-still-haunts-us/.

24. Lieber.

25. Lieber.

26. "Chants and Rants," *The Dallas Morning News,* September 1, 2008, 19a.

27. Knight, *Fort Worth,* 226.

28. Knight, 239.

29. McBeth, *The First Baptist Church of Dallas,* 27.

30. McBeth, 27.

31. "Our Story," First Baptist Fort Worth, accessed September 25, 2019, http://www.fbcfw.org/about.

32. Karen O'Dell Bullock, "First Baptist Church, Fort Worth," Texas State Historical Association, accessed January 26, 2021, https://tshaonline .org/handbook/online/articles/ibf01.

33. Correspondence between J. Frank Norris and President Harry Truman, folder 25236, AR 124, Southern Baptist Historical Library Archives, Nashville, TN.

34. Harold Rich, "Beyond Outpost: Fort Worth 1880–1918" (PhD diss., Texas Christian University, 2006), 202–05.

35. Wayne Short, *Luke Short: A Biography of One of the Old West's Most Colorful Gamblers and Gunfighters* (Tombstone, AZ: Devil's Thumb Press, 1996), 213.

36. "Largest Christian Denominations in the United States," ProCon .org, June 30, 2008, https://undergod.procon.org/background-resources /largest-christian-denominations-in-the-united-states/.

37. McBeth, *The First Baptist Church of Dallas*, 206.

38. McBeth, 206.

39. Truett Cathy, *Eat Mor Chikin: Inspire More People: Doing Business the Chick-fil-A Way* (Decatur, GA: Looking Glass Books, 2002), 12.

Chapter 2

1. Homer Ritchie, interview by the author, Fort Worth, TX, August 8, 2008. Ritchie was the handpicked pastoral successor of J. Frank Norris at the First Baptist Church in Fort Worth.

2. Robert A. Baker, *Tell the Generations Following: A History of the Southern Baptist Theological Seminary 1908–1983* (Nashville, TN: Broadman Press, 1983), 178.

3. Samuel Kyle Tullock, "The Transformation of American Fundamentalism: The Life and Career of John Franklyn Norris" (PhD diss., University of Texas at Dallas, 1997), 201.

4. "Norris Buys KFQB," *Fort Worth Record,* June 7, 1925, 1. This article relates that Norris was heard on a network of twenty-seven of the largest radio stations in America, covering every part of the country, and carries the story of Norris's purchase of "the largest and most powerful radio station in the Southwest with the best devices and equipment yet developed."

5. Roy Falls, *A Fascinating Biography of J. Frank Norris* (Euless, TX: First Baptist Church, 1975), 85.

6. James Gatewood, *J. Frank Norris, Top O' Hill Casino, Lew Jenkins and the Texas Oil Rich* (Garland, TX: Mullaney Publishers, 2006), 2.

7. These metaphors were used by Jesus Christ in the Sermon on the Mount to contrast those who build their lives on solid moral and biblical foundations (solid rock) with those who build their lives on less stable foundations (shifting sand). See Matthew 7:24–27.

8. J. Frank Norris, *Inside History of First Baptist Church, Fort Worth and Temple Baptist Church* (New York: Garland Publishing, 1938), 308.

9. While Catlett Smith became his first ministerial mentor, it is of interest that later, upon Norris's ordination to the gospel ministry at his first student pastorate at Mount Antioch Baptist Church in Hill County, Texas, Smith refused to take part in his ordination service because he saw Norris as being overly influenced by the "Haydenites," a somewhat derogatory term used to describe followers of S. A. Hayden, who advocated against denominationalism and in support of the supreme authority of the local church. Hayden was a Landmarker who looked upon all Baptist conventions with suspicion.

10. Gwin Morris, "J. Frank Norris: Rascal or Reformer?" *Baptist History and Heritage* 3, no. 3 (Fall 1998): 25.

11. Gatewood, *J. Frank Norris, Top O' Hill Casino, Lew Jenkins and the Texas Oil Rich*, 3–4.

12. E. Ray Tatum, *Conquest or Failure: Biography of J. Frank Norris* (Dallas: Historical Foundation Publishers, 1966), 17.

13. Joseph Martin Dawson, *A Thousand Months to Remember* (Waco, TX: Baylor University Press, 1964), 57.

14. J. Frank Norris, "A Visit to My Boyhood Home and My Mother's Grave," *The Fundamentalist,* September 16, 1949, 1, 8.

15. Tatum, *Conquest or Failure*, 18.

16. Guy Thompson, interview by author, Fort Worth, TX, October 8, 2008. Thompson, owner of Harveson and Cole Funeral Home, was a Fort Worth fixture for decades and conducted the funerals of most of the Fort Worth notables, including Dr. and Mrs. Norris and many of their family.

17. *Handbook of Texas Online*, Texas State Historical Association, accessed October 2, 2019, http://www.tshaonline.org/handbook/online/archives/hlh67.

18. Louis Entzminger, *The J. Frank Norris I Have Known for 34 Years* (Fort Worth, TX: Self Published, undated), 35–36.

19. R. Albert Mohler, interview by author, Nashville, September 17, 2019. Although Norris would mention his valedictorian status through the years, Mohler indicates there is no official record at Southern Seminary that this was the case. He might well have been, or it might have been the embellishment of his own achievements as they grew through the years.

20. Norris, *Inside History*, 24.

21. Norris, 26.

22. John M. Brown, "J. Frank Norris: The Sin-Hating Sensationalist" (MDiv project, Liberty University), 6.

23. Tatum, *Conquest or Failure*, 81.

24. Entzminger, *Norris I Have Known*, 69–70.

25. Leon McBeth, "Two Ways to Be a Baptist," *Baptist History and Heritage* (April 1997): 27.

26. This strange death raised suspicions about how such a healthy middle-aged man as J. M. Gaddy could fall from the back of a train in the middle of the night. No formal inquiry or charges were ever made because there were no witnesses to the tragedy. While historians like Leon McBeth in "Two Ways to Be a Baptist" question Norris's part in the death, Gaddy's widow and Norris's mother-in-law had no such doubts. She testified passionately for Norris as a character witness at his arson trial in 1912 and happily lived in the Norris home the rest of her life.

27. Clovis Gwin Morris, "He Changed Things: The Life and Thought of J. Frank Norris" (PhD diss., Texas Tech University, 1973), 48.

28. Dr. Homer G. Ritchie, *The Life and Legend of J. Frank Norris: The Fighting Parson*, (Fort Worth, TX: self published, 1991), 43.

29. Ritchie, 461.

30. Flemmons, *Amon*, 173.

31. Norris, *Inside History*, 38.

32. Flemmons, *Amon*, 173–74.

33. Norris, *Inside History*, 40.

34. J. Frank Norris, editorial, *The Baptist Standard*, August 27, 1908, 1.

35. Norris, *Inside History*, 40.

36. Norris, 41.

37. Tatum, *Conquest or Failure*, 115.

38. Flemmons, *Amon*, 176.

39. Flemmons, 178.

40. Barry Hankins, *God's Rascal: J. Frank Norris and the Beginnings of Southern Fundamentalism* (Lexington: The University Press of Kentucky, 1996), 14–15.

41. Flemmons, *Amon*, 175.

42. Harry Keeton was the great uncle of the author, and this story was often told at family gatherings and reunions though the years. It is recorded as heard on numerous occasions.

43. Entzminger, *Norris I Have Known*, 147.

44. Norris, *Inside History*, 43.

45. Norris, 43.

46. Frank Norris's ecclesiology adhered to "congregational rule" when it suited his purposes. However, after this church-wide vote there is no record that the church ever voted on anything in a church-wide vote again. His insistence on complete pastoral authority, as opposed to congregational rule, was a key reason First Baptist Church was later expelled from the Tarrant Baptist Association in 1922. Information related to expulsion from TBA can be found in Morris, "He Changed Things," 117.

47. Hankins, *God's Rascal*, 42.

48. McBeth, "Two Ways to Be a Baptist," 31.

49. McBeth, 31.

50. McBeth, 31.

51. Michael E. Schepis, *J. Frank Norris: The Fascinating, Controversial Life of a Forgotten Figure of the Twentieth Century* (Nashville, TN: WestBow, 2012), 45.

52. Brown, "J. Frank Norris," 10.

53. Schepis, *J. Frank Norris*, 2.

54. "Norris indicted on two counts arson, one count perjury," *The Fort Worth Record*, March 2, 1912, 1.

55. J. B. Gambrell, editorial, *The Baptist Standard*, May 2, 1912, 1.

56. Entzminger, *Norris I Have Known*, 88.

57. McBeth, "Two Ways to Be a Baptist," 35.

58. Correspondence between J. Frank Norris and President Harry Truman, folder 23, AR 124, Southern Baptist Historical Library Archives, Nashville, TN.

59. Tatum, *Conquest or Failure*, 155.

60. Norris, *Inside History*, 64.

61. Norris, 65.

62. "First Baptist Pastor Speedily Cleared of Arson-Crowd Cheers Verdict," *Fort Worth Star-Telegram*, January 24, 1914, 1.

63. "Dr. Norris Slays D. E. Chipps," *Fort Worth Star-Telegram*, July 18, 1926, 1.

64. Tatum, *Conquest or Failure*, 215.

65. Flemmons, *Amon*, 185.

66. Ritchie, *Life and Legend*, 160. Ritchie was quoting from Norris's words recorded in his weekly tabloid, *The Searchlight*, July 16, 1926, 2, 5.

67. Entzminger, *Norris I Have Known*, 107.

68. Fannie Tom Greer, affidavit before C. W. Braselton, folder 292, Frank Norris Papers AR 124, Southern Baptist Historical Library Archives, Nashville, TN. This sworn affidavit took place in Tarrant County, Texas.

69. James Bryant, phone interview by author, September 11, 2008. Bryant said that Kathryn Jackson, First Baptist's children's worker, often told the account of hearing this consistent claim that several eyewitnesses including L. H. Nutt and Jane Hartwell, the pastor's secretary, saw a gun lying beside the body of Chipps on the floor of the office. Bryant, now deceased, was associate pastor of the First Baptist Church in Dallas in the 1960s and pastor of Sagamore Hill Baptist Church in Fort Worth in the 1970s.

70. Affidavit of Jane Hartwell before C. W. Braselton, folder 292, Norris Papers AR 124, Southern Baptist Archives. Sworn in Braselton, Tarrant County, Texas.

71. Ritchie, *Life and Legend*, 165.

72. Flemmons, *Amon*, 187.

73. "Meacham Hires Special Prosecutors," *Dallas News*, October 31, 1926, 1–2.

74. Ritchie, *Life and Legend*, 168.

75. Ritchie, 170.

76. "Word for Word Transcript of Norris Trial," *Austin Statesman*, July 21, 1927, jfnorris.net.

77. Tatum, *Conquest or Failure*, 240–41, quoting *The Fundamentalist*, January 28, 1927, 1.

78. J. Frank Norris, editorial, *The Searchlight*, January 28, 1927, 2.

79. Tatum, *Conquest or Failure*, 241, quoting *New York American*, January 27, 1927, 1.

80. Norris, *Inside History*, 94.

81. Norris, 95.

82. See chapter 4 for detailed accounts of the major controversies and conflicts between Norris and Truett involving the entire SBC, which raged for almost four decades.

83. Bill Swank Papers, folder 61, Norris Collection, archives, Southwestern Baptist Theological Seminary, Fort Worth, TX.

84. Bill Swank Papers.

85. Norris, *Inside History*, 99.

86. Falls, *Fascinating Biography*, 94.

87. Entzminger, *Norris I Have Known*, 1.

88. The remnants of Norris's seminary still exists today, now known as Arlington Baptist University located in Arlington, Texas. A large bronze statue of J. Frank Norris greets everyone entering the campus.

89. Thompson, interview by the author.

90. "Son Is Named Pastor—But Norris Has Not Resigned," *Fort Worth Press*, June 19, 1944, 1.

91. Although this famous quote is universally attributed to Horace Greeley, these originally were the words of John B. L. Soule. "Go West, Young Man, Go West," Encyclopedia.com, November 22, 2019, https://www.encyclopedia.com/history/dictionaries-thesauruses-pictures-and-press-releases/go-west-young-man-go-west.

92. Ritchie, interview by the author.

93. Correspondence from J. Frank Norris to George Norris, January 9, 1945, folder 1372, J. Frank Norris Papers AR 124, Southern Baptist Historical Library Archives, Nashville, TN.

94. Correspondence from J. Frank Norris to George Norris, January 9, 1945.

95. Correspondence from J. Frank Norris to George Norris, January 11, 1945, folder 1372, J. Frank Norris Papers AR 124, Southern Baptist Historical Library Archives, Nashville, TN.

96. Ritchie, interview by the author.

97. Correspondence from Harry Keeton to George Norris, January 12, 1945, folder 1372, J. Frank Norris Papers AR 124, Southern Baptist Historical Library Archives, Nashville, TN.

98. Correspondence from J. Frank Norris to George Norris, January 25, 1945, folder 1372, J. Frank Norris Papers AR 124, Southern Baptist Historical Library Archives, Nashville, TN.

99. Correspondence from J. Frank Norris to George Norris, January 25, 1945.

100. Correspondence from George Norris to the First Baptist Church in Fort Worth, January 26, 1945, folder 1372, J. Frank Norris Papers AR 124, Southern Baptist Historical Library Archives, Nashville, TN.

101. "Absalom's revolt" is a common expression in ecclesiological language related to how King David's son, Absalom, revolted against David's leadership, betrayed his father, and tried unsuccessfully to take the kingdom away from his father. The encounter is recorded for posterity in 2 Samuel 15.

102. Correspondence from J. Frank Norris to George Norris, June 5, 1945, folder 1372, J. Frank Norris Papers AR 124, Southern Baptist Historical Library Archives, Nashville, TN.

103. George Norris Jr., phone interview by author, Vernon, TX, September 9, 2008. Norris, now deceased, was the son of George Norris and the grandson of J. Frank Norris.

104. Beauchamp Vick served as the campus pastor at Temple Baptist Church in Detroit, administered the church, and preached when Norris was absent. He was later appointed by Norris to head the Bible Baptist Seminary in Fort Worth.

105. Morris, "He Changed Things," 470.

106. J. Frank Norris, editorial, *The Fundamentalist*, February 10, 1950, 1–5.

107. Correspondence from Ralph Pew to Temple Baptist Church in Detroit, June 14, 1950, folder 1911, J. Frank Norris Papers AR 124, Southern Baptist Historical Library Archives, Nashville, TN.

108. Correspondence from Ralph Pew to Temple Baptist Church in Detroit.

109. Correspondence from Beauchamp Vick to J. Frank Norris, May 17, 1950, folder 1910, Southern Baptist Historical Library Archives, Nashville, TN.

110. Morris, "He Changed Things," 480.

111. Jerry Falwell, Bible Baptist College's most famous graduate, was the founder of the megachurch Thomas Road Baptist Church in Lynchburg, Virginia, as well as the founder of Liberty University, now among the world's largest Christian universities.

112. Ritchie, interview by author.

113. Morris, "J. Frank Norris," 37.

114. Billy Graham, *Just As I Am: An Autobiography* (San Francisco: HarperCollins Publishers, 1997), 158.

115. Correspondence from J. Frank Norris to Billy Graham, March 2, 1950, folder 778, J. Frank Norris Papers AR 124, Southern Baptist Historical Library Archives, Nashville, TN.

116. Correspondence from J. Frank Norris to Billy Graham, June 7, 1950, folder 778, J. Frank Norris Papers AR 124, Southern Baptist Historical Library Archives, Nashville, TN.

117. Correspondence from J. Frank Norris to Billy Graham.

118. Correspondence from J. Frank Norris to Billy Graham, March 24, 1951, folder 779, J. Frank Norris Papers AR 124, Southern Baptist Historical Library Archives, Nashville, TN.

119. Correspondence from J. Frank Norris to Luther C. Peak, February 14, 1952, folder 1513, J. Frank Norris Papers AR 124, Southern Baptist Historical Library Archives, Nashville, TN.

120. Correspondence from Luther C. Peak to Membership of First Baptist Church, June 8, 1952, folder 1513, J. Frank Norris Papers AR 124, Southern Baptist Historical Library Archives, Nashville, TN.

121. Hankins, *God's Rascal,* 125.

122. Ritchie, author interview.

123. Ritchie.

124. "Norris Is Praised by Long Time Associate," *Fort Worth Star-Telegram,* August 21, 1952, 1.

125. Ritchie, *Life and Legend,* 264.

126. David Stokes, *Apparent Danger: The Pastor of America's First Mega Church and the Texas Murder Trial of the Decade of the 1920s* (Minneapolis, MN: Bascom Hill Books, 2010), 19.

127. Tatum, *Conquest or Failure,* 281.

128. Tatum, 281.

129. Ritchie, interview by the author.

130. Morris, "He Changed Things," 448.

131. Correspondence from J. Frank Norris to the First Baptist Church in Fort Worth, July 21, 1951, 1, 8428, J. Frank Norris Papers AR 124, Southern Baptist Historical Library Archives, Nashville, TN.

132. Schepis, *J. Frank Norris*, 220–21.

133. Correspondence from J. Frank Norris to Luther C. Peak, July 8, 1952, folder 1513, J. Frank Norris Papers AR 124, Southern Baptist Historical Library Archives, Nashville, TN.

134. Ritchie, interview by the author.

135. Harry Heineke, "Body of Norris Archives," *Fort Worth Star-Telegram*, August 22, 1952, Box 2, L. R. Scarborough Collection, Southwestern Baptist Theological Seminary, Fort Worth, TX.

136. Thompson, interview by author.

137. Thompson, interview by author.

138. "J. Frank Norris Dies on Florida Visit," *Fort Worth Star-Telegram*, August 21, 1952, 1.

139. George Norris, audio recording, n.d., Heritage Collection, Arlington Baptist College, Arlington, TX.

140. Ritchie, interview by the author.

Chapter 3

1. Powhatan James, *George W. Truett A Biography* (Nashville: Broadman Press, 1939), 21.

2. James, 21.

3. James, 21.

4. James, 25.

5. James, 25.

6. James, 37.

7. James, 40.

8. McBeth, *The First Baptist Church of Dallas,* 119.

9. McBeth, 119.

10. McBeth, 120.

11. James, *George W. Truett*, 52.

12. George W. Truett, "The Preacher as a Man" (address, Southwestern Baptist Theological Seminary, Fort Worth, TX, February 18, 1914), 11, file 1916, MF 1909-1972:2 (F.3.12), George W. Truett Collection, A. W. Roberts Library, Southwestern Baptist Theological Seminary, Fort Worth, TX.

13. Correspondence from George W. Truett to B. H. Carroll, February 18, 1891, Southwestern Baptist Theological Seminary, file 815, George W. Truett Collection, A. W. Roberts Library, Southwestern Baptist Theological Seminary, Fort Worth, TX.

14. Durso, *Thy Will Be Done*, 273.

15. Durso, 42.

16. Rosalee Mills Appleby, "The Price of Power," typed manuscript, n.d., 3, Truett Baptist History File, Southern Baptist Historical Library Archives, Nashville, TN.

17. Durso, *Thy Will Be Done*, 45.

18. James, *George W. Truett*, 9–10.

19. McBeth, *The First Baptist Church of Dallas*, 123.

20. J. B. Cranfill, *Dr. J. B. Cranfill's Chronicle* (New York: Fleming H. Revell, 1916), 487.

21. McBeth, *The First Baptist Church of Dallas*, 112.

22. James, *George W. Truett*, 81.

23. McBeth, *The First Baptist Church of Dallas*, 114.

24. McBeth, *The First Baptist Church of Dallas*, 352.

25. *Fort Worth Record*, September 13, 1919, Norris Archives, Fort Worth Public Library, Fort Worth, TX.

26. Trevin Wax, "Lessons from the Megachurch Pastor Who Killed a Man," *The Gospel Coalition*, May 29, 2012, https://thegospelcoalition .org/blogs/trevin-wax/lessons-from-the-megachuch-pastor-who-killed-a -man/.

27. "J. Frank Norris by the Numbers," Baptistbasics.org, https://www .baptistbasics.org/baptists/norris7.php; McBeth, *The First Baptist Church of Dallas*, 352.

28. W. A. Criswell succeeded George W. Truett as pastor of the First Baptist Church in 1944 and within a year reversed a steady twenty-year decline in attendance and membership by adding 888 new members in just his first year of ministry. The church saw explosive growth throughout the

Criswell years, reaching a zenith of more than twenty-five thousand members in the 1970s.

29. These details of the Arnold incident come from excerpts of George W. Baines's diary, which can be found in McBeth, *The First Baptist Church of Dallas*, 135–37.

30. J. M. Dawson, "Truett's Gethsemane Now Revealed" (1958), 2, TC 629/MF 628-657:1.

31. McBeth, *The First Baptist Church of Dallas*, 137.

32. James, *George W. Truett*, 88.

33. Durso, *Thy Will Be Done*, 58.

34. McBeth, *The First Baptist Church of Dallas*, 137.

35. McBeth, 137.

36. McBeth, 133.

37. J. M. Carroll, *A History of Texas Baptists* (Dallas: Baptist Standard Publishing Company, 1923), 785.

38. Carroll, 800–801.

39. B. F. Riley, *History of Baptists in Texas* (Dallas: self-published, 1907), 457.

40. Newspaper clipping [unidentifiable], file 33, George W. Truett Collection, Southwestern Baptist Theological Seminary.

41. George W. Truett, diary, July 19, 1919, file 33, George W. Truett Collection, A. W. Roberts Library, Southwestern Baptist Theological Seminary.

42. Leon McBeth, "George W. Truett: Baptist Statesman," *Baptist History and Heritage* 32, no. 2 (April 1997): 17.

43. McBeth, "George W. Truett," 17.

44. Southern Baptist Convention Annual, 1920, 115.

45. Douglas Blount and Joseph Woodall, *The Baptist Faith and Message 2000: Critical Issues in America's Largest Denomination* (Louisville, CO: Rowman and Littlefield Publishers, 2007), 153.

46. Blount and Woodall, *Baptist Faith and Message*, 153.

47. W. A. Criswell, interview by author, Dallas, TX, August 25, 1994.

48. Michael Stone, "Megachurch Pastor Robert Jeffress: 'There's No Such Thing as Separation of Church and State,'" *Progressive Secular Humanist*, September 27, 2019, https://www.patheos.com/blogs/progressive secularhumanist/2019/09/megachurch-pastor-Robert-Jeffress-theres-no-such -thing-as-separation-of-church-and-state/.

49. Darwin Payne, "When Dallas Was the Most Racist City in America," *D Magazine*, June 2017, https://www.dmagazine.com/publications/d-magazine/2017/June/when-DALLAS-was-the-most-racist-city-in-America/.

50. Payne, "When Dallas Was Racist," 3.

51. Dawson, *Thousand Months to Remember*, 165.

52. Joseph Davis, "Embrace Equality: Texas Baptists, Social Christianity, and Civil Rights in the Twentieth Century" (Master's thesis, University of North Texas, 2013), 75.

53. George W. Truett, "Baptists and Religious Liberty," May 16, 1920, accessed December 5, 2019, https://bjconline.org/baptists-and-religious-liberty-2/, 3.

54. McBeth, *The First Baptist Church of Dallas*, 209.

55. Hankins, *God's Rascal*, 166.

56. Davis, "Embrace Equality," 68.

57. James, *George W. Truett*, 169.

58. Durso, *Thy Will Be Done*, 69.

59. W. A. Criswell, "Dr. Truett and Baylor Hospital," June 6, 1980, W. A. Criswell Sermon Library, https://www.wacriswell.com/sermons/1980/dr-truett-and-Baylor-hospital/, 3.

60. Criswell, 4.

61. Wendy Hermes, interview by author, Dallas, TX, October 11, 2019.

62. Robert Baker, *The Thirteenth Check: The Jubilee History of the Annuity Board* (Nashville: Broadman Press, 1968), 4.

63. William Lunsford succeeded B. H. Carroll as pastor of the First Baptist Church in Waco in 1901. Succeeding the legendary Carroll as pastor of this prominent pulpit enabled Lunsford to become personally acquainted with all the major leaders in Texas Baptist life, including the likes of J. M. Dawson, George W. Truett, and others.

64. Baker, *Thirteenth Check*, 14.

65. *GuideStone 100: Celebrating 100 Years of Service* (Dallas: self published, 2018), 11.

66. McBeth, *The First Baptist Church of Dallas*, 207.

67. McBeth, 191.

68. Josephine Nash, interview by author, Dallas, September 18, 2008. Josephine Nash was the niece of Dr. and Mrs. Truett and the namesake of Mrs. Truett. She was a lifelong, faithful member of the First Baptist Church.

69. McBeth, *The First Baptist Church of Dallas*, 236.

70. McBeth, 236.

71. McBeth, "George W. Truett," 21.

72. Joe Wright Burton, *Prince of the Pulpit: A Pen Picture of George W. Truett at Work* (Grand Rapids, MI: Zondervan, 1946), 35.

73. Durso, *Thy Will Be Done*, 248.

74. Correspondence from A. B. Tanco to W. A. Criswell, December 27, 195, box 11, "Speeches on FBC, Texas Baptists" folder, H. Leon McBeth Collection, Texas Baptist Historical Collection, Waco, TX.

75. McBeth, *The First Baptist Church of Dallas*, 233.

76. Kelly David Pigott, "Comparison of the Leadership of George W. Truett and J. Frank Norris in Church, Denominational, Interdenominational and Political Affairs" (PhD diss., Southwestern Baptist Theological Seminary, 1993), 71.

77. McBeth, *The First Baptist Church of Dallas*, 352.

78. W. A. Criswell, *Standing on the Promises* (Dallas: Word Publishing, 1990), 178–79.

79. Criswell, interview by author.

80. Nash, interview by author.

81. Entzminger, *Norris I Have Known*, 186.

82. Entzminger, 186.

83. A. B. Tanco, interview by author, Dallas, November 15, 1993. When the author became pastor of the First Baptist Church in Dallas, several reports came related to the remarkable memory of Mr. Tanco, who was then in his nineties. This former lawyer and decades-long deacon resided at Buchner's Retirement Center.

84. McBeth, *The First Baptist Church of Dallas*, 215.

85. Durso, *Thy Will Be Done*, 265.

86. George W. Truett, *On Eagle Wings*, ed. Powhatan W. James (Grand Rapids, MI: William B. Eerdmans Publishing House, 1953).

87. McBeth, *The First Baptist Church of Dallas*, 352.

88. McBeth, 216.

89. Each year for fifty years on the anniversary of Truett's death in July, Criswell would preach a message lauding the many accomplishments of his distinguished predecessor. In his autobiography *Standing on the Promises*, Criswell tells of the warm and wonderful manner in which he

and his wife were initially welcomed by Mrs. Truett. Criswell, *Standing on the Promises*, 172.

90. Criswell, interview by author.

91. Joel Gregory, *Too Great A Temptation* (Fort Worth, TX: Summit Group Publishers, 1994), 44.

92. McBeth, *The First Baptist Church of Dallas*, 215.

93. Durso, *Thy Will Be Done*, 272.

94. Criswell, interview by author. This account was repeatedly heard by the author at various times and in the presence of many SBC notables such as Jack Graham, Jack Pogue, and Mac Brunson, who readily attest to its validity today.

Chapter 4

1. Leon McBeth, "J. Frank Norris and His Relationship with Southwestern Seminary," paper, Founder's Day Chapel at Southwestern Baptist Theological Seminary, March, 12, 1987, Box 2, Norris Collection, Southwestern Baptist Theological Seminary, Fort Worth, TX.

2. Nash, interview by author.

3. Norris and Truett clashed on such denominational controversies as the move of Southwestern Baptist Theological Seminary from Waco to Fort Worth, the evolution controversy at Baylor University in the early 1920s, and the 75 Million Campaign from 1919 to 1924. For further study of these, see Leon McBeth, "J. Frank Norris and Southwestern Seminary," *Southwestern Journal of Theology* 30, no. 3 (Summer 1988): 16; James, *George W. Truett*.

4. McBeth, *The First Baptist Church of Dallas*, 190.

5. Landmarkism was a brand of Baptist ecclesiology that arose in the later years of the nineteenth century. It was committed to a strong version of the perpetuity theory of Baptist origins, suggesting an unbroken line between modern-day Baptists and the apostolic period. It favored strong local church authority over denominational loyalty. For further study, see Kristian Pratt, *The Father of Modern Landmarkism: The Life of Ben M. Bogard* (Macon, GA: Mercer University Press, 2013).

6. Pigott, "Comparison of Leadership," 8.

7. Tullock, "Transformation of American Fundamentalism," 33.

8. Tullock, 9.

9. Tullock, 241.

10. Correspondence from J. Frank Norris to Louis Entzminger, January 6, 1931, folder 1228, J. Frank Norris Papers AR 124, Southern Baptist Historical Library Archives, Nashville, TN.

11. Correspondence from J. Frank Norris to Victor Masters, December 16, 1932, folder 1230, J. Frank Norris Papers AR 124, Southern Baptist Historical Library Archives, Nashville, TN.

12. Correspondence from Victor Masters to J. Frank Norris, May 8, 1949, folder 1230, J. Frank Norris Papers AR 124, Southern Baptist Historical Library Archives, Nashville, TN.

13. Norris, *Inside History*, 32.

14. McBeth, "Two Ways to Be a Baptist," 43.

15. Durso, *George W. Truett*, 175.

16. Correspondence from J. Frank Norris to George W. Truett, March 9, 1940, file 1133, MF 736-1336:35, George W. Truett Collection, A. W. Roberts Library, Southwestern Baptist Theological Seminary, Fort Worth, TX.

17. Durso, *George W. Truett*, 241.

18. Durso, 240.

19. Brown, "J. Frank Norris," 6.

20. Durso, *George W. Truett*, 79.

21. Dawson, *A Thousand Months to Remember*, 121.

22. Durso, *George W. Truett*, 93.

23. Brown, "J. Frank Norris," 6.

24. Morris, *He Changed Things*, 62.

25. Presnall Wood and Floyd Thatcher, *Prophets and Pens* (Dallas: Baptist Standard Publishing Company, 1969), 61–63.

26. Norris, *Inside History*, 24.

27. Morris, "Rascal or Reformer," 22.

28. J. B. Gambrell, "The Growing of a Great Religious Paper," *The Baptist Standard* 19, no. 17.

29. J. B. Gambrell, "Some Observations Concerning Denominational Loyalty," *The Baptist Standard*, 19, no. 29.

30. Durso, *George W. Truett*, 93.

31. Norris, *Inside History*, 32.

32. Morris, *He Changed Things*, 79.

33. Glenn Carson, "Lee Rutland Scarborough: Architect of a New Denominationalism within the Southern Baptist Convention" (PhD diss., Southwestern Baptist Theological Seminary, July 1992), 43.

34. McBeth, "Norris and Southwestern Seminary," 16.

35. McBeth, 16.

36. Leon McBeth, *Texas Baptists: A Sesquicentennial History* (Dallas: Baptist Way Press, 1998), 148.

37. Correspondence from B. H. Carroll to George W. Truett, March 30, 1909, B. H. Carroll Archives, Southwestern Baptist Theological Seminary, Fort Worth, TX.

38. Schepis, *J. Frank Norris*, 36.

39. Entzminger, *Norris I Have Known*, 77.

40. Entzminger, 78.

41. McBeth, "Norris and Southwestern Seminary," 16.

42. McBeth, 16.

43. Baker, *Tell the Generations Following*, 154.

44. "Dr. Norris Accepts First Baptist's Call," *Fort Worth Star-Telegram*, October 9, 1909, 8.

45. *Fort Worth Star-Telegram*, October 11, 1909, 2.

46. McBeth, "Norris and Southwestern Seminary," 16.

47. Alan Lefever, *Fighting the Good Fight: The Life and Work of Benajah Harvey Carroll* (Fort Worth, TX: Eakin Press, 1994), 120.

48. Pigott, "Comparison of Leadership," 79.

49. L. R. Scarborough, *A Modern School of the Prophets* (Nashville: Broadman Press, 1939), 90.

50. Scarborough, 90.

51. Pigott, "Comparison of Leadership," 79.

52. McBeth, "Norris and Southwestern Seminary," 18.

53. Durso, *George W. Truett*, 175.

54. Alan Lefever, interview by author, August 27, 2019.

55. Bobby D. Compton, "J. Frank Norris and Southern Baptists," *Review and Expositor* 79, no. 1 (Winter 1982): 72.

56. Samuel Dow, *Introduction to Sociology* (New York: Thomas Y. Crowell, Co.), 1920.

57. Compton, "J. Frank Norris and Southern Baptists," 72.

58. Gwin Morris, "No Love Lost: J. Frank Norris and Texas Baptists, 1921–1925," *Baptist History and Heritage* 21 (2001): 86.

59. Thomas Nettles, *By His Grace and for His Glory* (Grand Rapids, MI: Baker Book House, 1986), 244.

60. Samuel Tullock, *The Transformation of American Fundamentalism: The Life and Career of John Franklyn Norris* (Dallas: The University of Texas at Dallas, 1997), 114–15.

61. Durso, *George W. Truett*, 189.

62. W. W. Barnes, "Denominational Leader," *Southwestern News III* (May 1945): 2.

63. Morris, "He Changed Things," 492.

64. Tatum, *Conquest or Failure*, 181–82.

65. Tatum, 186.

66. Norris, *Inside History* [1938], 6-7.

67. Tullock, *Transformation of American Fundamentalism*, 221.

68. John Davies, "Science and the Sacred: The Evolution Controversy at Baylor, 1920–1929," *East Texas Historical Journal* 29, no. 2 (1991): 43.

69. Pigott, "Comparison of Leadership," 110.

70. Gambrell, "Some Observations."

71. For a more detailed summary of the 75 Million Campaign, see Durso, *Thy Will Be Done*, 166–75.

72. Barnes, "The Norris Affair."

73. Pigott, "Comparison of Leadership," 94.

74. Pigott, 91.

75. Morris, "Rascal or Reformer," 31.

76. Morris, 30. This statement was sworn and authorized before L. H. Nutt, notary public, on October 16, 1922, in Tarrant County, Texas.

77. Jess Fletcher, *The Southern Baptist Convention: A Sesquicentennial History* (Nashville: Broadman Press), 1994, 148–49.

78. Entzminger, *Norris I Have Known*, 179.

79. Morris, "He Changed Things," 131–49.

80. Correspondence from J. Matthew Harder to George W. Truett, November 2, 1923, file 934, MF 736-1336:21, George W. Truett Collection, A. W. Roberts Library, Southwestern Baptist Theological Seminary, Fort Worth, TX.

81. Entzminger, *Norris I Have Known*, 278.

82. Nate Adams, "The Baptist 75 Million Campaign," SBC Life, May 1, 1999, http://www.sbclife.net/article/448/the-baptist-75-million-campaign.

83. Pigott, "Comparison of Leadership," 92.

84. Pigott, 92.

85. Pigott, 97.

86. Morris, "Rascal or Reformer," 31.

87. Annual, Baptist General Convention of Texas, 1924, 25.

88. Durso, *George W. Truett*, 175.

89. Ron Sayles, *Old Time Radio Digest* 2009, no. 51.

90. The Truett-Scarborough coalition timed what would later be termed "The Radio Hate Fest" just months after Norris's notorious murder trial, in which he was eventually acquitted for the slaying of D. E. Chipps.

91. Norris, *Inside History*, 198.

92. Durso, *George W. Truett*, 70.

93. Correspondence from J. Frank Norris to George W. Truett, March 9, 1940.

94. Nash, interview by author.

95. McBeth, *The First Baptist Church of Dallas*, 194.

96. Pigott, "Comparison of Leadership," 145.

97. Norris, *Inside History* [1938], 198, quoting G. Beauchamp Vick.

98. Norris, 162.

99. Norris, 198.

100. Norris, 199.

101. Ritchie, *Life and Legend*, 135–36.

102. Entzminger, *Norris I Have Known*, 282.

103. Entzminger, 282.

104. Entzminger, 281.

105. Entzminger, 281.

106. Correspondence from J. Frank Norris to L. R. Scarborough, December 1, 1927, box 37, folder 1683, J. Frank Norris Papers AR 124, Southern Baptist Historical Library Archives, Nashville, TN.

107. Correspondence from J. Frank Norris to F. S. Groner, December 15, 1927, box 17, folders 10365–10367, J. Frank Norris Papers AR 124, Southern Baptist Historical Library Archives, Nashville, TN.

108. These letters can be viewed at the Southern Baptist Historical Library Archives and are found in J. Norris Papers AR 124, Southern Baptist Historical Library Archives, Nashville, TN: J. Frank Norris to Frank Groner, April 19, 1928, folder 10370; Frank Groner to J. Frank Norris, April 26, 1928, folder 10371; J. Frank Norris to Frank Groner, October 11, 1928, folder 10373; Frank Groner to J. Frank Norris, October 15, 1928, folder 10374; J. Frank Norris to Frank Groner, October 19, 1928, folder 10376.

109. Glenn Carson, *Calling out the Called: The Life and Work of Lee Rutland Scarborough* (Austin, TX: Eakin Press, 1996), 131.

Chapter 5

1. Brown, "J. Frank Norris," 6.

2. Nash, interview by author. Mrs. Nash, niece of George W. Truett, related that Dr. Truett would never mention Norris's name, publicly or privately. When forced to refer to him, he would simply call him "that man in Fort Worth."

3. Matthew Lyon, "J. Frank Norris: No Independent," Founder's Ministries, July 1, 2013, https://founders.org/2013/07/01/j-frank-norris-no-independent.

4. McBeth, "Two Ways to Be a Baptist," 52.

5. Paul Pressler, *A Hill on Which to Die: One Southern Baptist's Journey* (Nashville: B&H Publishers, 1999); Pigott, "Comparison of Leadership," 246; Morris, "Frank Norris," 27. The so-called Conservative Resurgence in the Southern Baptist Convention refers to the period from 1979, with the election of Adrian Rogers as president, to 2000. During this time the conservative wing elected a series of presidents who appointed strategic committees to appoint various boards of SBC entities to ensure that, in time, they had a major majority so as to determine a more conservative trajectory in the SBC's theology and practice. Those "denominational loyalists" who opposed this movement called themselves "moderates" and saw this movement more as a takeover than a resurgence. For further information on the Conservative Resurgence, see Pressler, *A Hill on Which to Die*, 246.

6. Paige Patterson, interview by author, Dallas, October 4, 2018. Patterson, one of the two recognized architects of the Conservative

Resurgence along with Judge Paul Pressler, stated that Norris proved a model for them of how it could not be done (i.e., from without) and how it could be done by reestablishing majorities on the various boards from within by electing the kind of presidents who would appoint like-minded committees.

7. The faculties of all six of the Southern Baptist seminaries are required to sign the confessional statement known as the Baptist Faith and Message approved in 2000 by the SBC.

8. Arthur Flake, *Building a Standard Sunday School* (Nashville: The Sunday School Board, 1934).

9. Flake, 29–55.

10. Charles Kelley, *Fuel the Fire* (Nashville: B&H Academic Publishers, 2018), 94.

11. Kelley, 94.

12. Ritchie, interview by author.

13. Leon McBeth, "The Texas Tradition: A Study in Baptist Regionalism," *Baptist History and Heritage* (January 1981): 53.

14. Jimmy Draper, *Lifeway Legacy: A Personal History of Lifeway Christian Resources* (Nashville: B&H Publishers, 2006), 147.

15. "Paid Advertisement," *Fort Worth Star-Telegram*, March 22, 1919, 2.

16. Entzminger, *Norris I Have Known*, 264.

17. McBeth, "Two Ways to Be a Baptist," 52.

18. McBeth, "The Texas Tradition," 52.

19. McBeth, "Two Ways to Be a Baptist," 52.

20. McBeth, *Baptist Heritage*, 622.

21. Hankins, *God's Rascal*, 27.

22. J. Frank Norris, "To Avert National Calamity," *The Searchlight*, June 16, 1921.

23. Durso, *Thy Will Be Done*, 164.

24. W. W. Barnes, *The Southern Baptist Convention, 1845–1953* (Nashville: Broadman Press, 1954), 223–24.

25. Durso, *Thy Will Be Done*, 168.

26. George W. Truett, *Christian Education* (Birmingham, AL: Education Board, Southern Baptist Convention, 1926), 9, file 1929, MF 1909-1970:6-7, George W. Truett Collection, A. W. Roberts Library, Southwestern Baptist Theological Seminary, Fort Worth, TX.

27. Durso, *Thy Will Be Done*, 175.

28. Durso, 192.

29. McBeth, "Two Ways to Be a Baptist," 52.

30. Durso, *Thy Will Be Done*, 188.

31. J. Frank Norris, "Denominational Nightmare," *The Searchlight*, March 24, 1922, 1.

32. Morris, "No Love Lost," 84.

33. James Thompson Jr., *Tried As By Fire: Southern Baptists and the Controversies of the 1920s* (Macon, GA: Mercer University Press, 1982), 101–36.

34. Durso, *Thy Will Be Done*, 188.

35. Barry Hankins, *Uneasy in Babylon: Southern Baptist Conservative and American Culture* (Tuscaloosa: University of Alabama Press, 2002), 212.

36. Ritchie, *Life and Legend*, 256.

37. While the term "Conservative Resurgence" has been commonly used to describe the succession of a number of conservative presidents elected to serve the SBC—who in turn appointed more conservative board members for the various entities, thereby changing the trajectory of the SBC—the more denominationally loyal moderates rejected this term, preferring instead the title "Fundamentalist Takeover."

38. The initial leaders of the Conservative Resurgence were Paige Patterson, president of Criswell College, Paul Pressler, a state appeals court judge from Houston, and prominent pastors W. A. Criswell, Adrian Rogers, Charles Stanley, Homer Lindsey, Jerry Vines, and Jimmy Draper.

39. Paige Patterson, "An Interview with Judge Paul Pressler," *The Theological Educator*, special edition (1985): 15-17.

40. Pressler, *A Hill on Which to Die*, 60.

41. Adrian Rogers, "Adrian Rogers Analyzes Convention Issues from Conservative Perspective," *Indiana Baptist*, June 2, 1992, 21.

42. Ralph Elliott, *The Message of Genesis* (Nashville: Broadman Press, 1961).

43. Paige Patterson, *Anatomy of a Reformation: The Southern Baptist Convention 1978–2004* (Fort Worth, TX: Seminary Hill Press, 2004), 1.

44. James A. Smith, "Prof's Doubts about 1 & 2 Kings Show Why SBC Needed Reformation," *Baptist Press*, May 10, 2001, 4.

45. Roy Honeycutt, ed., *The Broadman Bible Commentary*, vol. 3 (Nashville: Broadman Press, 1970), 242.

46. Fisher Humphreys, *The Death of Christ* (Nashville: Broadman Press, 1978), 61.

47. Noel Wesley Hollyfield Jr., "A Sociological Analysis of the Degrees of 'Christian Orthodoxy' among Selected Students in the Southern Baptist Theological Seminary" (ThM thesis, Southern Baptist Theological Seminary, 1976); Paul1611, May 15, 2006, comment on "Old Survey Concerning Southern Baptist Theological Seminary," Baptist Board, https:// www .baptistboard.com/threads/old-survey-concerning -southern -baptist -theological -seminary.3242/#post-74066; Michael Foust, "25 Years Ago, Conservative Resurgence Got Its Start," *Baptist Press*, June 15, 2004, http:// bpnews.net/18486/25-years-ago-conservative-resurgence-got-its-start.

48. Daniel Akin, *Contrasting and Comparing: Conservatives and Moderates in the Southern Baptist Convention* (Louisville: Southern Baptist Theological Seminary, n.d.). Akin wrote this booklet while serving as vice president and dean of the School of Theology at Southern Seminary in Louisville, Kentucky. He presently serves as president of the Southeastern Baptist Theological Seminary in Wake Forest, North Carolina.

49. Patterson, interview by author.

50. Barnes, *Southern Baptist Convention*, 209.

51. Norris, *Inside History*, 32.

52. Patterson, interview by author.

53. "Moderate" was the term that the established and entrenched leaders of the SBC chose to describe themselves. Often, when conservatives were referring to moderates they would use the term "liberals." Conversely, when the more moderate persuasion of the SBC referred to those in the conservative camp, they favored the pejorative term "fundamentalists." Randall Lolley, president of Southeastern Seminary, resigned in 1987 after trustees voted to hire only faculty members who adhered to the Baptist Faith and Message Statement. Al Shackleford and Dan Martin of *Baptist Press* were fired in 1990 for perceived bias against conservatives in their press coverage. Lloyd Elder, president of the Sunday School Board, resigned under pressure in 1991. Roy Honeycutt resigned as president of Southern Seminary in 1992 after being accused by the board's chairman, Jerry Johnson, of not

believing the Bible. Russell Dilday, president of Southwestern Seminary, was abruptly fired in 1994.

54. W. A. Criswell, "Whether We Live or Die," June 10, 1985, W. A. Criswell Sermon Library, https://wacriswell.com /sermons/1985/whether -we-live-or-die-SBC/. This message, as well as more than four thousand of W. A. Criswell's sermons on video, audio, and in manuscript form, can be found at www.wacriswell.com free of charge.

55. Criswell.

56. Criswell.

57. Although recognized as a "denomination," there is a real sense in which the Southern Baptist Convention is not a denomination in the purest expression of the term. There is no hierarchical system in Southern Baptist life. Every local church is completely autonomous. In essence, the SBC only exists for two days a year during its annual meeting and is a loose fellowship of independent, autonomous churches cooperating in ministry and missions.

58. James C. Hefley, *The Conservative Resurgence in the Southern Baptist Convention* (Hannibal, MO: Hannibal Books, 1991), 219.

59. Thomas J. Nettles, *The Baptists: Key People Involved in Forming a Baptist Identity*, vol. 3 (Fearn, Scotland: Christian Focus Publishers, 2007), 235.

60. For a more detailed and extensive analysis of Norris's part in the Conservative Resurgence, see Hankins, *Uneasy in Babylon*.

61. Criswell, interview by author.

62. Pigott, "Comparison of Leadership," 246.

63. McBeth, "Two Ways to Be a Baptist," 52.

64. Morris, "J. Frank Norris," 27.

65. Dwight A. Moody, "The Conversion of J. Frank Norris: A Fresh Look at the Revival of 1910," *Baptist History and Heritage Journal* 45, no. 3 (Summer/Fall 2010): 59.

66. Daniel Akin, David Allen, and Ned Matthews, *Text-Driven Preaching* (Nashville: B&H Academic Publishers, 2010), 8.

67. J. Frank Norris, *Gospel of John* (Plano, TX: Calvary Baptist Publications, n.d.), 31. Author's emphasis on Norris's use of the second-person singular.

68. George W. Truett, *Follow Thou Me* (Nashville: Broadman Press, 1932), 87.

69. Dewitt Talmadge Holland, "A Rhetorical Analysis of the Preaching of George W. Truett" (PhD diss., Northwestern University, 1956), 413.

70. See Simon Peter's first recorded sermon at Pentecost recorded in Acts 2 and Paul's first recorded sermon at Pisidian Antioch recorded in Acts 13; Norris, *Gospel of John*, 36.

71. Truett, *Follow Thou Me*, 91.

72. B. H. Carroll, "The Twentieth-Century Pastor; or, Lectures on Pastoral Theology," *Southwestern Journal of Theology* 58, no. 2 (Spring 2016): 214.

73. Carroll, 215.

74. David Larsen, *The Company of Preachers*, vol. 2 (Grand Rapids, MI: Kregel Publishers, 1998), 741.

75. Robert Rohm, *Dr. C* (Chicago: Moody Press, 1990), 80.

76. Criswell, interview by author.

77. Rohm, *Dr. C*, 81.

78. Criswell, interview by author. Criswell indicated that his first few months in the Dallas pulpit, all he saw as he stood in the pulpit were the backs of empty wooden pews, thus his comment, "I just preached to wood." Rohm, *Dr. C*, 81.

79. McBeth, "George W. Truett," 21.

80. McBeth, 21.

81. Clyde Fant Jr. and William Pinson Jr., *20 Centuries of Great Preaching: An Encyclopedia of Great Preaching* (Waco, TX: Word Publishers, 1971), 137

82. J. Frank Norris, *A Commentary on Genesis* (Fort Worth, TX: Calvary Publications, n.d.); J. Frank Norris, *Lectures on Revelation* (n.d., repr., Fort Worth, TX: Calvary Publications, 1984); J. Frank Norris, *Studies on Isaiah* (Fort Worth, TX: Bible Baptist Institute, 1942); J. Frank Norris, *Practical Lectures on Romans* (Fort Worth, TX: Calvary Publications n.d.).

83. Ritchie, *Life and Legend*, 263. Here Ritchie quotes Dr. J. B. Leavell, the well-known and well-respected pastor of the First Baptist Church in Houston.

84. Larsen, *The Company of Preachers*, 741.

85. McBeth, *The First Baptist Church of Dallas*, 194.

86. McBeth, 196.

87. Ritchie, interview by author.

88. Schepis, *J. Frank Norris*, ix.

89. Criswell, *Standing on the Promises*, 55–56.

90. Akin, Allen, and Matthews, *Text-Driven Preaching*, 8.

91. Ritchie, *Life and Legend*, 227.

92. Rick Warren, *The Purpose Driven Life* (Grand Rapids, MI: Zondervan Publishers, 2002).

93. J. Josh Smith, "The Necessity of Exhortation in Preaching: A Biblical and Theological Defense" (DMin diss., Southwestern Baptist Theological Seminary, 2015), 116.

94. Joel Gregory, interview by author, Waco, TX, December 14, 2018.

95. Paul Enns, *Moody Handbook of Theology* (Chicago: Moody Press, 1989), 384–85.

96. Durso, *Thy Will Be Done*, 38–39.

97. Tullock, *The Transformation of American Fundamentalism*, 174, 187.

98. Tullock, 187.

99. Correspondence from J. Frank Norris to Harry S. Truman, October 2, 1947, folder 25229, J. Frank Norris Papers AR 124, Southern Baptist Historical Library Archives, Nashville, TN.

100. Correspondence from J. Frank Norris to Harry S. Truman, telegram, February 1948, folder 25238, J. Frank Norris Papers AR 124, Southern Baptist Historical Library Archives, Nashville, TN.

101. Correspondence from J. Frank Norris to Harry S. Truman, May 16, 1948, folder 25242, J. Frank Norris Papers AR 124, Southern Baptist Historical Library Archives, Nashville, TN.

102. John Snetzinger, *Truman: The Jewish Vote and the Creation of Israel* (Stanford, CA: Hoover Institute Press, 1974), 102–11.

103. "Baptist Meeting Bans Joint Move," *The New York Times*, May 20, 1948, 1.

104. David Roach, "Israel Embassy Protests Draw Baptist Reactions," *Baptist Press*, May 14, 2018.

105. *Fort Worth Record*, September 13, 1919, Norris Archives, Fort Worth Public Library, Fort Worth, TX.

106. Wax, "Lessons from the Megachurch Pastor Who Killed a Man."

107. Moody, "Conversion of J. Frank Norris," 5.

108. Schepis, *J. Frank Norris*, 163.

109. McBeth, "Two Ways to Be a Baptist," 52.

110. Tullock, *The Transformation of American Fundamentalism*, 251.

111. Tullock, 16.

112. Tullock, 16.

113. Pressler, *A Hill on Which to Die*, xi.

114. Pigott, "Comparison of Leadership," 244.

115. McBeth, "Two Ways to Be a Baptist," 52.

116. Morris, "J. Frank Norris," 27.

Chapter 6

1. McBeth, "George W. Truett," 22.

2. Morris, "He Changed Things," 496.

3. Keith Durso, "George W. Truett: Making a Life Versus Making a Living," *Journal of the Texas Baptist Historical Society* 29 (2009): 80.

4. McBeth, "Two Ways to Be a Baptist," 35.

5. Entzminger, *Norris I Have Known*, 107.

6. Greer, affidavit before C. W. Braselton.

7. Ritchie, *Life and Legend*, 176–77, quoting from *The Austin Statesman*, January 21, 1927.

8. Mark Toulouse, "A Case Study in Schism: J. Frank Norris and the Southern Baptist Convention" (paper, The University of Chicago Divinity School, 1981), Foundations: 24:32–48, 9.

9. McBeth, "Two Ways to Be a Baptist," 52.

10. Morris, "He Changed Things," 507.

11. Ritchie, *Life and Legend*, 256.

12. McBeth, "Two Ways to Be a Baptist," 53.

13. Pigott, "Comparison of Leadership," 246.

14. Morris, "J. Frank Norris," 27.

15. Norris, *Inside History*, 32.

16. McBeth, "Two Ways to Be a Baptist," 52.

17. *Fort Worth Record*, September 13, 1919, Norris Archives, Fort Worth Public Library, Fort Worth, TX.

18. J. Frank Norris, *The Fundamentalist*, February 10, 1950, 1–5.

19. *Fort Worth Star-Telegram*, October 30, 1949, Norris Archives, Fort Worth Public Library, Fort Worth, TX.

20. Pigott, "Comparison of Leadership," 240.

21. The author was converted to Christ at Sagamore Hill Baptist Church in Fort Worth on January 3, 1965, as a seventeen-year-old senior in high school. Several of these men and women mentioned were his first Bible teachers and leaders in the Christian faith.

22. Entzminger, *Norris I Have Known*, 186.

23. Entzminger, 186.

24. Entzminger, 180–81.

25. Entzminger, 180–81.

26. Entzminger, 182.

27. In 1947, this cemetery was located west of Fort Worth. As the city has grown over the decades, Greenwood Memorial Park is today Fort Worth's largest cemetery and located well within the city limits.

28. Raymond Barber, interview by author, Fort Worth, TX, October 8, 2008.

29. Correspondence from J. Frank Norris to L. R. Scarborough, October 28, 1924, file 261, L. R. Scarborough Collection, Southwestern Baptist Theological Seminary, Fort Worth, TX.

30. Carson, *Calling out the Called*, 50.

31. Morris, "J. Frank Norris," 38.

32. McBeth, "Norris and Relationship with Southwestern," 1.

33. Ritchie, interview by author. Ritchie was the hand-picked pastoral successor of J. Frank Norris at the First Baptist Church in Fort Worth.

34. McBeth, "Two Ways to Be a Baptist," 52.

35. Morris, "J. Frank Norris," 38.

BIBLIOGRAPHY OF PRIMARY SOURCES

Annual. Baptist General Convention of Texas. 1924.

Annual. Southern Baptist Convention. 1920.

Appleby, Rosalee Mills. "The Price of Power." Typed manuscript, n.d. Truett Baptist History File. Southern Baptist Historical Library Archives, Nashville, TN. "Baptist Meeting Bans Joint Move." *The New York Times*, May 20, 1948.

Carroll, B. H. "Our Seminary." Compiled by J. W. Crowder. Fort Worth, TX: Southwestern Baptist Theological Seminary, 1957.

———, to George W. Truett. March 30, 1909. B. H. Carroll Archives. Southwestern Baptist Theological Seminary, Fort Worth, TX.

Criswell, W. A. "Dr. Truett and Baylor Hospital." June 6, 1980. W. A. Criswell Sermon Library. https://wacriswell.com/sermons/1980/dr-truett -and-baylor-hospital/.

———. "Whether We Live or Die." June 10, 1985. W. A. Criswell Sermon Library. https://wacriswell.com/sermons/1985/whether-we-live-or-die -SBC/.

"Dr. Norris Accepts First Baptist's Call." *Fort Worth Star-Telegram*, October 9, 1908.

"Dr. Norris Slays D. E. Chipps." *Fort Worth Star-Telegram*, July 18, 1926.

Entzminger, Louis. *The Fundamental Baptist Bible Institute Begins Its First Session*. Fort Worth, TX: self-published, 1939.

———. *The J. Frank Norris I Have Known for 34 Years*. Fort Worth, TX: self-published, 1948.

"First Baptist Pastor Speedily Cleared of Arson—Crowd Cheers Verdict." *Fort Worth Star-Telegram*, January 24, 1914.

Flake, Arthur. *Building a Standard Sunday School*. Nashville: The Sunday School Board, 1934.

Folder 1, 8428. J. Frank Norris Papers AR 124. Southern Baptist Historical Library Archives, Nashville, TN.

Folder 23. J. Frank Norris Papers AR 124. Southern Baptist Historical Library Archives, Nashville, TN.

Folder 25236. J. Frank Norris Papers AR 124. Southern Baptist Historical Library Archives, Nashville, TN.

Fort Worth Record, September 13, 1919. Norris Archives. Fort Worth Public Library, Fort Worth, TX.

The Fort Worth Register, October 8, 1901, 1.

Fort Worth Star-Telegram, October 11, 1909.

Fort Worth Star-Telegram, October 30, 1949. Norris Archives. Fort Worth Public Library, Fort Worth, TX.

Gambrell, J. B. Editorial. *The Baptist Standard*, May 2, 1912.

———. "The Growing of a Great Religious Paper." *The Baptist Standard* 19, no. 17.

———. "Some Observations Concerning Denominational Loyalty." *The Baptist Standard* 19, no. 29.

Greer, Fannie Tom. Affidavit before C. W. Braselton. Folder 292. J. Frank Norris Papers AR 124. Southern Baptist Historical Library Archives, Nashville, TN.

Groner, Frank Shelby. *A Discussion Concerning Attacks Now Being Made on Our Organized Work*. Dallas: n.d.

———, to J. Frank Norris. April 26, 1928. Folder 10371. J. Frank Norris Papers AR 124. Southern Baptist Historical Library Archives, Nashville, TN.

———, to J. Frank Norris. October 15, 1928. Folder 10374. J. Frank Norris Papers AR 124. Southern Baptist Historical Library Archives, Nashville, TN.

Harder, J. Matthew, to George W. Truett. November 2, 1923. File 934. MF 736-1336:21. George W. Truett Collection. A. W. Roberts Library, Southwestern Baptist Theological Seminary, Fort Worth, TX.

Hartwell, Jane. Affidavit before C. W. Braselton. Folder 292. J. Frank
    Norris Papers AR 124. Southern Baptist Historical Library Archives,
    Nashville, TN.

Heineke, Harry. "Body of Norris Arrives." *Fort Worth Star-Telegram*, August
    22, 1952. Box 2. L. R. Scarborough Collection. Southwestern Baptist
    Theological Seminary, Fort Worth, TX.

"J. Frank Norris Dies on Florida Visit." *Fort Worth Star-Telegram*, August
    21, 1952.

Keeton, Harry, to George Norris. January 12, 1945. Folder 1372. J. Frank
    Norris Papers AR 124. Southern Baptist Historical Library Archives,
    Nashville, TN.

Masters, Victor, to J. Frank Norris. May 8, 1949. Folder 1230. J. Frank
    Norris Papers AR 124. Southern Baptist Historical Library Archives,
    Nashville, TN.

"Meacham Hires Special Prosecutors." *Dallas News*, October 31, 1926.

"Norris Buys KFQB." *Fort Worth Record*, June 7, 1925.

Norris, George, to the First Baptist Church in Fort Worth. January 26,
    1945. Folder 1372. J. Frank Norris Papers AR 124. Southern Baptist
    Historical Library Archives, Nashville, TN.

"Norris Indicted on Two Counts Arson, One Count Perjury." *Fort Worth
    Record*, March 2, 1912.

"Norris Is Praised by Long Time Associate." *Fort Worth Star-Telegram*,
    August 21, 1952.

Norris, J. Frank. *Americanism: An Address to the Texas Legislature*. Fort
    Worth, TX: Seminary Bible and Book House, 1949.

———. *Anniversary Message*. N.d., 1936.

———. *The Battle of Armageddon*. Fort Worth, TX: self-published, n.d.

———. *The Battle of Armageddon, Why the Believer, 24 Truths Set Forth by
    Baptism*. N.d.

———, to Billy Graham. March 2, 1950. Folder 778. J. Frank Norris Papers
    AR 124. Southern Baptist Historical Library Archives, Nashville, TN.

———, to Billy Graham. June 7, 1950. Folder 778. J. Frank Norris Papers
    AR 124. Southern Baptist Historical Library Archives, Nashville, TN.

———, to Billy Graham. March 24, 1951. Folder 779. J. Frank Norris Papers
    AR 124. Southern Baptist Historical Library Archives, Nashville, TN.

————. *"But God" & Other Sermons*. N.d.

————. *Christ's Second Coming: Pre-millennial or Amillennial*. N.d.

————. *The Church That Is Different and Why: What the First Baptist Church Believes*. Fort Worth, TX: First Baptist Church, 1934.

————. *Commentary on the Book of Revelation*. N.d.

————. *Commentary on Colossians*. N.d.

————. *Commentary on Galatians*. N.d.

————. *A Commentary on Genesis*. Fort Worth, TX: Calvary Publications, n.d.

————. *Commentary on the Gospel of John*. N.d.

————. *Commentary on Isaiah*. N.d.

————. *Commentary on Second Corinthians*. N.d.

————. *Confession of Faith*. N.d.

————. "Denominational Nightmare." *The Searchlight*, March 24, 1922.

————. *Did the Jews Write the Protocols?* N.d.

————, ed. *Dr. Louie Newton—A Modern Jehoshaphat*. Fort Worth, TX: self-published, n.d.

————. Editorial. *The Baptist Standard*, August 27, 1908.

————. Editorial. *The Searchlight*, January 28, 1927.

————. Editorial. *The Fundamentalist*, February 10, 1950.

————. *The Federal Council of Churches Unmasked*. Fort Worth: self-published, n.d.

————. *The Federal Council of Churches Unmasked*. Detroit: Temple Baptist Church, 1939.

————. *"The Four Horsemen are Riding Fast" and Five Other Outstanding Messages*. Plano, TX: Calvary Baptist Church, n.d.

————. "Fort Worth Gives $200,000 to Seminary." *The Baptist Standard*, November 11, 1909.

————. *The Gospel of Dynamite*. N.d.

————. *Gospel of John*. Plano, TX: Calvary Baptist Publications, n.d.

————. *Greatest Annual Church Report in Modern Times*. N.d. 1937.

————. *The Holy Spirit and Soul Winning Power*. N.d.

————. *Infidelity among Southern Baptists Endorsed by Highest Officials*. Fort Worth, TX: self-published, 1945.

————. *Inside Facts and Figures of the Unparalleled and Unpublished History of the First Baptist Church, Fort Worth, Texas*. N.d.

————. *Inside History of First Baptist Church, Fort Worth and Temple Baptist Church, Detroit.* New York: Garland Publishing, 1988.

————. *The Inside History of the First Baptist Church of Fort Worth.* Fort Worth, TX: Gospel Witness Publishers, 1938.

————. *Inside the Cup.* N.d., 1930.

————. *Inside the Cup—Norris-Martin Debate.* N.d.

————. *Is America at the Crossroads?* N.d.

————. *Largest Combined Membership in the World Under One Pastorate—17,000 Members.* N.d., 1939.

————. *Lectures on Revelation.* N.d. Reprint, Fort Worth, TX: Calvary Publications, 1984.

————, to F. S. Groner. December 15, 1927. Box 17. Folders 10365–10367. J. Frank Norris Papers AR 124. Southern Baptist Historical Library Archives, Nashville, TN.

————, to F. S. Groner. April 19, 1928. Folder 10370. J. Frank Norris Papers AR 124. Southern Baptist Historical Library Archives, Nashville, TN.

————, to F. S. Groner. October 11, 1928. Folder 10373. J. Frank Norris Papers AR 124. Southern Baptist Historical Library Archives, Nashville, TN.

————, to F. S. Groner. October 19, 1928. Folder 10367. J. Frank Norris Papers AR 124. Southern Baptist Historical Library Archives, Nashville, TN.

————, to George Norris. January 9, 1945. Folder 1372. J. Frank Norris Papers AR 124. Southern Baptist Historical Library Archives, Nashville, TN.

————, to George Norris. January 25, 1945. Folder 1372. J. Frank Norris Papers AR 124. Southern Baptist Historical Library Archives, Nashville, TN.

————, to George Norris. June 5, 1945. Folder 1372. J. Frank Norris Papers AR 124. Southern Baptist Historical Library Archives, Nashville, TN.

————, to George W. Truett. March 9, 1940. File 1133. MF 736-1336:35. George W. Truett Collection. A. W. Roberts Library, Southwestern Baptist Theological Seminary, Fort Worth, TX.

————, to Harry S. Truman. October 2, 1947. Folder 25229. J. Frank Norris Papers AR 124. Southern Baptist Historical Library Archives, Nashville, TN.

————, to Harry S. Truman. May 16, 1948. Folder 25242. J. Frank Norris Papers AR 124. Southern Baptist Historical Library Archives, Nashville, TN.

————, to Harry S. Truman. Telegram. February 1948. Folder 25238. J. Frank Norris Papers AR 124. Southern Baptist Historical Library Archives, Nashville, TN.

————, to L. R. Scarborough. October 28, 1924. File 261. L. R. Scarborough Collection. Southwestern Baptist Theological Seminary, Fort Worth, TX.

————, to L. R. Scarborough. December 1, 1927. Box 37. Folder 1683. J. Frank Norris Papers AR 124. Southern Baptist Historical Library Archives, Nashville, TN.

————, to Louis Entzminger. January 6, 1931. Folder 1228. J. Frank Norris Papers AR 124. Southern Baptist Historical Library Archives, Nashville, TN.

————, to Luther C. Peak. February 14, 1952. Folder 1513. J. Frank Norris Papers AR 124. Southern Baptist Historical Library Archives, Nashville, TN.

————, to Luther C. Peak. July 8, 1952. Folder 1513. J. Frank Norris Papers AR 124. Southern Baptist Historical Library Archives, Nashville, TN.

————, to Victor Masters. December 16, 1932. Folder 1230. J. Frank Norris Papers AR 124. Southern Baptist Historical Library Archives, Nashville, TN.

————. *My Fifth Trip to Palestine*. Fort Worth, TX: The Fundamentalist Press, 1948.

————, ed. *New Dealism Exposed: Communism in Baptist Circles*. Fort Worth, TX: The Fundamentalist Publishing Company, n.d.

————. *Norris-Martin Debate*. N.d.

————. *The Norris-Wallace Debate*. N.d.

————. *Practical Lectures on Daniel*. Fort Worth, TX: self-published, 1945.

————. *Practical Lectures on Romans*. Fort Worth, TX: Calvary Publications, n.d.

————. *Practical Lectures on Romans*. Fort Worth, TX: self-published, 1945.

————. *The Prophesied Alliance of America and England on One Side versus All of Europe on the Other*. N.d., 1940.

————. *The Return of the Saloon and the Doom of America*. Fort Worth, TX: self-published, 1933.

————. *Six Reasons Why Al Smith Should Not Be President of the United States*. Fort Worth, TX: Protestant Press of America, n.d.

————. *Sovietizing American through Churches, Colleges, and Consumer's Cooperatives*. Rochester, NY: Interstate Evangelistic Association, 1936.

————. *Studies on Isaiah*. Fort Worth, TX: self-published, n.d.

————. *Studies on Isaiah*. Fort Worth, TX: Bible Baptist Institute, 1942.

————. *Three Sermons*. N.d.

————. "To Avert National Calamity." *The Searchlight*, June 16, 1921.

————. *The Triple Major Operation in Detroit*. N.d.

————. "A Visit to My Boyhood Home and My Mother's Grave." *The Fundamentalist*, September 16, 1949.

————. *The Wages of Sin and How to Be Saved*. N.d.

————. *What Do Fundamentalist Baptists Believe?* N.d., 1935.

————. *What Does the Bible Teach Concerning Baptism?* N.d.

————. "Why America Will Not Go under a Dictatorship." Archives, A. Webb Roberts Library, Southwestern Baptist Theological Seminary, Fort Worth, TX.

————, and J. L. Hines. *The Norris-Hines Debate: A Discussion*. Dallas: J. L. Hines, 1946.

"Paid Advertisement." *Fort Worth Star-Telegram*, March 22, 1919.

Peak, Luther C., to First Baptist Church. June 8, 1952. Folder 1513. J. Frank Norris Papers AR 124. Southern Baptist Historical Library Archives, Nashville, TN.

Pew, Ralph, to Temple Baptist Church in Detroit. June 14, 1950. Folder 1911. J. Frank Norris Papers AR 124. Southern Baptist Historical Library Archives, Nashville, TN.

"Son Is Named Pastor—But Norris Has Not Resigned." *Fort Worth Press*, June 19, 1944.

Tanco, A. B., to W. A. Criswell. December 27, 1954. Box 11. "Speeches on FBC, Texas Baptists" folder. H. Leon McBeth Collection. Texas Baptist Historical Collection, Waco, TX.

Truett, George W. "An Adequate Gospel for a Lost World." In *Third Baptist World Congress: Stockholm, July 21–27, 1923*, ed. W. T. Whitley, 114–23. London: Kingsgate, 1923.

————. *After His Likeness*. Edited by Powhatan W. James. Grand Rapids, MI: William B. Eerdmans Publishing House, 1954.

————. *The Baptist Message and Mission for the World Today*. Nashville: Sunday School Board, 1939.

————. "Baptists and Religious Liberty." May 16, 1920. https://bjconline .org/baptists-and-religious-liberty-2/.

————. *Be Still and Know That I Am God*. Atlanta: Radio Committee, Southern Baptist Convention, 1943. Box 5.6. Baptist Hour Sermons. Southern Baptist Historical Library Archives, Nashville, TN.

————, to B. H. Carroll. February 18, 1981. File 815. George W. Truett Collection. A. W. Roberts Library, Southwestern Baptist Theological Seminary, Fort Worth, TX.

————. "Charles Haddon Spurgeon Centenary." http://members.aol.com /pilgrimpub/centnary.htm.

————. *Christian Education*. Birmingham, AL: Education Board, Southern Baptist Convention, 1926. File 1929. MF 1909-1970:6-7. George W. Truett Collection. A. W. Roberts Library, Southwestern Baptist Theological Seminary, Fort Worth, TX.

————. *Christmas Messages*. Chicago: Moody Bible Institute, 1945.

————. *Christ's Answer to World Need*. Atlanta: Radio Committee, Southern Baptist Convention, 1943. Box 1.3b. Baptist Hour Sermons. Southern Baptist Historical Library Archives, Nashville, TN.

————. "Closing Words." In *Fifth Baptist World Congress, Berlin, August 4–10, 1934*. Edited by J. H. Rushbrooke, 215–17. London: Baptist World Alliance, 1934.

————. "The Coming of the Kingdom in America." In *The Baptist World Alliance, Second Congress, Philadelphia, June 19–25, 1911*, 421–29. Philadelphia: Harper & Brother Company, 1911. http://www.archive. org/details/recordofproceed 00unknuoft.

————. *The Conquest of Fear*. Atlanta: Radio Committee, Southern Baptist Convention, 1942. Box 1.1a. Baptist Hour Sermons. Southern Baptist Historical Library Archives, Nashville, TN.

————. Diary, July 19, 1919. File 33. George W. Truett Collection. A. W. Roberts Library, Southwestern Baptist Theological Seminary, Fort Worth, TX.

————. *Follow Thou Me*. Nashville: Broadman Press, 1932.

———. Foreword. In *Golden Years: An Autobiography*, Mrs. William L. Williams, 7–9. Dallas: Baptist Standard Publishing Company, 1921.

———. *George W. Truett Library*. Edited by Powhatan W. James. 4 vols. Nashville: Broadman Press, 1980.

———. *God's Call to America*. Edited by J. B. Cranfill. Philadelphia: Judson Press, 1923.

———. *The Inspiration of Ideals*. Edited by Powhatan W. James. Grand Rapids, MI: William B. Eerdmans Publishing House, 1950.

———. Introduction. In *The Doctrines of Our Faith*, E. C. Dargan, 9–16. Nashville: Sunday School Board, Southern Baptist Convention, 1905.

———. Introduction. In *Young People's Pilgrim's Progress*, John Bunyan, ed. S. J. Reid, 7–8. New York: Fleming H. Revell Company, ca. 1914.

———. *The Larger Day for Texas Baptists*. N.p.: 1906. File 1581. MF 1576–1595:2. George W. Truett Collection. A. W. Roberts Library, Southwestern Baptist Theological Seminary, Fort Worth, TX.

———. "Loyal to the Name." In *No Other Name: Proceedings of the First Southwide B.Y.P.U. Conference, Memphis, Tennessee, December 31, 1929–January 2, 1930*, 79–85. Nashville: Sunday School Board, Southern Baptist Convention, 1930.

———. *On Eagle Wings*. Edited by Powhatan W. James. Grand Rapids, MI: William B. Eerdmans Publishing House, 1953.

———. *On Preachers and Preaching*. N.p.: 1934. File 1940. MF 1909–1970:9. George W. Truett Collection. A. W. Roberts Library, Southwestern Baptist Theological Seminary, Fort Worth, TX.

———. *Our Adequate and Abiding Gospel*. Atlanta: Radio Committee, Southern Baptist Convention, 1942. Box 1.1a. Baptist Hour Sermons. Southern Baptist Historical Library Archives, Nashville, TN.

———. "Paper Read by George W. Truett." In Annual, Baptist General Convention of Texas, 1917, 19.

———. "The Preacher as a Man." February 18, 1914. Address. Southwestern Baptist Theological Seminary, Fort Worth, TX, File 1916. MF 1909–1972:2 (F.3.12). George W. Truett Collection. A. W. Roberts Library, Southwestern Baptist Theological Seminary, Fort Worth, TX.

———. *The Prophet's Mantle*. Edited by Powhatan W. James. Grand Rapids, MI: William B. Eerdmans Publishing House, 1948.

————. *A Quest for Souls*. Edited by J. B. Cranfill. New York: George H. Doran Company, 1917. http://www.archive.org/details/questforsouls00 9583mbp.

————. "Remarks during the 'Young People's Session,' June 20, 1911, at the Baptist World Alliance Congress in Philadelphia." In *The Baptist World Alliance, Second Congress, Philadelphia, June 19–25, 1911*, 95–99. Philadelphia: Harper & Brother Company, 1911. http://www.archive .org/details/ recordofproceed00unknuoft.

————. "Response to Greetings, July 21, 1923, at the Baptist World Alliance Congress in Stockholm." In *Third Baptist World Congress: Stockholm, July 21–27, 1923*, ed. W. T. Whitley, 6. London: Kingsgate, 1923.

————. *The Salt of the Earth*. Edited by Powhatan W. James. Grand Rapids, MI: William B. Eerdmans Publishing House, 1949.

————. *Sermons from Paul*. Edited by Powhatan W. James. Grand Rapids, MI: William B. Eerdmans Publishing House, 1947.

————. *Some Vital Questions*. Edited by Powhatan W. James. Grand Rapids, MI: William B. Eerdmans Publishing House, 1946.

————. *The Supper of Our Lord*. Dallas: B. J. Robert Book Company, n.d. File 1873. MF 1809-1880:17. George W. Truett Collection. A. W. Roberts Library, Southwestern Baptist Theological Seminary, Fort Worth, TX.

————. "The Texas Baptist Memorial Sanitarium." N.p.: n.d. File 1913. MF 1909–1970:1. George W. Truett Collection. A. W. Roberts Library, Southwestern Baptist Theological Seminary, Fort Worth, TX.

————. *These Gracious Years: Being the Year-End Messages and Addresses of Dr. George W. Truett*. Nashville: Sunday School Board of the Southern Baptist Convention, 1929.

————. *Tribute of the Church to Scouting*. Atlanta: Radio Committee, Southern Baptist Convention, 1943. Baptist Hour Sermons. Box 5.6. Southern Baptist Historical Library Archives, Nashville, TN.

————. *We Would See Jesus*. Edited by J. B. Cranfill. New York: Fleming H. Revell Company, 1915. http://www.archive.org/details /we wouldseejesusa00trueuoft.

————. *Who Is Jesus?* Edited by Powhatan W. James. Grand Rapids, MI: William B. Eerdmans Publishing House, 1952.

————, et al. "Christian Union: A Deliverance by the Baptist General Convention of Texas." In *Christian Union Relative to Baptist Churches*, ed. J. M. Frost, 35–42. Nashville: Sunday School Board of the Southern Baptist Convention, 1915.

————, J. H. Rushbrooke, and Clifton D. Gray. "A Postscript to the Congress." In *Fifth Baptist World Congress, Berlin, August 4–10, 1934*, ed. J. H. Rushbrooke, 251. London: Baptist World Alliance, 1934.

Vick, Beauchamp, to J. Frank Norris. May 17, 1950. Folder 1910. Southern Baptist Historical Library Archives, Nashville, TN.

"Word for Word Transcript of Norris Trial." *Austin Statesman*, July 21, 1927. jfnorris.net.

BIBLIOGRAPHY OF SECONDARY SOURCES

Books

Akin, Daniel. *Contrasting and Comparing: Conservatives and Moderates in the Southern Baptist Convention*. Louisville, KY: Southern Baptist Theological Seminary, n.d.

Akin, Daniel, David Allen, and Ned Matthews. *Text-Driven Preaching*. Nashville: B&H Academic Publishers, 2010.

Alter, Judy, and James Ward Lee. *Literary Fort Worth*. Fort Worth: TCU Press, 2002.

Baker, Robert. *Tell the Generations Following: A History of Southwestern Baptist Theological Seminary: 1908–1983*. Nashville: Broadman Press, 1983.

————. *The Thirteenth Check: The Jubilee History of the Annuity Board*. Nashville: Broadman Press, 1968.

Barber, Raymond W. *A Man among Men: J. Frank Norris*. Fort Worth: n.p.,1986.

Barber, Raymond W., and Wayne Martin. *The Man and the Movement: J. Frank Norris and the World Baptist Fellowship*. Arlington: World Baptist Fellowship.

Barnes, W. W. *The Southern Baptist Convention 1845–1953*. Nashville: Broadman Press, 1954.

Bartlett, Billy Vick. *A History of Baptist Separatism*. Springfield, MO: Baptist Bible Fellowship Publications, 1972.

Beale, David O. *In Pursuit of Purity: American Fundamentalism Since 1850*. Greenville, SC: Bob Jones University Press, 1986.

Blount, Douglas, and Joseph Woodall. *The Baptist Faith and Message 2000: Critical Issues in America's Largest Denomination*. Louisville, CO: Rowman and Littlefield Publishers, 2007.

Bonam, Claud J. *Blazing the Trail: My Experiences Working with Dr. J. Frank Norris*. San Antonio: Huisache Avenue Baptist Church, 1993.

Burton, Joe Wright. *Prince of the Pulpit: A Pen Picture of George W. Truett at Work*. Grand Rapids: Zondervan, 1946.

Carroll, J. M. *A History of Texas Baptists*. Dallas: Baptist Standard Publishing Company, 1923.

Carson, Glenn Thomas. *Calling out the Called: The Life and Work of Lee Rutland Scarborough*. Austin, TX: Eakin Press, 1996.

Cathy, Truett. *Eat Mor Chikin: Inspire More People: Doing Business the Chick-fil-A Way*. Decatur, GA: Looking Glass Books, 2002.

Chambers, Claude E. *The Rise and Fall of J. Frank Norris*. Shelbyville, TN: Bible and Literature Missionary Foundation, 1997.

Cole, Stewart G. *The History of Fundamentalism*. New York: Richard R. Smith, Inc., 1931.

Combs, James O. *Roots and Origins of Baptist Fundamentalism*. Springfield, MO: John the Baptist Press, 1984.

Cranfill, J. B. *Dr. J. B. Cranfill's Chronicle*. New York: Fleming H. Revell, 1916.

Criswell, Wallie A. *Standing on the Promises*. Dallas: Word Publishing, 1990.

———. *Fifty Years of Preaching at the Palace*. Grand Rapids: Zondervan, 1969.

Dana, H. E. *Lee Rutland Scarborough: A Life of Service*. Nashville: Broadman Press, 1942.

Daniel, J. C. *A History of the Baptists of Hill County, Texas*. Waco, TX: Hill-Kellner-Frost Co., 1907.

Dawson, Joseph Martin. *A Thousand Months to Remember*. Waco, TX: Baylor University Press, 1964.

Delnay, Robert George. *A History of the Baptist Bible Union*. Winston-Salem, NC: Piedmont Bible College, 1974.

Dollar, George W. *A History of Fundamentalism in America*. Greenville, SC: Bob Jones University Press, 1973.

Dow, Samuel. *Introduction to Sociology*. New York: Thomas Y. Crowell, Co., 1920.

Dowell, W. E. *The Birth Pangs of the Baptist Bible Fellowship, International*. Springfield, MO: Temple Press, 1977.

Draper, Jimmy. *Lifeway Legacy: A Personal History of Lifeway Christian Resources*. Nashville: B&H Publishers, 2006.

Durso, Keith. *Thy Will Be Done: A Biography of George W. Truett*. Macon, GA: Mercer University Press, 2009.

Elliott, Ralph. *The Message of Genesis*. Nashville: Broadman Press, 1961.

Enns, Paul. *Moody Handbook of Theology*. Chicago: Moody Press, 1989.

Falls, Roy Emerson. *A Biography of J. Frank Norris 1877–1952*. Euless, TX: self-published, n.d.

———. *A Fascinating Biography of J. Frank Norris*. Euless, TX: First Baptist Church, 1975.

Fant, Clyde, Jr., and William Pinson Jr. *20 Centuries of Great Preaching: An Encyclopedia of Great Preaching*. Waco, TX: Word Publishers, 1971.

Flemmons, Jerry. *Amon: The Life of Amon Carter, Sr. of Texas*. Austin, TX: Jenkins Publishing Company, 1978.

Fletcher, Jess. *The Southern Baptist Convention: A Sesquicentennial History*. Nashville: Broadman Press, 1994.

Garrett, Julia Kathryn. *Fort Worth: A Frontier Triumph*. Austin, TX: Encino Press, 1972.

Gatewood, James. *J. Frank Norris, Top O' Hill Casino, Lew Jenkins and the Texas Oil Rich*. Garland, TX: Mullaney Publishers, 2006.

Graham, Billy. *Just As I Am: An Autobiography*. San Francisco: HarperCollins Publishers, 1997.

GuideStone 100: Celebrating 100 Years of Service. Dallas: self-published, 2018.

Haldeman-Julius, Marcet. *A Report of the Rev. J. Frank Norris' Trial*. Girard, KS: Haldeman-Julius Publications, 1927.

Hankins, Barry. *God's Rascal: J. Frank Norris and the Beginnings of Southern Fundamentalism*. Lexington: University of Kentucky Press, 1996.

————. *Uneasy in Babylon: Southern Baptist Conservative and American Culture*. Tuscaloosa: University of Alabama Press, 2002.

Hawkins, O. S. *VIP: How to Influence with Vision, Integrity and Purpose*. Nashville: Thomas Nelson Publishers, 2016.

Hefley, James C. *The Conservative Resurgence in the Southern Baptist Convention*. Hannibal, MO: Hannibal Books, 1991.

————. *The Truth in Crisis*, vol. 2. Hannibal, MO: Hannibal Books, 1987.

————. *The Truth in Crisis*, vol. 5. Hannibal, MO: Hannibal Books, 1990.

Honeycutt, Roy, ed. *The Broadman Bible Commentary*, vol. 3. Nashville: Broadman Press, 1970.

Humphreys, Fisher. *The Death of Christ*. Nashville: Broadman Press, 1978.

Hyles, Jack. *Fundamentalism in My Lifetime*. Hammond, IN: Hyles Publications, 2002.

James, Powhatan. *George W. Truett: A Biography*. Nashville: Broadman Press, 1939.

Kelley, Charles. *Fuel the Fire*. Nashville: B&H Academic Publishers, 2018.

Kemp, Roy A. *Norris Extravaganza! My Reminisce: A Biography of J. Frank Norris: "The Fighting Parson."* Fort Worth: n.d., 1991.

Kirkland, Bootsie, Geneva Kirkland, and Mary Doherty. *A History of the First Baptist Church: Mt. Calm, Texas, 1878–1978*. Mt. Calm, TX: self-published, 1978.

Knight, Oliver. *Fort Worth: Outpost on the Trinity*. Fort Worth: Texas Christian University Press, 1990.

Kutilek, Doug. *J. Frank Norris and His Heirs: The Bible Translation Controversy*. Pasadena, TX: Pilgrim Publication, 1999.

Larsen, David. *The Company of Preachers*, vol. 2. Grand Rapids: Kregel Publishers, 1998.

Lefever, Alan. *Fighting the Good Fight: The Life and Work of Benajah Harvey Carroll*. Fort Worth: Eakin Press, 1994.

Marsden, George M. *Fundamentalism and American Culture: The Shaping of Twentieth Century Evangelicalism: 1870–1925*. New York: Oxford University Press, 1980.

Martin, T. T. *Inside the Cup Turned Out*. Jackson, TN: McCowat-Mercer Co., 1932.

————. *Shall We Kill Our Mission Boards, Seminaries, and Leaders?* N.d.

McBeth, H. Leon. *A Sourcebook for Baptist Heritage*. Nashville: B&H Academic, 1990.

———. *The Baptist Heritage: Four Centuries of Baptist Witness*. Nashville: B&H Academic Publishing, 1987.

———. *The First Baptist Church of Dallas*. Grand Rapids: Zondervan Publishers, 1968.

———. *Texas Baptists: A Sesquicentennial History*. Dallas: Baptist Way Press, 1998.

Nettles, Thomas J. *The Baptists: Key People Involved in Forming a Baptist Identity*, vol. 3. Fearn, Scotland: Christian Focus Publishers, 2007.

———. *By His Grace and for His Glory*. Grand Rapids: Baker Book House, 1986.

Patterson, Paige. *Anatomy of a Reformation: The Southern Baptist Convention 1978–2004*. Fort Worth: Seminary Hill Press, 2004.

Pratt, Kristian. *The Father of Modern Landmarkism: The Life of Ben M. Bogard*. Macon, GA: Mercer University Press, 2013.

Pressler, Paul. *A Hill on Which to Die*. Nashville: B&H Publishers, 1999.

Riley, B. F. *History of Baptists in Texas*. Dallas: self-published, 1907.

Ritchie, Homer. *The Life and Legend of J. Frank Norris: The Fighting Parson*. Fort Worth: self-published, 1991.

Rohm, Robert. *Dr. C.* Chicago: Moody Press, 1990.

Russell, Allyn C. *Voices of American Fundamentalism*. Philadelphia: Westminster Press, 1976.

Sandeen, Ernest Robert. *The Origins of Fundamentalism*. Philadelphia: Fortress Press, 1968.

Sanders, Leonard. *How Fort Worth Became the Texasmost City 1849–1920*. Fort Worth: Texas Christian University Press, 1973.

Scarborough, L. R. *A Modern School of the Prophets*. Nashville: Broadman Press, 1939.

Schepis, Michael. *J. Frank Norris: The Fascinating, Controversial Life of a Forgotten Figure of the Twentieth Century*. Bloomington, IN: Westbow Books, 2012. Ebook.

Seller, Richard F. *Hell's Half Acre*. Fort Worth: Texas Christian University Press, 1991.

Sherman, Cecil. *By My Own Reckoning*. Macon, GA: Smith & Helwys Publishing, Inc., 2008.

Short, Wayne. *Luke Short: A Biography of One of the Old West's Most Colorful Gamblers and Gunfighters*. Tombstone, AZ: Devil's Thumb Press, 1996.

Shurden, Walter. *Not a Silent People: Controversies That Have Shaped Southern Baptists*. Nashville: Broadman Press, 1972.

Snetzinger, John. *Truman: The Jewish Vote and the Creation of Israel*. Stanford, CA: Hoover Institute Press, 1974.

Stokes, David. *Apparent Danger: The Pastor of America's First Megachurch and the Texas Murder Trial of the Decade in the 1920s*. Minneapolis, MN: Bascom Hill Books, 2010.

———. *The Shooting Salvationist: J. Frank Norris and the Murder Trial That Captivated America*. Hanover, NH: Steerforth, 2011.

Tatum, Ray. *Conquest or Failure: Biography of J. Frank Norris*. Dallas: Historical Foundation Publishers, 1966.

Thompson, James J. *Tried as by Fire: Southern Baptists and Religious Controversies of the 1920s*. Macon, GA: Mercer University Press, 1982.

Tullock, Samuel. *The Transformation of American Fundamentalism: The Life and Career of John Franklyn Norris*. Dallas: The University of Texas at Dallas, 1997.

Waldor, Milton A. *Peddlers of Fear*. Newark, NJ: Lynnross Publishing Co., 1966.

Warren, Rick. *The Purpose Driven Life*. Grand Rapids: Zondervan Publishers, 2002.

Wood, Presnall, and Floyd Thatcher. *Prophets and Pens*. Dallas: Baptist Standard Publishing Company, 1969.

Articles

"Amazing Achievements of Dr. George W. Truett's Ministry, 1897–1941." *Quarterly Review* 10 (October–December 1941): 59–65.

"Amon Carter's Old Fort Worth Rivalry with Dallas Still Haunts Us." *Dallas Morning News*, September 15, 2019. Opinion section.

Barnes, W. W. "Denominational Leader." *Southwestern News III*, May 1945.

Burton, Joe Wright. "The Preacher and His Appointments." *Southern Baptist Home Missions* 13 (January 1942): 12–13.

————. "The Preacher and the Troubled." *Southern Baptist Home Missions* 13 (February 1942): 10–11.

Carroll, B. H. "The Twentieth Century Pastor; or, Lectures on Pastoral Theology." *Southwestern Journal of Theology* 58, no. 2 (Spring 2016): 183–282.

"Chants and Rants." *Dallas Morning News.* September 1, 2008, 19a.

Compton, Bobby D. "J. Frank Norris and Southern Baptists." *Review and Expositor* 79, no. 1 (Winter 1982): 63–84.

Cozzens, Katherine. "Church Growth: Fort Worth Style." *Texas Baptist History* 8 (1988): 32–48.

Davies, John. "Science and the Sacred: The Evolution Controversy at Baylor, 1920–1929." *East Texas Historical Journal* 29, no. 2 (1991): 41–53.

Durso, Keith. "George W. Truett: Making a Life Versus Making a Living." *Journal of the Texas Baptist Historical Society* 29 (2009): 80.

Hankins, Barry. "The Strange Career of J. Frank Norris: Or, Can a Baptist Democrat Be a Fundamentalist Republican?" *Church History* 61, no. 3 (September 1992): 373–92.

Hinkle, Don. "SBC Severs Ties with the BWA as Theological Concerns Remain." *Baptist Press.* June 15, 2004.

James, Powhatan W. "Truett, George Washington." In *Encyclopedia of Southern Baptists*, edited by Clifton Judson Allen and Norman Wade Cox. Nashville: Broadman Press, 1958.

McBeth, Leon. "George W. Truett: Baptist Statesman." *Baptist History and Heritage* 32, no. 2 (April 1997): 9–22.

————. "J. Frank Norris and Southwestern Seminary." *Southwestern Journal of Theology* 30, no. 3 (Summer 1988): 14–19.

————. "The Texas Tradition: A Study in Baptist Regionalism." *Baptist History and Heritage* (January 1981): 37–57.

————. "Two Ways to Be a Baptist." *Baptist History and Heritage* (April 1997): 39–53.

Moody, Dwight A. "The Conversion of J. Frank Norris: A Fresh Look at the Revival of 1910." *Baptist History and Heritage* 45, no. 3 (Summer/Fall 2010): 48–61.

Morris, C. Gwin. "J. Frank Norris: Rascal or Reformer?" *Baptist History and Heritage* 3, no. 3 (Fall 1998): 21–38.

———. "No Love Lost: J. Frank Norris and Texas Baptists, 1921–1925." *Baptist History and Heritage* 21 (2001): 86.

———. "The Pulpit and Politics: J. Frank Norris as a Case Study." *Texas Baptist History* 7 (1987): 1–19.

Patterson, Paige. "An Interview with Judge Paul Pressler." *The Theological Educator*, special edition (1985): 15–17.

Pratt, J. Kristian. "From 'Funnymentalist' to Friend: The Evolving Relationship of Ben M. Bogard and J. Frank Norris." *Baptist History and Heritage* 42, no. 2 (March 2007): 105–13.

Roach, David. "Israel Embassy Protests Draw Baptist Reactions." *Baptist Press*, May 14, 2018.

Rogers, Adrian. "Adrian Rogers Analyzes Convention Issues from Conservative Perspective." *Indiana Baptist*, June 2, 1992.

Smith, James A. "Prof's Doubts about 1 & 2 Kings Show Why SBC Needed Reformation." *Baptist Press*. May 10, 2001.

Academic Projects

Bates, David Keith. "Distinguishing Conservatism from Fundamentalism: The Approaches of J. Frank Norris and L. R. Scarborough to the Evolution Controversy." 1999.

Bevier, W. A. "A History of the Independent Fundamental Churches of America." PhD diss., Dallas Theological Seminary, 1957.

Bouldin, Donald G. "The J. M. Dawson–J. Frank Norris Controversy: A Reflection of the Fundamentalist Controversy among Texas Baptists." MA project, Baylor University, 1960.

Boyatt, Bernard C. "George W. Truett, Preacher and Public Speaker." Unpublished master's thesis, University of Tennessee, 1952.

Brannon, Richard Scott. "George Washington Truett and His Preaching." ThD diss., Southwestern Baptist Theological Seminary, 1956.

Brown, John M. "J. Frank Norris: The Sin Hating Sensationalist." MDiv project, Liberty Baptist Theological Seminary, 2014.

Bryant, Thurmon Earl. "The Ethics of George Washington Truett." ThD diss., Southwestern Baptist Theological Seminary, 1959.

Burlinson, B. E. "The Ecclesiology and Strategy of J. Frank Norris, from 1919 to 1950." MA thesis, University of Nebraska, 1960.

Burton, Joe Wright. "Oral Memoirs of W. A. Criswell." TMs. Religion and Culture Project, Baylor University, Program for Oral History, 1974.

Carpenter, Joel A. "The Renewal of American Fundamentalism, 1930–1945." PhD diss., Johns Hopkins University, 1984.

Carson, Glenn. "Lee Rutland Scarborough: Architect of a New Denominationalism within the Southern Baptist Convention." PhD diss., Southwestern Baptist Theological Seminary, July 1992.

Conolly, Kenneth. "The Preaching of J. Frank Norris." Unpublished MA thesis, University of Nebraska, 1960.

Curlew, Douglas James. "They Ceased Not to Preach: Fundamentalism Culture and the Revivalist Imperative at the Temple Baptist Church of Detroit." PhD diss., University of Michigan, 2001.

Davis, Joseph. "Embrace Equality: Texas Baptists, Social Christianity, and Civil Rights in the Twentieth Century." Master's thesis, University of North Texas, 2013.

Delnay, Robert George. "A History of the Baptist Bible Union." ThD diss., Dallas Theological Seminary, 1963.

Ferris, Charles J. "Southern Baptist and Evolution in the 1920s: The Roles of Edgar Y. Mullins, J. Frank Norris, and William Louis Poteat." 1973.

Gilbert, Timothy Dwain. "A Critical Analysis of the Development of the New Right in America with Particular Emphasis from 1964–1985." PhD diss., Southwestern Baptist Theological Seminary, 1987.

Hankins, Barry. "Saving America: Fundamentalism and Politics in the Life of J. Frank Norris." PhD diss., Kansas State University, 1990.

Hicks, Alfred Edward. "The Reverend J. Frank Norris of Texas and the Politics of Cataclysm." 1971.

Holland, Dewitt Talmadge. "A Rhetorical Analysis of the Preaching of George W. Truett." PhD diss., Northwestern University, 1956.

Hollyfield, Noel Wesley, Jr. "A Sociological Analysis of the Degrees of 'Christian Orthodoxy' among Selected Students in the Southern Baptist Theological Seminary." ThM thesis, Southern Baptist Theological Seminary, 1976.

Howe, Danny E. "An Analysis of Dispensationalism and Its Implications for the Theologies of James Robinson Graves, John Franklyn Norris, and Wallie Amos Criswell." PhD diss., Southwestern Baptist Theological Seminary, 1988.

Langley, Ralph. "The Preaching of George W. Truett." Unpublished master's thesis, Princeton Divinity School, 1949.

Lewis, Tom Tandy. "The Part of J. Frank Norris in the Fundamentalist Movement." 1965.

McBeth, Leon. "J. Frank Norris and His Relationship with Southwestern Seminary." Paper presented at Founder's Day Chapel at Southwestern Baptist Theological Seminary, Fort Worth, TX, March 12, 1987. Box 2. Norris Collection. Southwestern Baptist Theological Seminary, Fort Worth, TX.

McGlone, Lee Roy. "The Preaching of J. Frank Norris: An 'Apologia' for Fundamentalism." PhD diss., The Southern Baptist Theological Seminary, 1983.

Measures, Royce. "Men and Movements Influenced by J. Frank Norris." ThD Diss., Southwestern Baptist Theological Seminary, 1976.

———. "The Relation of J. Frank Norris to the Northern Fundamentalist Movement." ThM thesis, Southwestern Baptist Theological Seminary, 1970.

Morris, Clovis Gwin. "He Changed Things: The Life and Thought of J. Frank Norris." PhD diss., Texas Tech University, 1973.

Peak, Luther Campbell. "Oral Memoirs of Luther Campbell Peak." TMs. Texas Baptist Project, Baylor University, Institute for Oral History, 1985.

Pigott, Kelly David. "A Comparison of the Leadership of George W. Truett and J. Frank Norris in Church, Denominational, Interdenominational and Political Affairs." PhD diss., Southwestern Baptist Theological Seminary, 1993.

Rich, Harold. "Beyond Outpost: Fort Worth 1880–1918." PhD diss., Texas Christian University, 2006.

Ritchie, Homer. "The Life and Career of J. Frank Norris." MA thesis, Texas Christian University, 1967.

Shamburger, William M. "A History of Tarrant County Baptist Association 1886–1922." ThD diss., Southwestern Baptist Theological Seminary, 1953.

Smith, J. Josh. "The Necessity of Exhortation in Preaching: A Biblical and Theological Defense." DMin diss., Southwestern Baptist Theological Seminary, 2015.

Tatum, E. Ray. "The J. Frank Norris Murder Trial of 1927." MA project, Texas Tech University, 1968.

Terre-Blanche, Henry S. "The Life of J. Frank Norris." ThM project, Dallas Theological Seminary, 1966.

Toulouse, Mark. "A Case Study in Schism: J. Frank Norris and the Southern Baptist Convention." Paper, The University of Chicago Divinity School, 1981.

Tullock, Samuel Kyle. "The Transformation of American Fundamentalism: The Life and Career of John Franklyn Norris." PhD diss., The University of Texas at Dallas, 1997.

Vick, G. B. "Oral History of George Beauchamp Vick." TMs. Baylor University, Institute for Oral History, 1973.

Walker, Charles. "The Ethical Vision of Fundamentalism: An Inquiry into the Ethics of John Franklyn Norris." Unpublished diss., Southwestern Baptist Theological Seminary, 1985.

Wall, Eston Wayne. "The Effects of Controversy on Perceptions of Preaching Based on Methods of Dr. J. Frank Norris." 1989.

Interviews

Barber, Raymond. Interview by author. Fort Worth, October 8, 2008.

Bryant, James. Phone Interview by author. September 11, 2008.

Criswell, W. A. Interview by author. Dallas, August 25, 1994.

Gregory, Joel. Interview by author. Waco, TX, December 14, 2018.

Hermes, Wendy. Interview by author. Dallas, October 11, 2019.

Lefever, Alan. Interview by author. August 27, 2019.

Mohler, R. Albert. Phone interview by author. March 2, 2018.

———. Interview by author. Nashville, September 17, 2019.

Nash, Josephine. Interview by author. Dallas, September 18, 2008.

Norris, George, Jr. Phone interview by author. Vernon, TX, September 9, 2008.

Patterson, Paige. Interview by author. Dallas, October 4, 2018.

Ritchie, Homer. Interview by author. Fort Worth, August 8, 2008.

Tanco, A. B. Interview by author. Dallas, November 15, 1993.

Thompson, Guy. Interview by author. Fort Worth, October 8, 2008.

Web Sources

Adams, Nate. "The Baptist 75 Million Campaign." SBC Life. May 1, 1999. http://www.sbclife.net/article/448/the-baptist-75-million-campaign.

Bullock, Karen O'Dell. "First Baptist Church, Fort Worth." Texas State Historical Association. October 2, 2019. https://tshaonline.org /handbook/online/articles/ibf01.

"Dallas History." 2002. https://web.archive .org/web/20060422183559 /http://www.dallashistory.org/history/dallas/dallas_history.htm.

Foust, Michael. "25 Years Ago, Conservative Resurgence Got Its Start." *Baptist Press*, June 15, 2004. http://bpnews.net/18486/25 -years -ago -conservative-resurgence-got-its-start.

"Go West, Young Man, Go West." Encyclopedia.com. November 22, 2019. https://www.encyclopedia .com/history/dictionaries-thesauruses -pictures-and-press-releases/go-west-young-man-go-west.

Handbook of Texas Online. Texas State Historical Association. http://www .tshaonline.org/handbook/online/archives/hlh67.

"J. Frank Norris by the Numbers." Baptistbasics.org. https://www .baptistbasics.org/baptists/norris7.php.

"Largest Christian Denominations in the United States." ProCon .org. June 30, 2008. https://undergod .procon.org/view.additional -resource .php?resourceID=000087.

Lyon, Matthew. "J. Frank Norris: No Independent." Founders Ministries. July 1, 2013. https://founders .org /2013 /07 /01 /j -frank -norris -no -independent.

McElhaney, Jackie, and Michael V. Hazel. "Dallas, TX." Texas State Historical Association. November 3, 2015. https://tshaonline.org/hand book/online/articles/hdd01.

"*Our Story*." First Baptist Fort Worth. http://www.fbcfw.org/about/.

Paul1611. Comment, May 15, 2006. On "Old Survey Concerning Southern Baptist Theological Seminary." Baptist Board. https://www.baptistboard.com /threads /old -survey -concerning -southern -baptist -theological -seminary .3242/#post-74066.

Payne, Darwin. "When Dallas Was the Most Racist City in America." *D Magazine*. June 2017. https://www.dmagazine .com/publications/d-magazine /2017/June/when-DALLAS-was-the-most-racist-city-in-America/.

Scudder, Charles. "Why Is Fort Worth Called Panther City?" *The Dallas Morning News*, June 6, 2018. https://www.dallasnews.com/news/curious-texas/2018/06/06/why-is-fort-worth-called-panther-city-curious-texas-investigates-a-regional-rivalry/.

Stone, Michael. "Megachurch Pastor Robert Jeffress: 'There's No Such Thing as Separation of Church and State.'" Progressive Secular Humanist. September 27, 2019. https://www.patheos.com/blogs/progressivesecular humanist/2019/09/megachurch-pastor-Robert-Jeffress-theres-no-such-thing-as-separation-of-church-and-state/.

Stringer, Tommy. "How Did Dallas Get Its Name?" *Corsicana Daily Sun*, April 12, 2008. https://www.corsicanadailysun.com/news/local_news/stringer---how-did-dallas-get-its-name/article_10df5bb3-45e1-5e6d-abf4-cc5b233cab15.html.

Wax, Trevin. "Lessons from the Megachurch Pastor Who Killed a Man." *The Gospel Coalition*. May 29, 2012. https://thegospelcoalition.org/blogs/trevin-wax/lessons-from-the-megachurch-pastor-who-killed-a-man/.

Winters, Adam. "The Broadman Bible Commentary Controversy: From Genesis to the Conservative Resurgence." *Towers*. June–July 2016. http://equip.sbts.edu/wp-content/uploads/2016/06/Towers-June-July-2016.pdf.

Other

Barnes, W. W. "The Norris Affair." Founder's Day Address, undated. Baker Archives. Southwestern Baptist Theological Seminary, Fort Worth.

Bill Swank Papers. Folder 61. Norris Collection. Archives. Southwestern Baptist Theological Seminary, Fort Worth.

Dawson, J. M. "Truett's Gethsemane Now Revealed." 1958. File 629. MF 628-657:1. George W. Truett Collection. A. W. Roberts Library, Southwestern Baptist Theological Seminary, Fort Worth.

Newspaper clipping [unidentifiable]. File 33. George W. Truett Collection. A. W. Roberts Library, Southwestern Baptist Theological Seminary, Fort Worth.

Norris, George. Audio recording. N.d. Heritage Collection. Arlington Baptist College, Arlington, TX.

NAME AND SUBJECT INDEX

ABOUT THE AUTHOR

O. S. Hawkins, a native of Fort Worth, Texas, is a graduate of TCU (BBA) and Southwestern Baptist Theological Seminary (MDiv, PhD). He is the former pastor of the First Baptist Church in Dallas, Texas, and since 1997 has served as President/CEO of GuideStone Financial Resources, the world's largest Christian-screened mutual fund with assets approaching $20 billion. Hawkins is the author of more than forty books, including the best-selling Code Series of devotionals published by HarperCollins/ThomasNelson with sales of more than two million copies. He is married to his wife, Susie, and has two daughters, two sons-in-law, and six grandchildren.